Hugo Wolf's *Lieder* and Extensions of Tonality

Studies in Musicology, No. 82

George Buelow, Series Editor

Professor of Music
Indiana University

Other Titles in This Series

Hugo Wolf's *Lieder* and Extensions of Tonality

by
Deborah J. Stein
Assistant Professor of Music Theory
Eastman School of Music
Rochester, New York

UMI RESEARCH PRESS
Ann Arbor, Michigan

From *Structural Hearing* by Felix Salzer. Figure 382 of Volume II used by permission of Dover Publications, Inc., New York.

From *FREE COMPOSITION (Der freie Satz)* by Heinrich Schenker, translated and edited by Ernst Oster. Copyright © 1979 by Longman Inc. Reprinted by permission of Longman Inc., New York.

Copyright © 1985
Deborah Jane Stein
All rights reserved

Produced and distributed by
UMI Research Press
an imprint of
University Microfilms International
A Xerox Information Resources Company
Ann Arbor, Michigan 48106

Library of Congress Cataloging in Publication Data

Stein, Deborah J.
   Hugo Wolf's Lieder and extensions of tonality.

   (Studies in musicology ; no. 72)
   Revision of the author's thesis (Yale University,
1982.)
   Bibliography: p.
   Includes index.
   1. Wolf, Hugo, 1860-1903. Songs. 2. Tonality.
I. Title.
ML410.W8S8 1985   784.3'0092'4   85-1166
ISBN 0-8357-1469-1 (alk. paper)

LIBRARY
ALMA COLLEGE
ALMA, MICHIGAN

To the memory of my parents, Aaron and Henrietta Stein, who would have greatly enjoyed what I have discovered in Wolf's songs, and whom I dearly miss at this special moment of my life.

LIBRARY
ALMA COLLEGE
ALMA, MICHIGAN

Contents

Acknowledgments

This book culminates a rich and gratifying period of work begun at Yale University. I have been most fortunate during these years, as I have studied with and come to know many wonderful people, including some extraordinary musicians and scholars. As an undergraduate at the University of Michigan, I had the privilege of studying with Professor Wallace T. Berry, who, as my teacher and mentor, helped establish the musical and intellectual foundation of this book. While at Yale, it was my great fortune to study with Professor Allen Forte, a man who is uniquely responsible for creating the climate for theoretical research at Yale that both encourages and supports studies such as this. As my advisor, Allen was unfailing in his insight, interest, and encouragement; in addition, he was—and continues to be—a supportive and caring friend.

It is a pleasure for me to thank a number of people who contributed to the completion of this project. I thank Martha Hyde and Leon Plantinga, for their encouragement. I also thank Robert Freeman and Jon Engberg of the Eastman School of Music for their financial assistance; and David Beach for his support and counsel. I also wish to thank Joan Harissis and Robert Taylor of the University of Rochester Computing Center for their patient assistance in teaching me how to use the word processor. Eastman graduate students Richard Cohn, Jeanne Golan, Jean Janes, and bruce mcclung were remarkably tenacious and insightful in proofreading chapters of the book at various stages of completion; and Eastman colleagues Robert Bailey and Patrick McCreless were especially generous in sharing with me their remarkable understanding of nineteenth-century music. Roseanne Scheuermann was most supportive and helpful in preparing parts of the text, and in generally keeping the rest of my professional world intact. I wish to thank Michael Torke for copying the musical examples and Hali Fieldman for special help in final copying and editing when the project was in the throes of completion.

It is a special pleasure for me to be able to acknowledge here my family and those friends who have nurtured and sustained me over the years. George V.

Rose was the first to encourage me to become a musician. Years later in Ann Arbor, Joanne Murphy Horn and George B. Wilson shared in developing my creative abilities. In New Haven, Raphael Atlas and Susan Blaustein were especially important colleagues; and most recently, during my first years at the Eastman School of Music, Leah Fygetakis, Steven Laitz, Daniel McMullin, and Deborah Modrak gave me constant support and encouragement. Special thanks are due to my sisters Leslie, Maggie, and Vicky, and to my brother-in-law Clark for their continued love and faith. They sustained me from the beginning and gave me the courage to persist.

Finally, I must single out three individuals who have had the most impact on the substance of this book. Roger Graybill was a wonderful colleague at Yale who helped the development of this study. Through hours of intense discussion, Roger helped me come to appreciate the oftentimes tortuous process of learning to communicate original ideas. Jenny Kallick has been a most cherished friend for over a decade. Her nurturance and assistance has been constant; she edited endless drafts and debated with me countless issues. Jenny supported me during the bad times and celebrated with me during the good. As a superb musician and scholar, she taught me how to conceptualize more clearly, write more effectively, and love music more dearly. Finally, David Lewin's impact on this study is almost ineffable. Much of this study was inspired by his course on text-setting at Yale, and many more insights arose from his much-appreciated willingness to read this book in draft form. More than that, however, David taught me to treasure my creative imagination—and then provided for me a safe place in which to test out my least defined, but most daring, ideas.

1

Introduction to the
Music and the Methodology

This study considers the harmonic language of the late nineteenth century as an expansion of common-practice tonality. Late-nineteenth-century romantic composers explored such an extended-tonal language through a variety of styles, techniques, and genres ranging from large-scale symphonic works and grandiose operas to miniature piano pieces and intimate art songs. A special component of late-nineteenth-century tonal expansion was the use of extramusical elements such as theatre, literary allusions or references, and poetic verse. Our investigation of extended-tonal composition considers the role of the extramusical element in late-nineteenth-century music: Was the musical innovation a response to poetic or theatrical structure, or did the extramusical element offer a conventional framework for progressive musical ideas?

Despite the immense volume of music written in the late nineteenth century, the selection of music appropriate for demonstrating the use of extended-tonal procedures during this period was problematic. The music had to fulfill three important conditions: it had to incorporate some extramusical element, preferably a text; it had to be concise enough to allow for the greatest possible study of detail; and, in its demonstration of extended-tonal procedures, it had to offer the greatest amount of diversity and variety. Despite the lure of Wagner's operas and Mahler's symphonies, the *Lieder* of Hugo Wolf (1860-1903) proved to be ideal. Wolf composed over 260 miniature masterworks from which one could choose the most cogent examples of extended-tonal technique. Beyond that, *Lieder* generally represent one of the most expressive late-nineteenth-century genres, and Wolf's *Lieder* specifically exemplify some of the most highly personal and idiomatic art songs ever created.

This study will be neither a comprehensive examination of Hugo Wolf's songs nor an exhaustive survey of late-nineteenth-century tonal expansion. Rather, each of the next three chapters will isolate one technique of tonal expansion, explore the musical and theoretical foundation of that technique, and exemplify the resultant extended-tonal structures with carefully selected Wolf songs. Following that, the fifth chapter will examine those special Wolf songs that combine several extended-tonal techniques within a single musical work. The examination here incorporates only about two dozen songs chosen because they best depicted the theoretical or analytical issues at hand. (Scores to songs examined in this study are found at the end of the chapter in which they are discussed.) As a result, some of Wolf's most well-known and most popular songs were not included, and the study explores a mere sampling of Wolf's remarkable *œuvre*.

Two other factors contribute to the scope of this study: Wolf's unique relationship to Richard Wagner and to Wagner's revolutionary musical language; and the similarities between Wolf's music and that of his contemporaries. Wolf's songs represent a deliberate application of Wagner's harmonic language.[1] To Wolf, Wagner's music represented the quintessence of contemporary music, both in its harmonic and melodic language and in its musical relationship to the text and drama. For the purposes of the present study, the fact that Wolf modeled his music after that of Wagner suggests that the Wolfian extended-tonal language is one possible extrapolation of Wagner's own extended-tonal discourse. In this way, the study of Wolf songs offers a glimpse of the impact of Wagner's musical language on the music of his contemporaries and successors.

Even though this study confines its focus and scope to one composer and one genre, some of the compositional techniques identified here with Wolf can be considered part of a more universal late-nineteenth-century extended-tonal language. Many of the harmonic innovations cited here can also be found in the music of Wolf's contemporaries: in the symphonies of Mahler and Bruckner, in the piano works of Liszt, and in the operas of Wolf's beloved mentor, Richard Wagner.

Analytical Methodology: Use of Schenkerian Analysis

The theory and methodology of Heinrich Schenker (1868-1935) will be the analytical point of departure for this study.[2] In addition, Schenker's analytical system will serve two other special functions. First, Schenker's analytic framework will depict the common-practice tonal system as a norm of syntax that was expanded upon in the late nineteenth-century; second, the tonal norm established by Schenker's system will function as a standard against which extended-tonal techniques can be gauged for harmonic conformity or innovation. The applicability of Schenker will be an ongoing concern throughout this study: each extended-tonal technique explored will be examined in light of the usefulness or inappropriateness of Schenkerian analysis. Where Schenkerian analysis remains applicable, the extended-tonal technique can be characterized as relatively conservative. Where Schenkerian analysis becomes inapplicable and inappropriate, the extended-tonal technique can be considered unusual and innovative.

Schenker's System as a Tonal Norm

Schenker's analytical methodology is a remarkable conceptualization of common-practice tonality. No other theorist has Schenker's insight and vision, and no other analytical system offers as much depth and scope of analytical perception. In order to set the foundation for the use of Schenkerian analysis, let us review the basic assumptions that underlie Schenker's system.

Schenker's conceptualization of common-practice tonality is predicated upon two fundamental premises. First, common-practice tonality is structurally diatonic; chromaticism functions to elaborate or embellish—on a foreground or middleground level—a diatonic background. Second, common-practice tonality exists within a framework of monotonality wherein one background tonality is embellished by surface modulations that emphasize structurally important scale steps within that singular tonal region.[3] Schenker's concept of diatonic monotonality is the basic foundation upon which his notion of the *Ursatz*—and the attending tenets of *Urlinie* and *Bassbrechung*—are constructed. The concept of the *Ursatz* is in turn founded upon the premise of a primary structural and inherently cohesive relationship between the tonic and its dominant, the so-called "tonic-dominant axis."[4] The structural power of the tonic-dominant axis is unparalleled within the tonal system, and Schenker's depiction of the contrapuntal horizontalization of this structure— the *Ursatz*—is compelling and persuasive.

While this study does not propose to appraise Schenker's theories in a systematic way, it will occasionally be necessary to ascertain whether some of Schenker's concepts are wholly relevant or applicable to a particular late-nineteenth-century extended-tonal technique. In such cases, the purpose is not to criticize Schenker, but rather to indicate that his system (which he himself did not apply extensively to music beyond that of Brahms) ceases to be completely useful for analyzing the music at hand. This will involve several of Schenker's most important concepts, such as the *Kopfton* (see chapter 4), the *Bassbrechung* (see chapter 3), and the *Urlinie* (see chapters 2 and 5). In such cases, what is called an inapplicability of Schenker asserts only that some of Schenker's concepts cannot be used faithfully to depict the music being examined. Whether that inapplicability is due to problems inherent in the extended-tonal musical structure or to limitations within Schenker's analytical system are questions that cannot be fully addressed at this time.

Schenker's System as a Gauge for Tonal Innovation

Once the degree of conformity of a given extended-tonal structure to common-practice tonality has been established, some Schenkerian precepts can demonstrate how the tonal syntax is being altered. Specific Schenkerian concepts such as *Ursatz, Urlinie, Bassbrechung, Kopfton,* and *Schichten*[5] will serve as models of tonal design that offer specific criteria for tonal cohesion. Even where Schenker's system is inapplicable—for instance, when a *Kopfton* does not descend—many of the components of that system continue to function as prototypes for new, late-nineteenth-century harmonic structures, structures that will cohere and achieve tonal clarity in either analogous or in wholly alternative ways.

Modification of Schenker's System

Since 1945, various theorists have attempted to apply Schenker's ideas to music which he himself did not extensively explore.[6] This study resists such a modification of Schenker's methodology for two reasons. First, Schenker's analytical framework is invaluable to this study precisely because it depicts a specific tonal language, namely that of the common-practice period. To alter Schenker's system would result in undermining the tonal norm whose extension is being evaluated. Second, the value of this study will not be restricted solely to the application of Schenkerian analysis, but rather will explore alternative, non-Schenkerian analytical ideas as well.

Schenker's system will be modified in that it will not be used in totality: even when some elements of Schenker's analytical framework are no longer applicable to the present study, others will be retained. In chapter 4, for example, a form of double tonality is described that simply cannot be comprehended in Schenker's terms. Nonetheless, even though Schenker's concept of monotonality is undermined, use will be made of a *Kopfton* and other components of Schenker's system. This retention of some elements of Schenker in the absence of others will prove invaluable in that it will show the extent to which common-practice tonality can continue to exist within innovative, extended-tonal structures.

Wolf's Relation to the Text

Because of his special reverence for poetry and his painstaking adherence to textual demands, many consider Wolf to be the greatest songwriter of the formidable *Lied* tradition.[7] In his 1907 study, Ernest Newman discusses at great length the intimate and intense relationship between Wolf and the poetry he set. Newman reports, for instance, that "Wolf, at his recitals, first read and expounded the poem to his auditors before he allowed a note of the music to be heard."[8] Newman also discusses both Wolf's refusal to set to music any poetry but that of the greatest poets, his unwillingness to compose a song based on poetry already set to music unless the existent setting failed to convey adequately the meaning of the verse. In his more recent (1968) biography, Frank Walker confirms much of the information cited by Newman. Walker further details Wolf's determination to publish his songs as a tribute to the poet rather than to the composer: "when the volume was published, the title page did not read '53 Songs by Hugo Wolf, words by Mörike,' but 'Poems by Eduard Mörike, for voice and piano, set to music by Hugo Wolf.'"[9] Walker also notes Wolf's insistence that the photograph included in his published volumes be that of the poet rather than of the composer.

Musical Innovations Resulting from Text Depiction

The oftentimes colorful accounts of Wolf's devotion to his poets are revealing. One wonders, for instance, to what extent many of Wolf's harmonic innovations resulted from his preoccupation with text depiction rather than from any interest in harmonic experimentation *per se*. This view is especially intriguing when Wolf's reverence for poetry is considered together with his allegiance to Wagnerian concerns about text. For example, Wolf developed (partly in reaction to Wagner's operatic style) a highly idiomatic *parlando* vocal line, which clearly enunciated a poetic text irrespective of a complex or ambiguous piano accompaniment. The ultimate consequence of this style was the unprecedented independence of vocal line and accompaniment in some of Wolf's most complex songs—in particular, the occasional setting of voice and piano parts in different keys. This technique vividly conveyed a dramatic conflict between the poet/singer and some opposing force represented by the piano accompaniment.[10]

The Ambiguity Principle

One of Wolf's most characteristic methods for depicting text is his exploitation of harmonic and/or tonal ambiguity. He created harmonic ambiguity in a variety of ways, for example through textural extremes, chromatic third relations, or several forms of double tonality. These specific types of ambiguity will be explored later in greater detail. Meanwhile, a brief introduction to Wolf's use of harmonic ambiguity as a general principle of formal design will be offered.

The term "ambiguity principle" will be used to denote the following compositional procedure: a song begins with some form of musical ambiguity or confusion; over time, the ambiguity is resolved with appropriate musical clarification. The term "ambiguity" is used in its broadest possible sense to mean lack of clarity. In this way, "ambiguity" can be identified with psychological dissonance, and the complementary term "clarification" can be identified with psychological consonance. While the creation of psychological dissonance and its resolution into psychological consonance are basic to many forms of art, the principle of ambiguity offered here will predominantly focus upon harmonic and tonal ambiguity. The former occurs when the function of a given chord is unclear or ambivalent; and the latter occurs when the tonal orientation of a given segment of music is somehow undefined or indeterminate. The "clarification" of such harmonic or tonal ambiguity, then, involves a precise articulation of harmonic function or tonal focus.

The creation and resolution of tonal or harmonic ambiguity is certainly not a phenomenon first seen in the songs of Wolf: tonal or harmonic ambiguity was created and resolved in a variety of ways in the music of many of Wolf's predecessors. The very act of modulation outside a given tonality, for instance, creates a dissonant polarity or conflict that ultimately requires resolution with a clear return to the original tonic.[11] Charles Rosen and Donald Tovey, among other scholars, have described in great detail the unusual harmonic relations used to create harmonic or tonal dissonance in the music of Haydn, Mozart, Beethoven, Schubert, Schumann, and Brahms.[12]

Wolf's exploitation of tonal ambiguity thus belongs within a rich tradition. In extending that tradition to a new level, Wolf created musical tension that paralleled to a remarkable extent the conflicts of his texts. Indeed, in some cases, Wolf's harmonic ambiguities can be considered musical analogs to poetic metaphors or dramatic conflicts. In this sense, the establishment and resolution of ambiguity is an expansion or a replacement of traditional common-practice formal schemes that used the tonic-dominant polarity, I-V-I, to express the dramatic rhythm of tension and resolution. In the chapters that follow, the use of ambiguity as a formal principle will not only exemplify Wolf's fidelity to the text but will demonstrate Wolf's innovation in the area of musical form.

Two Special Characteristics of Wolf's Harmonic Language: Double Tonality and Harmonic Substitution

The remainder of this chapter will focus upon two special features of Wolf's tonal expansion. The first involves Wolf's innovative concept of tonality which accommodates more than one tonal focus, here called "double tonality." The second involves an inventive manipulation of harmonic function which traditionally has been called "harmonic substitution." Both of these features are intimately related to text depiction and both have become hallmarks of Wolf's musical language.

Double Tonality

As used in this study, the term "double tonality" refers to any musical situation where two different tonalities potentially function as governing "tonic." One type of double tonality, directional tonality, will be explored in detail in chapter 4. A different type, one that occurs in various musical contexts, involves a complex formal design in which the traditional common-practice polarity of two closely related harmonies is replaced by a tension between two opposing and remotely related tonalities. The Wolf song, "In dem Schatten meiner Locken," exemplifies this latter type. In that song, Wolf's desire to capture the tensions between the two lovers is depicted through a conflict between the tonic, B♭ major, and an opposing tonality, D major. While D major may be understood as III♯ in B♭,[13] the relationship of B♭ to D is not I to III♯, but rather is one of two different keys which function at different times as the tonic. In this case, the key of D major does not simply create a polarity to the tonic, B♭ major, but threatens to usurp B♭'s role as tonic altogether. The resulting tonal ambiguity conveys the tension and ambivalence surrounding the two lovers; aural confusion as to the function of D major within a song seemingly in B♭ major lingers on even after the song's conclusion. A more extensive interpretation of this song is presented in chapter 3.

Harmonic Substitution

In addition to exploring large-scale harmonic and/or tonal ambiguity (including the use of double tonality), Wolf exploits small-scale or local harmonic ambiguity in the form of harmonic substitution. Harmonic substitution occurs when an anticipated harmony is replaced by a different, but closely related, harmony. One expects the original harmony because of the norm of harmonic syntax; the substituting harmony is accepted despite the use of an alternate harmonic entity because the original harmonic function is still maintained. The use of closely related chords as harmonic substitutes is a crucial feature of this phenomenon: in order for one chord to substitute for another, there must be at least one and preferably two common tones. The often-used term "third substitution" is, in effect, a synonym for the term harmonic substitution.

   Whereas no comprehensive study of harmonic substitution exists to this date, there has been some theoretical discourse on the subject. Harmonic substitution is related to the traditional restriction of harmonic function to three main chords: the tonic, subdominant, and dominant. This framework of harmonic relations began with the writings of Rameau and was more fully developed in the theories of Riemann.[14] Riemann's theoretical system is itself predicated on harmonic substitution in that his various chord derivations

(Scheinkonsonanten, Parallelklänge, and *Leittonwechselklänge)* are based on the idea that a derived chord is in some sense a substitute for one of the three main harmonic functions.[15] Whereas some of Riemann's chord derivations may seem prompted by theoretical rather than actual musical concerns, others are convincing in their roles as secondary substitutes for primary harmonic functions: e.g., II as a *Parallelklang* to IV can substitute for the subdominant (see chapter 2, "The Plagal Domain").

The notion of primary and secondary harmonies is echoed in later theoretical works. In Louis and Thuille's *Harmonielehre* of 1906, the authors reiterate Riemann's position and illustrate musically the substitution of II for IV, III for V, and VI for I.[16] Louis and Thuille's discussion is invaluable; the authors interpret these substitutions and demonstrate how theoretical substitutions do, in fact, create unusual musical structures in late-nineteenth-century compositions.

Although the use of harmonic substitution varies extensively, two general types of harmonic substitution can be identified: (1) simple substitution of the basic harmonic functions, I, IV, or V; and (2) substitution within the deceptive cadence. The second type can be further subdivided into several subcategories that range from the traditional common-practice deceptive cadence to several innovative, chromatic deceptive cadences of the later nineteenth century. The various types of this category are distinguished by the extent of tonal clarity that is maintained during harmonic substitution.

The most common example of the first category is the aforementioned use of II or VI—or a chord of mixture, ♭II, IV♭, or ♭VI—in the subdominant's role of dominant preparation. Here the function is clear, but the harmonic representation of that function is variable. See example 1-1. The equally common but potentially more disruptive second category, the deceptive cadence, occurs traditionally with VI substituting for I. This is an altogether different type of harmonic substitution because the substitution denies the anticipated harmonic resolution. Rather than closure, the substitute chord causes cadential interruption. See example 1-2.

Ex. 1-1. Simple Harmonic Substitution

I   II7   V
         for

         IV

Ex. 1-2. Harmonic Substitution within the Deceptive Cadence

I   V   VI for I

Wolf uses both basic categories of harmonic substitution in the well-known Mörike song, "Das verlassene Mägdlein." The song demonstrates the deceptive cadence in m. 9, where the F-A-C-E sonority can be understood as either a tonic with added sixth or a tonic substitute, VI, with added seventh. The listener hears a resolution of the preceding V, but the resolution is ambiguous. In this instance, the deceptive cadence becomes a more complex phenomenon: the case for hearing an embellished tonic is undermined by the fact that the embellishing chord sounds like the traditional substitute chord, VI, with its own embellishment. As the text translation below suggests, this ambiguity is altogether in keeping with the confusions of awakening at dawn after a difficult night.[17] This unusual deceptive cadence recurs in m. 42, and

Text to "Das verlassene Mägdlein"
[Mörike, 24 March 1888]

Früh, wann die Hähne krähn,	Early, when the cocks crow
Eh' die Sternlein schwinden,	Before the stars fade away,
Muss ich am Herde stehn,	I must stand before the hearth,
Muss Feuer zünden.	I must kindle the fire.
Schön ist der Flammen Schein,	Beautiful is the light of the flames,
Es springen die Funken;	The sparks leap about;
Ich schaue so darein,	I gaze into it,
In Leid versunken.	Engulfed in sorrow.
Plötzlich, da kommt es mir,	Suddenly, it comes to me,
Treuloser Knabe,	Faithless boy,
Dass ich die Nacht	That all night
Von dir geträumet habe.	I dreamed of you.
Träne auf Träne dann	Tear upon tear then
Stürzet hernieder	Tumbles down;
So kommt der Tag heran	So begins the day
O ging' er wieder!	Oh, would it go back!

the ambiguity of function, I or VI, is finally resolved, first in the vocal line of m. 46 and then in an echo of that gesture in the RH piano part of m. 47, where F resolves down to E and the song ends on the first and only clear tonic chord.

An example of simple harmonic substitution occurs in mm. 14, 16, and 18, where the C$\sharp^4_2$ chord appears as a substitute for V of A major.[18] Here the function of V is understood even as the precise meaning of the substitute chord is enigmatic. In addition to being a chord of harmonic substitution, the C$\sharp^4_2$ chord also depicts a specific textual element and generates much of the piece that follows. Both the registral shifts of the section beginning at m. 13 and the dense voicing of the C$\sharp^4_2$ chord (in addition to the analogous augmented triads that follow later) depict the flames of the early morning fire and the awakening consciousness of the young girl. The C$\sharp^4_2$ chord thus helps to signal the emergence of the central issue in the text—the dream of the faithless lover—and the ambiguous substitution chord, in addition to the mere fact of substitution, initiates a shift from tentative early-morning music to intense, chromatic recollection music.

As mentioned earlier, there are several chromatic variants of the deceptive cadence. In one variant, an expected resolution of V occurs with a substitute chromatic chord that leads out of the given tonality, either briefly or for a lengthy period of time. In this case, a deceptive cadence might lead into a prolongation of a region such as ♭VI, which in a major mode piece forms a chromatic third relation with the tonic. See example 1-3. The third relations that result from this type of substitution will be explored in detail in chapter 3, Third Relations.

Ex. 1-3. Deceptive Cadence Using a Chromatic Third Relation

A special type within this category of harmonic substitution results from a chromatically altered deceptive cadence where the shift away from the tonic creates tonal ambiguity. An example of a Wolf song from the *Spanischesliederbuch* collection, "Führ' mich, Kind," illustrates this dramatic type of substitution. The song opens with a simple harmonic progression (I-IV-II) in A major, which creates the expectation of V, E major, in m. 4. Wolf substitutes a C♯ major triad for the E major dominant and the song shifts tonal focus to the relative minor, F♯. The C♯ major triad of m. 4 is reinterpreted as V of F♯, the tonal shift being reinforced by the half cadences (in F♯) of mm. 8-9. The ensuing section, mm. 10-14, prolongs F♯ minor and the transitional bars 15-17 lead back to V of A and a reprise of the opening nine measures. The remarkable effect of the harmonic substitution is that while the dominant function remains constant, the tonality changes: the listener expects V and the C♯ chord is heard as V, but V of a new key. The substitute chord thus undermines the opening tonality and establishes a tonal ambiguity that continues until the song's final cadence in A major. This is, of course, related to the text, which is as follows:

Text to "Führ' mich, Kind"
[*Spanischeslieder*, 15 December 1889]

Führ' mich, Kind, nach Bethlehem!
Dich, mein Gott, dich will ich sehn.
Wem geläng' es, wem,
Ohne dich zu dir zu gehn!

Rüttle mich, dass ich erwache,
Rufe mich, so will ich schreiten;
Gib die Hand mir, mich zu leiten,
Dass ich auf den Weg mich mache.

Dass ich schaue Bethlehem,
Dorten meinen Gott zu sehn.
Wem geläng' es, wem,
Ohne dich zu dir zu gehn!

Von der Sünde schwerem Kranken
Bin ich träg und dumpf beklommen.
Willst du nicht zu Hülfe kommen,
Muss ich straucheln, muss ich schwanken.

Leite mich nach Bethlehem,
Dich, mein Gott, dich will ich sehn.
Wem geläng' es, wem,
Ohne dich zu dir zu gehn!

Lead me, Child, to Bethlehem!
You, my God, you do I wish to see.
Who could succeed, who
Without you to come to you!

Shake me, that I may awaken,
Call me, so I will set forth;
Give me your hand to lead me
That I may start on my way.

That I may behold Bethlehem,
There my God to see.
Who could succeed, who
Without you to come to you!

From sin's heavy sickness
Am I weighted and oppressed.
If you will not come to my aid,
Then must I stumble, must I waver.

Lead me to Bethlehem,
You, my God, you must I see.
Who will succeed, who
Without you to come to you!

The singer pleads for salvation; without God's help, the sinner cannot be saved. Notice that the pivotal chord C♯ is associated with several words that refer to the Lord: "Gott" (mm. 4, 21, 38); "wem" (which refers to God; mm. 5, 6, 22, 23, 39, 40); and "zu gehn" (meaning to reach God; mm. 8 and 25). Note as well that the phrase "gib die Hand mir" is on a C♯ dominant pedal and that the final phrase "zu dir zu gehn" ends not on C♯ as V but on A as I. The key of A major becomes the key of salvation, while the key of F♯ minor functions as the key of earthly struggle. The spiritual being who can lead from earthly sin to eternal salvation is symbolized by the pivot chord, C♯, whose function is initially a substitute for V.

As will be seen in later chapters, harmonic substitution occurs in Wolf's music for a number of reasons. It is sometimes present to create variety or ambiguity, while at other times it occurs to weaken or obscure a particular tonal or harmonic relationship. In all cases, no matter how closely or remotely the substitute is related to the expected harmony, the meaning of the original harmonic function still remains.

Conclusion

In addition to presenting the analytical methodology for this study, chapter 1 has attempted to suggest the extraordinary influence of the poetic text upon both the form and the musical language of Wolf's songs. While we cannot be precise about how much influence the poetry had in shaping the song, we cannot overstate the impact of Wolf's preoccupation with text depiction.

In our introductory forays into particular features of Wolf's musical language, the most important musical idea to emerge was Wolf's exploitation of musical ambiguity, either of tonal focus or of harmonic function. Wolf's use of musical ambiguity is pervasive, and with it he captures both poetic subtleties and dramatic confrontations. This study thus concerns itself as much about the impact of poetic depiction as about extension of common-practice tonality, and our analyses often will suggest that a particular harmonic innovation resulted not so much from a desire to expand the tonal system as from a need to express something in the poetic text.

Das verlassene Mägdlein
(The forsaken maiden)

Führ' mich, Kind, nach Bethlehem!
(Lead me, child, to Bethlehem!)

Ziemlich langsam

Führ' mich, Kind, nach Beth - - le -
Lead me, child, to Beth - - le -

3.

hem! dich, mein Gott, dich will ich sehn. Wem ge-
hem! Thee, my God, I long, to see. Come, sweet

6.

läng' es, wem, oh - ne dich zu dir — zu — gehn!
Sa - viour, come! lead thy serv - - ant un - to — Thee!

9.

Rütt - le mich, dass ich er - wa - che,
Wak - en me, lest sleep ensnare me,

12.

ru - fe mich, so will ich schrei - ten; gib die Hand mir,
call me, Lord, and do thou speed me, guard my foot-steps,

15.

mich zu lei - ten, dass ich auf den Weg___ mich ma - che.
Sa - viour, lead__ me, I would for the way_____ pre - pare me.

18.

Dass ich schau - e Beth - le - hem, dor - ten
Lead me on to Beth - le - hem, where my

34. muss ich strau - cheln, muss ich schwanken. Lei - te
lest I falt - er, grant sal - va - tion! Lead me

37. mich nach Beth - le - hem, dich, mein Gott, dich will ich
on to Beth - le - hem! Thee, my God, I long to

40. sehn. Wem ge - läng' es, wem, oh - ne dich zu
see. Come, sweet Sa - viour, come! let thy serv - ant

43. dir zu gehn!_____
wor - ship thee!_____

2

The Plagal Domain

This chapter will explore the expansion of the tonal system through an extended use of the subdominant, signified by the term "plagal domain." "Plagal domain" denotes both the subdominant harmony and a complex network of harmonic relationships which involve the subdominant and which transcend the traditional common-practice subdominant function.

During the eighteenth and early nineteenth centuries, the subdominant functioned as a subsidiary harmony within the powerful tonic-dominant axis. For the most part, it was either a preparation for the dominant or a neighboring harmony that prolonged the tonic; in both cases, it embellished harmonies that were structurally more important (see example 2-1). In the later nineteenth century, the subdominant acquired new functions and assumed more autonomous structural roles. Along with the change in status for the subdominant came a reassessment of the dominant and even of the tonic functions. Thus the development of the plagal domain is part of a larger nineteenth-century expansion upon several aspects of the tonal system.

Ex. 2-1. Common-Practice Functions of IV

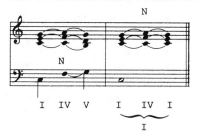

Historical Context for the Plagal Domain

Throughout the eighteenth and early nineteenth centuries, theorists offered a broad view of the subdominant. When, in 1726, Rameau bestowed upon the fourth scale step the name "sous dominant," he considered the subdominant to be co-equal with the dominant (he called V the "dominant-tonic"), the two "dominants" serving as harmonic pillars a fifth above and below the tonic.[1] Although Rameau conceded that the so-called irregular plagal cadence was subsidiary to the authentic dominant cadence, and although he was never able to offer adequate acoustical proof of the origin of the subdominant—a requirement that he deemed essential—he nevertheless maintained that the subdominant was a harmonic fact and that the harmonic system was a symmetrical one, with IV and V framing I. See example 2-2.[2]

Ex. 2-2. Rameau's Concept of Harmonic Function

The important theoretical status of the subdominant was sustained in the writings of such eighteenth-century theorists as Sorge (*Vorgemach der musikalischen Komposition*, 1745), Marpurg (*Handbuch bei dem Generalbasse*, 1755-58), and Kirnberger (*Die Kunst des reinen Satzes*, 1771-79). In the writings of such nineteenth-century theorists as Hauptmann and Riemann, the subdominant continued to be one of the three main chords of the tonal system, even though both theorists modified Rameau's various ideas about the source of the subdominant by invoking more contemporary theories. Hauptmann *(Natur der Harmonik und der Metrik*, 1888) related the subdominant, dominant, and tonic through the Hegelian dialectic: the triad "comes into opposition or contradiction with itself" by virtue of being in a "fifth duality" with its dominants: I is IV of V and V of IV; through this opposition the tonic triad reemerges as a unity or synthesis.[3] Meanwhile, in *Die Natur der Harmonik* of 1882 and *Vereinfachte Harmonielehre* of 1893, Riemann offered a basis for the subdominant through an analog to the overtone series which he called the undertone series, and which he claimed had acoustical validity.

The continuous insistence on an equivalent status between the subdominant and dominant reflected the speculative nature of most eighteenth- and nineteenth-century theoretical discourse. In musical practice, however, the subdominant never functioned in a manner that was correlative to the dominant. This discrepancy between theory and practice was finally noted and dramatized in Schenker's theories where, in contrast to the speculation of his predecessors, Schenker demonstrated that in most common-practice tonal music, the subdominant maintained a subsidiary status to the more structurally important dominant. Schenker's opposition to the traditional view of the subdominant is persuasive: he shows that for almost two centuries theoretical speculation about the function of the subdominant was misguided, and that the subdominant fulfilled a much more limited function than earlier theorists had suggested.

Schenker's view of the subdominant could well have been a refutation of the earlier theories of Rameau and Riemann were it not for a problem inherent in his theoretical system. Where earlier theorists had perhaps too expansive a view of the subdominant, Schenker seems to have had one that remained too narrow. Schenker's preoccupation with refining his complex analytical system seems to have prevented his consideration of nineteenth-century harmonic innovation; and at the time of his death many issues of contemporary practice unfortunately remained unexplored. Thus, while Schenker's analytical system accurately represents the limited function of the subdominant in most common-practice music, his system becomes less useful for depicting later nineteenth-century music.[4]

Wolf's Expansion of the Subdominant

In the discussion that follows, it will be shown that Wolf's expansion of the subdominant reflects the earlier, eighteenth-century view of a more structurally important subdominant. Wolf's innovative exploration of a new harmonic language within the plagal domain is best described as tentative. He tries to use plagal harmonies in new ways, but he does so in a relatively small number of songs. In most cases, Wolf's use of the plagal domain can be considered an enrichment of existing harmonic relations rather than an assertion of altogether new harmonic principles.

For the most part, Schenkerian analysis satisfactorily accommodates the expanded use of a traditionally limited subdominant function. However, when some of Wolf's harmonic innovations extend far beyond common-practice tonality (as in his use of dominant replacement), these new structures will prove incompatible with Schenkerian analysis, and modified Schenkerian or alternative non-Schenkerian readings will be offered instead.

Special Characteristics of the Plagal Domain

As figure 2-1 shows, the plagal domain encompasses two different types of harmonic procedures, one that remains within and another that extends beyond common-practice tonality. The exploration of certain types of ambiguity within the common-practice tonal system will be called plagal ambiguity; the innovative use of plagal harmonies to function as substitutions for the tonic-dominant axis will be called dominant replacement. In general, dominant replacement represents a radical departure from common-practice tonal syntax, while plagal ambiguity exemplifies a subtler expansion of

Fig. 2-1. The Plagal Domain

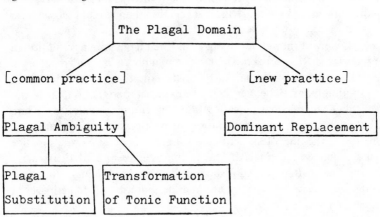

normative syntax—one which seems to retain at least some common-practice functions.

Plagal Ambiguity

The term plagal ambiguity denotes special and unique ambiguities inherent within the plagal domain. There are two basic types: (1) harmonic substitution amongst plagal elements, and (2) transformation of tonic function.

Harmonic substitution. On a simple level, harmonic substitution occurs within the plagal domain because a variety of chords can assume the subdominant function. Where no chord could adequately substitute for the common-practice dominant in its various cadential functions, II, ♭II, VI, and ♭VI can all assume many of the functions of IV.[5] The possibility of harmonic substitution—stemming from the common-practice use of II for IV as dominant preparation—leads to a broader definition of harmonic terms where II, IV, and VI (and their minor counterparts) are not necessarily separate chords but function as interchangeable parts of one harmonic function. The subdominant function becomes enlarged to include the deceptive cadence, and (through extension by the interrelationships within the plagal domain) becomes a more persuasive tonal element. The ultimate consequence of this subdominant enlargement is that the subdominant emerges as a tonal force that can compete with and eventually replace the dominant as a primary polarity to the tonic.

Two examples of subdominant expansion into the realm of the deceptive cadence will illustrate clearly that simple form of harmonic substitution. The first example occurs in the *Italienschesliederbuch* song "Gesegnet sei das

Grün" (13 April 1896). The opening (example 2-3) depicts a progression I-V⁷/VI-IV-V⁷-VI, where the deceptive cadence is extended by an interpolation of IV-V (m. 2). This interpolation in m. 2 suggests that IV is substituting for VI

Ex. 2-3. "Gesegnet sei das Grün": Harmonic Substitution

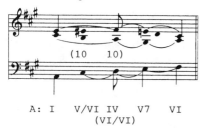

in resolving V⁷/VI of m. 1. This substitution recurs in mm. 3-4 (V/VI-IV⁶) and becomes intensified in mm. 5-6, where IV⁶ literally replaces VI twice in deceptive cadences. A second example (example 2-4) shows a similar use of IV for VI in the Mörike song "Schlafendes Jesuskind" (6 October 1888). In the piano part of mm. 6 and 28, IV functions clearly as if it were the customary VI within a deceptive cadence.

Ex. 2-4. "Schlafendes Jesuskind": Harmonic Substitution

Transformation of tonic function. As a second resource, the plagal domain offers a form of plagal ambiguity that will be called "transformation of tonic function." This transformation occurs when the tonic becomes the dominant of IV and a I-IV progression is transformed—with the addition of a single pitch—into a V⁷-to-I progression. The ambiguity that results from this transformation is especially powerful in that it not only creates harmonic ambiguity but also reverses the nature of harmonic motion from an opening to a closing progression. This will have important structural implications when, for instance, closure comes more quickly than originally anticipated or tonal shifts occur unexpectedly.

An example of the transformation of tonic function occurs within mm. 6-10 of the song "Wir haben beide lange Zeit geschwiegen" from the *Italienischesliederbuch* (16 December 1891). In a general sense, this song demonstrates the ambiguity principle defined in chapter 1, and the transformation of tonic function may be considered a component of that larger process. An analysis of the introductory first five measures of this song will be presented in chapter 5. For the present, suffice it to say that in m. 5 the passage concludes on an A♭ dominant seventh chord which strongly suggests a resolution to D♭ in m. 6 (example 2-5). A new section in D♭ begins in m. 6 with a simple harmonic progression I-IV⁶-II⁶-V⁷-I set above a double pedal on A♭ and D♭. While the harmonic progression and the D♭ pedal both clearly establish the tonality of D♭, the A♭ pedal creates harmonic ambiguity as the D♭ sonority is cast into a dissonant $\frac{6}{4}$ position. The replacement of the double A♭-D♭ pedal by a single D♭ pedal in mm. 8-9 signals the beginning of the transformation: the function of D♭ changes from a tonic in m. 8 to a V/IV in m. 9 which resolves to IV in m. 10.

Ex. 2-5. "Wir haben beide": Transformation of Tonic Function

The functional transformation of D♭ from I to V/IV can be understood on two levels. On a foreground level, mm. 6-7 contain simple I-IV⁶-II⁶-V⁷-I progressions in D♭ and m. 8 presents a I-V⁷/IV progression in D♭. With the resolution of V⁷/IV in m. 9, the simple secondary dominant becomes part of a tonal shift, as what was IV is really a cadential V_4^6 (with added ninth) that progresses to V⁷-I in the new key of G♭ major. Through a secondary dominant, the progression I to IV is transformed; the tonic is reinterpreted as V/IV in a new key. On a middleground level, mm. 6-10 can be understood as a large-scale

V-I progression in G♭. What appeared to be I/D♭ was really V/G♭. In this context, the use of the $^6_4$ position in mm. 6-8 is understood as an attempt to destabilize D♭ as tonic in order to prepare for its reinterpretation as dominant. It is an ingenious ploy, for while the $^6_4$ position renders D♭ a dissonance, it also implies a resolution to D♭, since a cadential $^6_4$ would presumably resolve to an authentic cadence in D♭. The overriding effect of the transformation is not just a shift in tonal focus from D♭ to G♭, but is also a change in the nature of the harmonic motion in mm. 6-10. Where the harmonic motion in mm. 6-8 had appeared to be that of an opening gesture, I-IV, the shift in function of D♭ transforms the gesture into a closing progression, V-I.

The text of "Wir haben beide" supports the use of the transformation technique. The text of mm. 6-10 states: "Die Engel, die herab vom Himmel fliegen,/Sie brachten nach dem Krieg den Frieden wieder." The music depicts the flight of angels to earth, bringing peace and resolving war: the use of the $^6_4$ position suggests in part the tension between earth and heaven, and the conflict between the two potential tonics, D♭ and G♭, depicts the "war" that is resolved by the peace-giving transformation. The interrelation of D♭ and G♭ is further enhanced by the text, where phrase 3 (mm. 10-14) is a variant of phrase 2 (mm. 6-10). The textual repetition is reflected in the music where the section in G♭ is a variant of the music in D♭, the piano part of mm. 10-12 being a literal transposition of the piano part of mm. 6-8.

Text to "Wir haben beide lange Zeit geschwiegen"
[*Italienischesliederbuch*, 16 December 1891]

Wir haben beide lange Zeit geschwiegen,	We have both long been silent,
Auf einmal kam uns nun die Sprache wieder.	Suddenly speech returned to us again.
Die Engel, die herab vom Himmel fliegen,	Angels, who fly down from heaven,
Sie brachten nach dem Krieg den Frieden wieder.	Bringing peace again after war.
Die Engel Gottes sind herabgeflogen,	God's angels have flown down
Mit ihnen ist der Frieden eingezogen.	Bringing with them peace.
Die Liebesengel kamen über Nacht	The angels of love came by night
Und haben Frieden meiner Brust gebracht.	And have brought peace to my breast.

The foregoing example demonstrates how the transformation of tonic function creates a form of dissonance unparalleled in the dominant region. The power of the subdominant to destabilize the tonic is as remarkable as the ability of the dominant to reinforce the tonic. Also, the transformation of function affects not only the subdominant and tonic harmonies, but the entire harmonic progression as well.

Dominant Replacement

Dominant replacement is a logical late-nineteenth-century step within the continuum of tonal expansion. The evolution of the tonal system had reached a plateau wherein the tonic-dominant axis was too commonplace: a stasis had occurred in the use of the now too-predictable tonic-dominant axis, and alternative cadence patterns and structural designs were needed. As is the case in any form of harmonic substitution, the use of the subdominant for the dominant is predicated upon some retention of the traditional dominant function. The success of dominant replacement depends, therefore, upon the ability of the plagal domain to provide a plagal analog for the dominant—to replace the tonic-dominant axis with what will be called a "plagal axis."

Before examining the nature of dominant replacement, let us review what is being replaced (i.e., the normative function of the dominant within the common-practical tonal system). Schenker offers a norm of dominant function in his model of the *Ursatz* and within his concept of structural levels. According to Schenker, the dominant functions on three levels. On the foreground level, the dominant divides music into discrete sections through half and authentic cadences. Within these cadences, the dominant also establishes either itself or the tonic as a local harmonic goal. On a middleground level—the large-scale I-V-I of the *Ursatz*—the dominant functions both as a harmonic goal and as a basic harmonic polarity to the opening and closing tonics. In addition, the dominant also offers crucial harmonic support for the primary melodic step $\hat{2}$ in the *Urlinie*. Lastly, on the deepest—or background—level, the dominant itself becomes subsumed by the tonic—it ceases to be an independent harmony and becomes instead a *Teiler*, or "divider," within the arpeggiation of the tonic chord.[6] The dominant functions, then, to define the tonic, to affirm the tonic on a local and large-scale level through authentic cadences or tonal polarity. The dominant also articulates the tonic—on the deepest and most abstract level—by participating in a horizontalization of the tonic triad through the *Bassbrechung*. Finally, the dominant provides a crucial counterpoint to the primary melodic motion, the *Urlinie* descent $\hat{2}$-$\hat{1}$.

Dominant replacement on the foreground. Dominant replacement can occur on the three different structural levels. On the foreground level, it occurs mostly in the substitution of the plagal for the authentic cadence. In historical terms, such a replacement has been noted for centuries; Rameau and his colleagues called the use of IV-I for V-I an "irregular" cadence and later theorists named the IV-I cadence "plagal." The early acknowledgment of the existence of a plagal cadence did not, however, signify that the plagal cadence was an actual substitute for the authentic cadence. In eighteenth- and early-nineteenth-century music, the plagal cadence rarely replaced the function of its authentic counterpart, but instead acted as a cadential afterthought or harmonic postlude. In these cases, the cadential subdominant could be considered an extension of the tonic rather than a replacement of the dominant, a use of the plagal cadence that might be considered a first step toward a later dominant replacement.[7] While this tonic prolongation through the plagal cadence neither replaced nor contradicted the tonic-dominant axis, the new role for IV did enlarge the subdominant function.

The lack of much dominant replacement on the foreground level is due to the problematic nature of such replacement, as is illustrated by a song from Wolf's Mörike collection, "Gesang Weylas" (9 October 1888). Example 2-6 shows how the song opens with the progression I-V-IV-I. This reversal of common-practice syntax suggests that the authentic cadence is either replaced by the plagal cadence or at least extended by the subdominant.[8] Several

Ex. 2-6. "Gesang Weylas": Dominant Replacement on the Foreground Level

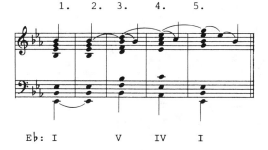

questions arise: Is the V of m. 3 a functional dominant or does it assume the dominant preparation role normally associated with the subdominant, the V becoming a contrapuntal harmony leading to the cadential IV-I of mm. 4-5? If V is structural, then what is the function of IV in m. 4? A Schenkerian response to these questions might be similar to the sketch of example 2-7. Here the tonic-

Ex. 2-7. "Gesang Weylas": Schenkerian Reading

dominant axis is preserved with the V remaining a structural goal. The IV of m. 4 is heard as a neighboring harmony to the tonic that expands the authentic cadence by prolonging the tonic.

In contrast to example 2-7, example 2-8 reverses this "Schenkerian" interpretation, making IV a dominant replacement and V either a subdominant replacement or a separate cadential function altogether. In example 2-8a, V becomes a contrapuntal embellishment (N) to the cadential IV; and in example 2-8b, V is a half cadence that yields to a plagal rather than to an authentic cadence. The readings in example 2-8a and example 2-8b pose a series of cumulative questions: If IV does replace V, is the plagal cadence an adequate, analogous replacement for V, or does IV offer a different type of cadence? If the plagal cadence is not analogous, is this different cadence less a replacement and more an alternative to the authentic cadence? Finally, if the plagal cadence is not simply a replacement but is a different sort of cadence, is this alternative to the authentic cadence less powerful?[9]

Ex. 2-8. "Gesang Weylas": Non-Schenkerian Interpretation

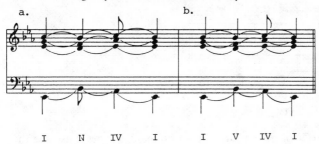

Some of the answers to the questions just raised are subjective. Wolf's own interpretation of this structure might be gleaned from the song's final phrase, mm. 14-17, which is illustrated in example 2-9. Wolf reverses the earlier syntax

Ex. 2-9. "Gesang Weylas": Traditional Harmonic Syntax, Last Phrase

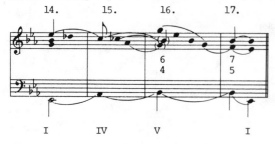

in this last phrase, placing IV and V in their more traditional roles. This suggests that in the opening gesture (mm. 1-5), a plagal cadence replaces the authentic because a strong cadence is not necessary—or maybe not even desirable. The cadence does close the phrase with a decrease in tension, but at the same time it creates a tonal diffuseness or ambiguity that urges the piece ahead. The plagal confusion is then amplified in the measures that follow, with such non-E♭ sonorities as G major, D major, and A minor. The resumption of normal syntax at the song's end can be understood in the same terms: the close of a piece requires a stronger cadence and more decisive tonal assertion; hence, the final cadence in example 2-9 is authentic, not plagal.

Voice-leading problems in the plagal cadence. The basic problem in foreground dominant replacement is that the plagal cadence is indeed weaker than the authentic—the subdominant does not define the tonic as strongly or precisely as does the dominant. The voice-leading problems that create a weak plagal cadence are demonstrated in example 2-10, which compares the voice leading in authentic and plagal cadences.

Example 2-10a shows the most powerful voice-leading possibilities for the authentic cadence, using only root position triads and no seventh chords: example 2-10a(1), shows the strong leading-tone resolution, $\hat{7}$ to $\hat{8}$, being supported by the V-I progression; example 2-10a(2) shows Schenker's *Urlinie* descent with dominant support; and example 2-10a(3), which combines the first and second, shows the full effect of combining all the voice-leading possibilities into one melodic/harmonic event. In all three cases, $\hat{1}$ is approached by step in a conclusive, tonic-defining melodic gesture.

Ex. 2-10a and b.   Voice Leading in Plagal and Authentic Cadences

In comparison to example 2-10a, the voice-leading possibilities for a plagal cadence are shown in example 2-10b. Rather than focusing upon $\hat{1}$, the melodic gestures embellish either $\hat{3}$ or $\hat{5}$ of the tonic triad, a factor that certainly supports the notion of a less definitive cadence. Further, when plagal half-step melodic gestures ($\hat{3}$-$\hat{4}$-$\hat{3}$ and $\hat{5}$-♭$\hat{6}$-$\hat{5}$) are compared to the authentic half step ($\hat{7}$-$\hat{8}$), the plagal voice leading is less conclusive. The melodic line could still descend further (from $\hat{3}$ or $\hat{5}$ to $\hat{1}$) and this ultimate conclusion would entail a passage through $\hat{2}$, which, of course, is supported by V.[10] Finally, example 2-10c uses seventh chords and harmonic inversion within a mixture of plagal and authentic voice-leading possibilities. Several new issues arise. First, both the V^7 and the II_5^6 allow for greater melodic dissonance, where $\hat{4}$ is a dissonant seventh in the

$$\hat{4}\text{-}\hat{3}$$
$$V^7\text{-}I$$

and $\hat{1}$ is a dissonant seventh in the

$$\hat{2}\text{-}\hat{1}$$
$$II_5^6\text{-}I\,.$$

Ex. 2-10c. Voice Leading in Plagal and Authentic Cadences (cont.)

The dissonance of the $\hat{4}$ in the V^7 chord reinforces the resolution of V to I, not so much by the melodic resolution of $\hat{4}\text{-}\hat{3}$, as by the tritone-enhanced resolution of $\hat{7}\text{-}\hat{8}$. In an even more dramatic way, the dissonant seventh of the II_5^6 (the seventh is $\hat{1}$) reinforces an authentic, not plagal resolution (see (3) of example 2-10c). This resolution (tenor voice, c to b) suggests a progression to the dominant, a use of V that was elided in example 2-10c(2). Example 2-10c(2) is a crucial step toward dominant replacement, for the only instance of plagal support for $\hat{2}\text{-}\hat{1}$ occurs with harmonic substitution, where II_5^6 substitutes for IV and where harmonic elision occurs, as the implied resolution of II to V is omitted.

A comparison of voice leading in plagal and authentic cadences may be summarized as follows: the plagal cadence is weaker because it does not confirm $\hat{1}$ in a strong, unequivocal stepwise motion; the plagal stepwise motion $\hat{4}\text{-}\hat{3}$ or $(\flat)\,\hat{6}\text{-}\hat{5}$ remains inconclusive (will a $\hat{2}\text{-}\hat{1}$ motion follow?) in comparison to the authentic half step $\hat{7}\text{-}\hat{8}$; the use of a plagal $\hat{4}\text{-}\hat{3}$ in a V^7-I cadence is not in itself a powerful cadential gesture, but rather reinforces the more definitive $\hat{7}$-$\hat{8}$ motion with which it resolves; and finally, the only feasible $\hat{2}$-$\hat{1}$ in a plagal cadence involves an elision of an authentic cadence (II^6_5-I for II^6_5-V^7-I), even though elision by definition makes that plagal cadence weaker and less conclusive.

It is clear, then, that a replacement of the cadential dominant is problematic and that the successful substitution of a plagal for an authentic cadence can only be accomplished with some sort of "compensation" for the inherent weakness of the plagal cadence. The necessity for such compensation within dominant replacement will be an ongoing concern throughout the rest of this chapter.

Dominant replacement on the middleground. The problem of a weak foreground authentic cadence translates on the middleground into a weak plagal axis, where a large-scale I-IV-I replaces the common-practice I-V-I. In this case, the relative weakness of the plagal axis threatens to obviate a clear tonal focus and, as well, undermines the formation of a self-contained, coherent tonal structure. Further, the power of the tonic-dominant axis as the middleground fulcrum of most common-practice music occurs partly because on the background level the dominant relates to the tonic within the *Bassbrechung.*[11] This crucial interpenetration of structural levels cannot occur analogously with the plagal axis, since no single tonal sonority emerges on a background level.

The lack of a cohesive background in music based on a plagal axis is a critical problem for a composer, who must compensate for such a middleground plagal structure. The following analysis will demonstrate how several repetitive devices counterbalance a weak plagal middleground, including the use of *foreground* authentic cadences.

Many of the issues involved in creating a plagal middleground are observed in the *Italienischesliederbuch* song "Sterb' ich so hüllt in Blumen meine Glieder" (13 April 1896). The compensatory techniques are so persistent and thorough that the middleground motion to the subdominant is almost elusive. As example 2-11 shows, Wolf's compensation involves two repetition devices: a two-bar piano ostinato and a bass pedal. The ostinato is continuous; it remains basically unchanged, except for a registral shift in mm. 6ff. and a transposition in mm. 10-13. Two factors preserve the vitality of the ostinato. First, the vocal line functions as a constantly changing set of variations above the repeated ostinato phrase. Second, the ostinato itself contains harmonic ambiguity (enhanced by the vocal line) which continuously challenges the listener. As line A of example 2-12 suggests, a change of harmony every beat results in the harmonic progression IV-VII-I-VI-II-V-I. Meanwhile, a different interpretation of the harmonic progression is also possible (line B), where the

Ex. 2-11. "Sterb' ich": Repetition Devices

Ex. 2-12. "Sterb' ich": The Ostinato

A: IV VII I VI II V I

B: VII7 I VI V7 I

descending thirds coalesce and form larger harmonic units which are grouped into a more complicated rhythm: ♩ ♩ ♩ | ♩ ♩ . This second reading can be understood as VII[7]-I-VI-V[7]-I. The aural confusion of the ostinato is due only in part to rhythmic factors; of more consequence is Wolf's use of incomplete triads which confound the listener by making the progression so implicit that the ear must continue to seek clarification in subsequent repetitions. In example 2-13, the vocal line is added to the ostinato; instead of elucidating the harmonic progression, the vocal line increases the ambiguity by altering the ostinato: IV becomes II[6] and II becomes VII[6].

The ostinato is ingenious in maintaining a delicate balance of repetition and change, while simultaneously existing with the other cohesive element, the

Ex. 2-13. "Sterb' ich": The Ostinato and the Vocal Line

A♭ pedal. The bass pedal is remarkable in itself, since it also persists—in this case with no change whatsoever—for the song's entirety. While the bass pedal can be thought of as compensatory, the constant reaffirmation of a single bass pitch can also be considered a problematic restricting element. A shift to the dominant is simply not possible with a recurrent tonic pedal; changing the pedal, say to E♭, would change the nature of the song, as would any digression from the key of A♭. Indeed, the subdominant is the only harmonic region the pedal will permit, and even though it is impossible to know whether Wolf planned the bass pedal or the middleground subdominant first, the interrelationship of the two is inescapable.

Example 2-14 demonstrates the harmonic shift from A♭ to D♭. The pedal

Ex. 2-14. "Sterb' ich": Middleground Shift to D♭ (IV)

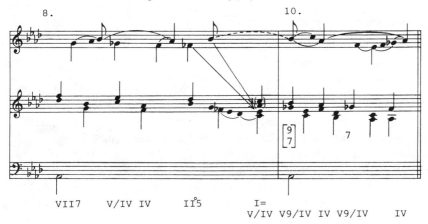

now assumes a new role: in m. 9, I/A♭ becomes V/D♭ and the tonic A♭ pedal becomes a dominant A♭ pedal. In a potently simple way, the motion to the middleground subdominant is achieved by one of the special features of the plagal domain—the transformation of tonic function in which I becomes V of IV.

A shift back to the key of A♭ occurs in mm. 13-14 (see example 2-15). In the first half of m. 13, VII⁷ of A♭ suggests a departure from D♭ with the crucial change of G♭ to G♮. When Wolf reintroduces the G♭ in the second half of m. 13, transforming D♭ into V/IV once again, he creates an elegant pun where a middleground return to I occurs through a foreground IV. This passage not only resolves the secondary dominant in m. 14 (V/IV to IV), but it also creates a smooth retransition back to the original ostinato (which begins on IV of A♭). The return to A♭ as tonic is not assured until the second beat of m. 14, where G♮ occurs as part of V/A♭. This return to A♭ is reinforced in the vocal line of m. 14, where, for the only time, Wolf places an E♭ in the vocal part above the ostinato third G/B♭. At this point in the ostinato, the voice previously had sung G♮ or D♭ and this had turned the piano's G/B♭ dyad into a form of the less stable VII chord.

Ex. 2-15. "Sterb' ich": Middleground Shift back to A♭ (I)

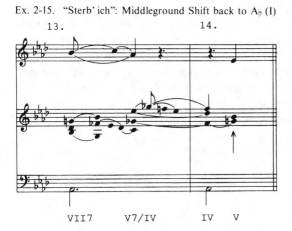

Several details in this middleground shift to the subdominant are worth noting. First, Wolf prepares for the shift to D♭ in m. 8, where he introduces V/IV on beat 3 as part of a chromatic descent in the voice. This is a wonderful example of a local detail foreshadowing a middleground event.[12] Second, Wolf accompanies the subtle shift in tonality with expressive manipulation of texture, rhythm, and chromatic density. In m. 9, the vocal line has a two-beat rest, the longest rest of the song. This silence in the voice signals a change in formal design, as it prepares for the change in tonal focus in m. 10. At the same time, the vocal line creates a transition from the $A\flat$ to the $D\flat$ region in mm. 9-10, as the vocal $B\flat$ in m. 9 has two diverse functions on the respective foreground and middleground levels. On the former level, the vocal $B\flat$ of m. 9 is resolved in the piano part in m. 9 (notated by an arrow in example 2-14), while on the middleground, the $B\flat$ remains unresolved and is restated immediately by the voice in m. 10 (notated by a dotted line). Despite its foreground resolution, the vocal $B\flat$ functions ultimately as a dissonant pivot between the regions of $A\flat$ and $D\flat$.

The piano part of m. 9 also uses silence to signal the tonal shift to $D\flat$, as the RH piano part rests for almost an entire beat. This is one of several ways that the $A\flat$ sonority of m. 9 is emphasized in anticipation of its functional transformation from I to V/IV. Another way occurs in the LH piano part, as the $A\flat$ pedal maintains its eighth-note motion on beat 4 in a telltale break with the rhythmic ostinato pattern. Wolf thus prepares the listener for the shift to $D\flat$ by reducing both the texture and most of the rhythmic motion, and by highlighting in various ways the pivotal $A\flat$ sonority.

The reduction of texture and overall complexity that occurred in mm. 9-10 is reversed with the return to $A\flat$ in m. 13. As already stated, the chromatic shifts between $G\natural$ and $G\flat$ cause both tonal ambiguity and a general tension that are only resolved with the resumption of the ostinato back in the original key of $A\flat$ (m. 14). Alternations between $F\natural/F\flat$ and $B\natural/B\flat$ also contribute to an increase of chromatic density. Finally, registral shifts in m. 13 intensify the climax of activity that leads to the return of $A\flat$. This increase in register and rhythmic activity in the RH piano is anticipated in m. 12, with the addition of a melodic fragment on the second and fourth beats; and this fragment, reintroduced in mm. 16-18, brings the song to its conclusion.

The middleground shift to the subdominant is reinforced by melodic factors. The vocal line achieves its climax within the region of $D\flat$ (m. 12), where it sings $E\flat$ on the word "gern." The melodic climax is intensified because it is set within the harmonic transformation and occurs within a dissonant context. As example 2-13 indicated earlier, the vocal line has two basic gestures, $B\flat$ to $A\flat$ and F to $E\flat$. These neighbor-note motions are reiterated throughout the first nine measures; $A\flat$ and $E\flat$ are always consonant pitches and $B\flat$ and F are always dissonant. With the shift to $D\flat$, the functions of $A\flat$ and $E\flat$ are transformed. While $A\flat$ remains consonant ($\hat{1}/A\flat \rightarrow \hat{5}/D\flat$), it is a less stable pitch, and $E\flat$ becomes the dissonant $\hat{2}/D\flat$. With the resolution $B\flat$ to $A\flat$ in m. 10, the $A\flat$ is consonant but the melodic motion is less decisive ($\hat{2}-\hat{1}\rightarrow\hat{6}-\hat{5}$). When $A\flat$ is reiterated in m. 11, it is again a resolution pitch (but one whose function is unclear) as the piano $A\flat$ shifts from I to V/$D\flat$ beneath the vocal $A\flat$. The normally consonant $E\flat$ of mm. 1-9 then becomes a poignant dissonance in m. 12, as it is now part of $V^9/D\flat$ within the transformation of $A\flat$. This last ambiguity is especially powerful because the vocal line is ending a phrase of text (along with the section in D♭) on the resolution of B♭ to A♭, which normally would be consonant. This is the only time Wolf ends a full line of text on the tonic pitch (m. 5 ends on E♭, m. 9 on B♭, and m. 17 on E♭), and he only does so because the tonal ambiguity renders the A♭ unstable.

In melodic terms, then, the recurrent gestures are interpreted in D♭ as either ambiguous, unstable, or dissonant. The climax of the song in m. 12 occurs within a general climax of melodic and harmonic tension and ambiguity, all of which is due to the use of the middleground subdominant.

The text of "Sterb' ich" offers its own rationale for a tonal shift in mm. 10 ff. The complete text may be divided into two sections: couplets 1 and 2 are set in m. 1-9 and couplets 3 and 4 are set in mm. 10-17. In couplets 1 and 2, the singer gives instructions to his beloved about his place of burial. In couplet 3, the singer begins to reflect upon the feelings of dying for love. The fourth couplet is a variant of the third, and the challenge to Wolf is that of repeating a couplet of text without merely repeating the musical setting—a challenge made all the more difficult in a song that already uses an extensive amount of musical repetition. Wolf's solution is ingenious: by placing the third couplet in D♭ he allows the fourth couplet to be a repetition of the third within the retransition back to A♭. The textual variation of couplets 3 and 4 becomes a vehicle for tonal shift: the connection between the two repetitive couplets is confirmed by the resolution of the middleground D♭ to A♭.

Text to "Sterb' ich, so hüllt in Blumen meine Glieder"
[*Italieneschesliderbuch,* 13 April 1896]

Sterb' ich, so hüllt in Blumen meine Glieder	If I die, cover my limbs with flowers;
Ich wünsche nicht, dass ihr ein Grab mir grabt.	I do not wish that you should dig me a grave.
Genüber jenen Mauern legt mich nieder,	Lay me beside that wall
Wo ihr so manchmal mich gesehen habt.	Where you have so often seen me.
Dort legt mich hin in Regen oder Wind;	There let me be laid in rain or wind;
Gern sterb' ich, ist's um dich, geliebtes Kind.	I die gladly if it is for you, beloved child.
Dort legt mich hin in Sonnenschein und Regen;	There let me be laid in sunshine and rain;
Ich sterbe lieblich, sterb' ich deinetwegen.	I die happy if I die for you.

The Plagal Axis

The use of the subdominant as a middleground harmonic goal is a most complicated phenomenon. In fact, the sketch in example 2-16 shows how the I-IV-I middleground structure might be understood as a series of embedded neighbor-note motions rather than as a large-scale harmonic progression. In

Ex. 2-16. "Sterb' ich": Neighbor-note Motion on the Middleground

order to evaluate this structure, questions raised earlier must be readdressed: Is the middleground plagal axis analogous to the tonic-dominant axis? Is this extended tonal plagal structure comparable to the Schenkerian *Ursatz*? The answer must be provisional: the plagal axis can replace the tonic-dominant axis on a middleground level, but only with adequate compensation that clarifies the plagal ambiguity. For instance, when example 2-17a sketches the large-scale plagal structure of "Sterb' ich," a basic tonal ambiguity prevails; the progression itself is actually more convincing in the key of D♭ than in A♭ because in the absence of V/A♭ the sonority A♭ is more readily heard as V/D♭ than as I/A♭. The compensations of this song have already been described. The

Ex. 2-17. "Sterb' ich": Middleground Plagal Structure

tonic pedal by itself is not sufficient compensation because it easily could be heard as a dominant pedal in D♭. That leaves the piano ostinato as the most compelling compensation, and what makes it effective is its use of foreground authentic cadences. The tonality of the ostinato is always clearly understood—despite the inherent ambiguity described earlier—by the continuous closure through V-I. The authentic cadence in m. 17 creates closure—of the section and of the song—in A♭ rather than D♭, and that authentic cadence is a foreground rather than a middleground event. Here Schenker's concept of structural levels becomes vital even as his *Ursatz* becomes inapplicable. There is no need, for instance, to posit a parenthetical middleground V in this song (see example 2-

17b), for the structure is viable without a middleground dominant. Two issues are operative: first, the tonal definition of the tonic and subdominant regions in this piece is achieved not by the interrelationship of the two harmonies but rather by authentic cadences within the separate tonal regions. Second, the basis for structural coherence in a plagal middleground is altogether different from that of Schenker's *Ursatz*. The nature of the tonic-dominant axis is the opposition of the tonic and dominant and the resolution of that opposition through the powerful authentic cadence. In contrast, the tonal opposition in the plagal axis is altogether different from that of its tonic-dominant counterpart, and the dissonance arises from ambiguity, not from polarity.

The plagal axis, then, creates a weaker tonal structure whose tonal definition is inherently unclear. While the necessity for compensation underscores the problematic nature of the plagal axis, that need also suggests that, in their efforts to investigate more complicated tonal relationships, composers in the later nineteenth century were willing to create more complex and possibly less cohesive musical structures.

Analyses of Songs Containing Plagal Ambiguity and Dominant Replacement: "Harfenspieler I" and "Begegnung"

Two songs demonstrate Wolf's innovative exploration of the plagal domain. Both songs exemplify some type of dominant replacement, and both exploit some form of plagal ambiguity. In particular, the Goethe song "Harfenspieler I" offers a tentative but revealing form of dominant replacement, while the Mörike song "Begegnung" explores a large-scale transformation of tonic function.

"Harfenspieler I"

"Harfenspieler I" of the Goethe songs (27 October 1888) utilizes the plagal domain in two ways: first, plagal ambiguity occurs with a diversified use of ♭II, IV, and ♭VI; and second, the song includes an initial step towards dominant replacement. The song is in G minor, and as plagal ambiguity develops, the harmonic areas of A♭ major (♭II), E♭ major (♭VI) and C minor (IV) all assume various subdominant functions. The harmonies of ♭II and ♭VI emphasize the subdominant region (C minor), and ♭VI undergoes a transformation of function, as ♭II/ G minor becomes ♭VI/ C minor. Dominant replacement occurs on two levels. A form of plagal cadence (♭VI/ IV-I) threatens to usurp the role of the authentic cadence, and the subdominant region (C minor) suggests itself as a potential polarity, along with the dominant (D major), in opposition to the tonic (G minor).

The minor mode and harmonic ambiguity. Before examining plagal ambiguity in "Harfenspieler I," let us pause briefly to consider how the minor mode creates harmonic ambiguity (both in general and within the plagal domain). It is well known that the minor mode contains more harmonic ambiguity than the major.[13] As the song in question aptly demonstrates, Wolf exploits the traditional harmonic ambiguity of the minor mode in the first two measures of "Harfenspieler I," as V/G minor in m. 1 is juxtaposed with ♭III/G minor in m. 2. In this case, ♭III serves as ♭VI/V going to V/V in an interpolated D major sequence of the opening G minor material. The juxtaposition of G minor and D major will be discussed in a later section. Suffice it to say here that the relative major, ♭III, becomes the connector between the two tonalities. When ♭III is transformed into a member of the plagal domain within the dominant region (♭III/G minor=♭VI/D major), the interconnections between the minor tonic, the dominant and the relative major—the three traditional harmonic centers of the tonal system—all become interwoven into a complex web of fifth and plagal relationships.

Example 2-18 shows the potential for harmonic substitution. Where the sonorities of E♭ (♭VI/G minor) and B♭ (♭III in G minor and ♭VI/D major) are clearly presented in a simple progression in G minor, they can also be interpreted in several other, closely related, tonalities. Members of the plagal domain connect the tonic and dominant in two ways: through the powerful fifth relation (e.g., ♭VI/G minor=♭II/D major) and through the relationship between the relative major and the plagal domain (e.g., ♭III/G minor=♭VI/D major). Note also that C minor, IV of G minor, is also a pivotal region, here between G minor and its submediant, E♭ major.

Ex. 2-18.   Harmonic Substitution and Ambiguity in the Minor Mode (G Minor)

```
                              6    5
                              4    3

   G :I  ♭VII ♭III♭VI   ♭II   V
   D :IV♭III ♭VI  ♭II         I
  ♭B♭:VI  V   I    IV
 [♭III]
   E♭:          V    I    IV
 [♭VI]
   C :          IV   VII  III   VI
 [IV]
```

Where normally ♭III would pose the most powerful polarity to a minor tonic, ♭VI is another harmonic area of potential force (example 2-19); the fact

Ex. 2-19.   The Submediant as Primary Harmonic Polarity in the Minor Mode

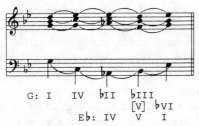

G: I   IV   ♭II   ♭III
                      [V] ♭VI
        E♭: IV   V   I

that ♭III and ♭VI are themselves related by fifth (♭III = V/♭VI) further intensifies the possibility for harmonic ambiguity. In mm. 9-11 of "Harfenspieler I," for instance, Wolf suggests the importance of ♭VI as he turns from IV (C minor) to ♭VI (E♭ major) through a typical late-nineteenth-century pivot chord (m. 9: half-diminished D-F-A♭-C♮ to full diminished D-F-A♭-C♭). Whereas the reference to E♭ in m. 10 is only fleeting, the return to C minor in m. 11 easily could have been deferred considerably longer while E♭ major remained the harmonic goal of mm. 9-10. Thus, what is usually considered a richness of harmonic relations in the minor mode might be considered a richness of the plagal domain as well.[14]

Harmonic substitution. On a specific level, harmonic ambiguity and plagal substitution in "Harfenspieler I" occur in several ways. First, ♭II and ♭III suggest themselves as ♭I of, respectively, the subdominant and the dominant. Second, ♭VI of G minor (E♭ major) undermines the tonal region of IV, C minor.

The harmonies ♭II and ♭III are both introduced in a straightforward manner. The chord ♭II occurs in m. 1 as a Neapolitan dominant preparation to V; ♭VI occurs in the same function in m. 2, within a transposition of m. 1 to the dominant region. As already stated, ♭III is the pivot between the tonalities of I and V (as it is reinterpreted in m. 2 as ♭VI/V) and continues in this function in mm. 2-3, 17, 28 (with the augmented sixth) and mm. 36-37. The role of ♭III as ♭VI/V is itself undermined in several instances where a seventh to the B♭ chord suggests V⁷/E♭, E♭ major being ♭II of D major and ♭VI of G minor. Such alternative usages of ♭III are found in mm. 10, 15, 21, and 26. The harmony ♭III never functions as a simple mediant in G minor, but vacillates between the roles of ♭VI/V and V/♭VI.

The role of the submediant, E♭, is also volatile. As already stated, this harmony is first heard in m. 2 as ♭II/V. It then recurs in m. 10 in an entirely different context. Measures 7-9 present a prolongation of the subdominant (C minor). The pivotal seventh chord already cited occurs on the last beat of m. 9, and E♭ suggests itself as a possible new tonal center in m. 10. While the motion to E♭ is, in fact, only transient (a shift back to C minor occurs in m. 11), the reference to E♭ does undermine the prolongation of C minor; the motion toward E♭ could signify a shift to ♭III/C minor (a common prolongation technique), or it could suggest a move away from C minor as IV and toward E♭ major as ♭VI. Thus, while IV remains the tonal focus of this section, ♭VI adds tension by threatening the stability of IV as a harmonic goal.

Dominant replacement. The piano introduction illustrates the central problem of key relations in this song, with both the relative major (♭III) and the Neapolitan (♭II) serving as pivots among the tonic, subdominant, and dominant regions (see example 2-20). A brief synopsis of mm. 1-4 goes as follows: m. 1 clearly states a I-V progression (with ♭II as dominant preparation); m. 2 recasts that progression into the dominant region, using ♭III/G minor as a substitute for the D as tonic (♭VI for I). A deceptive cadence carries D major into m. 3, but the chromatic interjection of B♮ shifts the tonal focus from the dominant to the subdominant in an analogous V⁷-♭VI progression in IV. The Neapolitan of G minor (m. 1) is now heard as ♭VI of C minor (m. 4), the G♭ seventh sounding strongly like an F♯ augmented sixth which could easily resolve to G♮ within an authentic cadence in the subdominant. (The rationale behind Wolf's spelling of the A♭ seventh chord is never clear.) The harmonic ambiguities of ♭II, ♭III, and ♭VI are cleverly exploited, and the song's tonal center, G minor, seems to have two potential polarities: D major (V) and C minor (IV). Measure 5 reasserts V as the harmonic goal of the opening, but not before a four-bar phrase is enlarged to five measures—an extension that is necessitated by the unusually strong reference to the subdominant.

Ex. 2-20. "Harfenspieler I": Harmonic Relations, mm. 1-5

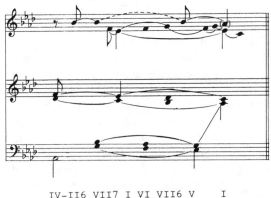

```
IV-II6 VII7 I VI VII6 V     I
```

Although the dominant seems to maintain its primacy over the subdominant in the basic structural design of mm. 1-4, the subdominant and its plagal domain ($\flat$VI/IV and $\flat$II) have an expanded role in what might best be described as a harmonic diversion away from the dominant. The subdominant does not actually replace the dominant in the piano introduction, though it does assume a greater structural role than the customary dominant preparation. Rather than functioning as a traditional dominant preparation, the harmony of mm. 3-4 moves not to V, but rather to V/IV. While the plagal harmonies in the piano introduction suggest a motion away from the dominant and toward the subdominant, the V[7] of G minor is interjected in m. 5. This reasserts the tonic-dominant axis, but not before a progression toward the subdominant severely undermines the role of the dominant.

A translation of the text of "Harfenspieler I" is offered below, and example 2-21 presents the setting of the first line of text. In one sense, mm. 7-15

Ex. 2-21. "Harfenspieler I": The Setting of Line I

enlarge upon the five-measure piano introduction's plagal expansion. In m. 6 and the first beat of m. 7, the first line of text is set to a repetition of the opening gesture: I-$\flat$II[6]-V. On the second beat of m. 7, the shift to IV occurs below the exclamation "Ach!", as Wolf depicts the subtle change and intensification of text through tonal shift. When the singer exclaims "Ach!" in reflecting upon his opening statement, the music diverges from the dominant and toward the subdominant. Another tonal shift occurs immediately in mm. 8-9, as the phrase "Der ist bald allein" is set again to a diverted cadence, V$^6_5$-V$^4_2$/IV-IV[6]. From m. 9 on, the remainder of the phrase develops the subdominant region, and a shift from IV to $\flat$VI is strongly suggested (but unfulfilled) in m. 10. The final phrase of text in this section, "und lässt ihn seiner Pein," is set entirely in IV (C minor), ending on $\flat$VI[7]/IV in m. 12. When the authentic cadence occurs in m. 13, the listener has been in the subdominant for almost five measures and the shift to the dominant seems interruptive. The vocal line of this first section supports the plagal rather than the customary tonic-dominant axis. From the word "Ach!" in m. 7, the vocal line is entirely in C minor and, as already stated, the chord in m. 12 easily could have closed in C minor (see example 2-22).

Ex. 2-22. "Harfenspieler I": Potential Cadence on the Subdominant

Text to "Harfenspieler I"
[Goethe, 27 October 1888]

Wer sich der Einsamkeit ergibt,
Ach! der ist bald allein;
Ein jeder lebt, ein jeder liebt,
Und lässt ihn seiner Pein.

He who devotes himself to solitude,
Ah, he is soon alone.
Men live and love
And leave him to his sorrow.

Ja! lasst mich meiner Qual!
Und kann ich nur einmal
Recht einsam sein,
Dann bin ich nicht allein.

Yes, leave me with my pain!
If I can once achieve
Utter solitude,
I shall not be alone.

Es schleicht ein Liebender lauschend sacht,
Ob seine Freundin allein?
So überschleicht bei Tag und Nacht
Mich Einsamen die Pein,
Mich Einsamen die Qual.
Ach, werd' ich erst einmal
Einsam im Grabe sein,
Da lässt sie mich allein!

A lover softly steals by,
Intent to know if his beloved is alone;
So, by day and night,
Sorrow and pain
Haunt my loneliness.
Ah, not until the day
I lie solitary in my grave
Will anguish leave me alone.

The text bolsters the idea that the subdominant and dominant regions are competing with one another as main polarity to the tonic. The opposition of the tonalities of G minor (I) and D major (V) is text-related: the verse depicts a conflict between the painful solitude of life without love (G minor) and the relief from this pain that can only be found in love or death (D major). The subdominant key of C minor and the other plagal keys of A♭ and E♭ major are also text-related, representing the pain involved in the conflict of a loveless life. As the following list shows, all the words of pain and anguish are associated with plagal harmonies: m. 6, "Einsamkeit"; m. 7, "Ach!"; m. 12, "Pein"; m. 14, "Qual"; and m. 16, "einsam." Just as the conflict between painful life (G minor) and death (D major) is resolved at the song's end, so the conflicts between life (G minor) and pain (C minor) and between death (D major) and pain (C minor) are resolved.

Associative tonality. Wolf's extensive use of several different tonalities outside the tonic is similar to Wagner's association of different key areas with specific ideas or emotions. Robert Bailey introduced the concept of "associative tonality" in his 1969 doctoral dissertation, and he later applied the term to Wagner's *Ring* in a 1977 article, "The Structure of the *Ring* and Its Evolution."[15] In the music of both Wagner and his follower Wolf, the appearance of associative tonal areas is not predicated upon a governing logic of tonal relations, but rather occurs in response to textual or dramatic exigencies. The resulting musical structures can be wholly unusual or idiosyncratic, and traditional tonal structures such as the tonic-dominant axis can be undermined or even replaced by nondominant harmonies such as third relations or harmonies of the plagal domain. In the use of associative tonality, the music is indeed mistress to the text, and the desire for musical continuity and coherence might well be superseded by the need for portraying poetic or dramatic tensions. In general, as Wolf's songs using associative tonality are examined, it can be presumed that harmonic innovation resulted first and foremost from text concerns, and that the composer had to construct unique musical coherence for such songs.

In "Harfenspieler I," the concept of associative tonality encourages yet another way of hearing the difficult mm. 12-13. If the song asserts a three-way polarity between G minor, C minor, and D major, then mm. 12-13 depict the conflict between the two associated ideas of the nontonic polarities: m. 12 represents the subdominant (pain of loveless life); m. 13, the dominant (relief through love or death). The tension between the two competing regions of IV and V is finally resolved in m. 14, as the phrase closes with a cadence to the tonic. The connector between the three tonalities is the chord on beat 1 of m. 13: F♯-A♭-C-E♭, which reinterprets the A♭ seventh chord of m. 12 (♭VI/IV) as an altered VII[7] in G minor (i.e., a substitute for V/G minor). The resolution of this chord to the D[7] chord a beat later is both a resolution of the conflict within G minor and, at the same time, a resolution of the "pain" within C minor.

The role of the subdominant. Thus far it has been demonstrated that the structural role of the traditional authentic cadence is undermined by the emphasis upon the subdominant. There are two ways to consider this unusual tension between the dominant and subdominant. First, the prolongation of the subdominant is not an elaboration of the dominant preparation function, but, rather, is a means of attempting to usurp the main structural role of the dominant. In this case, the extended use of the plagal axis reverses the customary metric design of the tonic-dominant axis from

I IV V

/ ⌣ /

(as in m. 1) to

V[V]IV V[V]

/ ⌣ / ⌣ /

(as in mm. 7ff.). This is not a literal dominant replacement; it is, however, a step toward that phenomenon.

A second view of the competition between the dominant and the subdominant involves reevaluating the function of the authentic cadence. Whereas the motion to V in m. 1 is unequivocal, other uses of V become less and less definitive. In m. 5, the cadential V is understood as a correction or redirection of harmonic motion that had been moving toward the subdominant in mm. 3-4. In m. 7, the clear progression to V is immediately undermined by a harmonic shift back to IV in an altered deceptive cadence where IV substitutes for VI. And in m. 13, the correction procedure cited in m. 5 (using the authentic cadence to return to V from IV) is at best an interruption of the subdominant in favor of the more traditional authentic cadence. It is possible, for instance, for the phrase to have closed in a plagal cadence: ♭VI/IV-I (example 2-23). This cadence formula is not as unlikely as it first appears, for ♭VI/IV can be reinterpreted once again as ♭II. The cadence ♭II-I is a logical step in the replacement of the dominant, where the semitonal ♭2̂-1̂ motion becomes a plagal analog to the authentic 7̂-8̂ motion.

Ex. 2-23. "Harfenspieler I": Possible Plagal Cadence of Line 1

♭VI/IV   V/IV IV   I

An important question arises at this point: If Wolf wants to replace the authentic with the plagal cadence, why does he add the authentic cadences of mm. 5 and 13, especially when the authentic cadence sounds more like an evasion of a goal than an arrival upon a goal? The answer is complex. The plagal axis becomes a middleground structural goal of the phrase, and the cadential V seems relegated to a local effect of closure. In fact, however, both the subdominant and the dominant are middleground goals and both participate in the cadences of mm. 5 and 13. If, for instance, the F♯-A♭-C-E♭ harmony of mm. 4-5 and 12-13 is understood as a plagal substitute for the dominant, then the actual authentic cadences of mm. 5 and 13 would seem more like vestigial cadential effects rather than actual harmonic goals. This view is supported by the dramatic shift in tessitura of mm. 5 and 13, where a four-way voice exchange suggests that the V^7-I cadences are dominant echoes of the plagal cadences begun in mm. 4 and 12.

While this view proposes a tentative form of dominant replacement, it does not deny the use of the authentic cadence. Though the dominant's function as traditional polarity is challenged and almost replaced, the dominant within the authentic cadence is retained. The role of the subdominant, meanwhile, has been considerably expanded.

The juxtaposition of plagal and authentic cadences reiterates the opposition of the dominant and subdominant harmonies that has occurred throughout the song: V-IV motions were heard in mm. 2-3 and 7-8. The unusual tension between the dominant and subdominant is finally resolved in m. 18 with a strong, unequivocal arrival on V. Despite this later traditional use of the dominant, the impact of earlier competition between the dominant and the subdominant in mm. 1-16 remains, and the subdominant region remains a viable harmonic goal. Finally, another way to hear the expanded subdominant in the song's opening measures is in the context of the dominant prolongation that ensues in mm. 18ff. The emphasis on the plagal domain prior to m. 18 enabled Wolf to deemphasize the dominant in order to preserve it for the contrasting section in mm. 18ff.

"Begegnung"

Wolf's Mörike song, "Begegnung" (22 March 1888), explores several types of plagal ambiguity. Transformation of tonic function occurs during the first half of the song and plagal substitution occurs during the second half, as VI (mm. 37-48) replaces IV (mm. 1-12) in a middleground plagal cadence. "Begegnung" also uses dominant replacement, where a plagal cadence on the middleground substitutes for the more customary authentic cadence. This occurs in part because the unusual tonal syntax depicts a strophic poem, where harmonic regions are juxtaposed together rather than integrated through harmonic progression. As noted in the song "Sterb' ich" (see p. 37), the middleground plagal axis here is articulated by foreground authentic cadences, which compensate for the inherent weakness of the plagal axis.

The correspondence between text and music in "Begegnung" is particularly complex. The poem describes a "meeting" of lovers after a stormy night. While the poem has the outward form of a strophic narrative, with each stanza depicting a new aspect of the lovers' encounter, the subtlety of poetic meaning and metaphor transforms a simple lovers' "Begegnung" ("Begegnung" meaning, simply, "meeting") into a complex sexual "Begegnung" ("Begegnung" meaning "encounter," with all the attending connotations of tension and potential conflict). The first stanza sets a foreboding tone—the raging storm of the previous night evokes a sense of frenzy and mystery, a scene of uncertainty in which the lovers' "Begegnung" takes place. The next two stanzas introduce the lovers: the girl is timid, the boy delighted, and the two meet with youthful embarrassment. In the final two stanzas, the complexity of the poetry comes to the fore. The references to the storm and to erotic dreams suggest that the storm is a metaphor for sex and the "Begegnung" is a story of sexual uncertainty. The reference back to the storm also casts doubt as to the temporal meaning of the "Begegnung": Is the title about the meeting in the street, or a meeting during the storm of the previous night, or both? As a final element of confusion, the last stanza also suggests that the "Begegnung" might be really in the imagination of the young boy, that the storm and the girl are imaginary components of a youthful sexual fantasy. The notion of "Begegnung" as a sexual encounter is reinforced by the latter two lines of both stanza 1 and stanza 4: "So unstet ihr Geschichen glüht... Derweil sie um die Ecke rauscht." Meanwhile, the idea of the "Begegnung" as an imaginary occurrence recasts the role of the girl as that of an illusive—and elusive— persona. In the musical analysis that follows, the examination of several extended-tonal techniques includes both the temporal and sexual uncertainty and the use of fantasy and illusion.

Text to "Begegnung"
[Mörike, 22 March 1888]

Was doch heut' Nacht ein Sturm gewesen,	What a storm there was last night,
Bis erst der Morgen sich geregt!	Raged until this morning!
Wie hat der ungebetne Besen	How that uninvited broom has
Kamin und Gassen ausgefegt!	Swept the streets and chimneys clean!
Da kommt ein Mädchen schon die Strassen,	Along the street a girl comes,
Das halb verschüchtert um sich sieht	Glancing about here, half-afraid,
Wie Rosen, die der Wind zerblasen,	Like roses tossed before the wind,
So unstet ihr Gesichtchen glüht.	Ever changing is her face's glow.
Ein schöner Bursch tritt ihr entgegen,	A handsome lad steps to meet her,
Er will ihr voll Entzücken nahn:	Would delightedly approach her:
Wie sehn sich freudig und verlegen	Oh, the joy and embarrassment
Die ungewohnten Schelme an!	In those novice rascals' looks!
Er scheint zu fragen, ob das Liebchen	He seems to ask if his beloved
Die Zöpfe schon zurechtgemacht,	Has put straight her plaits
Die heute Nacht im offnen Stübchen	Which, last night, in her open bedroom,
Ein Sturm in Unordnung begracht.	Were tousled by a storm.
Der Bursche träumt noch von den Küssen,	The lad's still dreaming of the kisses
Die ihm das süsse Kind getauscht,	Which that sweet child exchanged,
Er steht, von Anmut hingerissen,	And stands, captive to her charm,
Derweil sie um die Ecke rauscht.	While she whisks around the corner.

Transformation of tonic function. The ambiguity of tonal design in "Begegnung" occurs in the guise of a transformation of tonic function that takes place within the setting of the first and second stanzas of text. The opening stanza in A♭ minor anticipates this ambiguity when its opening function as tonic is cast into doubt by the progression to E♭ minor in mm. 8 and 12 (see ex. 2-24). Where A♭ minor had been understood as I in mm. 1-6, its function changes to IV♭ in E♭ minor, first by the half cadence of mm. 7-8 and then more emphatically by the authentic cadence in m. 12. This simple instance of shift in harmonic function from I to IV is a precursor of the more radical transformation in mm. 13ff., where the tonic, E♭, becomes V/IV. Further, the relatively simple functional shift of A♭ minor from I to IV♭ has the effect of disorienting the listener and thereby of foreshadowing the more intense transformation of A♭ minor that will occur in the second stanza.

Ex. 2-24. "Begegnung": Tonic Transformation

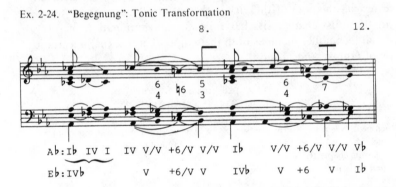

The function of A♭ minor, then, changes during the first stanza from a tonic to a dominant-preparation subdominant. This ambivalence of A♭ minor is reinforced in mm. 13ff., where the second stanza is set in E♭ major. The shift from the minor to the major mode has the unerring effect of suggesting that E♭ changes from a minor tonic to a major dominant.[16] The entire second stanza then revives the harmonic uncertainty: by m. 12, the function of A♭ minor has shifted from tonic to subdominant; in m. 13, the functional shift of E♭ from minor tonic to major dominant recasts the A♭ region once again, moving from a small-scale IV♭ to a large-scale I.

The interpretation of E♭ major as V (mm. 13ff.) is, of course, only one of two equally feasible readings. If the modal shift is considered merely innocuous, it is altogether possible to hear the E♭ of m. 13 as a major tonic. This reading retains A♭ minor's derived function of IV♭ and relates the first two stanzas as parts of a large-scale plagal cadence, IV♭-I.

The double reading of this section underscores how both the poem and the song "Begegnung" vividly exemplify transformational ambiguity. Whereas the transformation of tonic function always involves some degree of harmonic obscurity, it is usually resolved and the resultant harmonic relationships ultimately become clear. In the case of the song "Begegnung," however, the ambiguity remains, and A♭ minor and E♭ major each retain two possible harmonic functions.

Several factors contribute to the overall harmonic ambiguity of mm. 1-22. First, the strophic nature of the text setting has the effect of separating and isolating (rather than integrating) the two harmonic regions. This confuses the relationship between the first stanza in A♭ minor and the second in E♭ major, which at best can only be inferred. Second, Stanza 2 sounds like a transposed repetition of Stanza 1 (up a fifth), and this obscures rather than clarifies the harmonic focus. This ambiguity continues in the subsequent setting of Stanza 3, mm. 23-32, which is transposed up another fifth to B♭ major (see example 2-25). This second transposition to B♭ recasts the vague relationships of A♭ and E♭ into components of a circle-of-fifths progression, and the tonality remains unclear. The region of E♭ can be heard either as V of A♭ (with B♭ as V/V), or as a tonic whose weakened function within the plagal axis is compensated for by the subsequent appearance of its dominant in mm. 23ff. This latter interpretation is intriguing, for it dramatizes the power of the circle-of-fifths progression. Not only is the tonic weakened by its subdominant, but its closing function (in the plagal cadence) is deterred by the harmonic motion beyond the tonic to the powerful dominant. The tonic becomes a passing harmony rather than a harmonic goal, as the directed motion to the half cadence supersedes the closure of the plagal cadence.

Ex. 2-25. "Begegnung": Plagal Ambiguity

The use of the circle-of-fifths progression to intensify harmonic ambiguity is an extension of a common-practice circle-of-fifths usage that employs a weaker tonic in order to obtain a stronger dominant. An interesting common-practice example is found in J.S. Bach's *Well-tempered Clavier*, Volume I. In the third prelude (C♯ major), the subject is presented in pairs. It occurs first in the tonic and then immediately in the dominant. A second pair of entrances extends the fifth cycle from II to VI (mm. 17-31), and the fifth cycle functions in its traditional role of defining the tonality. After an unstable passage in mm. 32-

36, the subject recurs in the subdominant (mm. 47-54) as a preparation for the reprise of the subject in the tonic in m. 55. The pairing of the tonic subject with a subdominant instead of a dominant statement fulfills two formal requisites. First, the appearance of the subject in the reprise is varied: instead of being the first of a paired statement, it is the second, concluding, statement. Also, pairing the tonic with the subdominant allows the dominant region to assume a new function: rather than repeating the subject after the tonic, the dominant establishes a cadential pedal and initiates the prelude's closing. The use of the circle-of-fifths progression transforms a simple reprise into an elegant tonal structure wherein the tonic subject statement is deemphasized in favor of a more pronounced arrival on the structurally important dominant.

The function of the circle of fifths in the Wolf is similar to that in the Bach: the possible "tonic" E♭ is weakened by the motion to its dominant. Whether one hears mm. 1-32 as IV-I-V or as I-V-V/V, the net effect is the same: E♭ is heard as a passing harmony and B♭ as some sort of dominant to E♭, while the relation of A♭ to E♭ remains unclear.

As in every Wolf song, "Begegnung's" unusual harmonic design reflects the poetry. As stated earlier, "Begegnung" is a poem about the encounter of young lovers, with each of the first three stanzas depicting one facet of their "meeting." Wolf musically isolates each stanza of the poem by placing it in its own harmonic area. The harmony A♭ minor depicts the scene of the encounter—the streets in which a windswept storm had occurred the previous night. The "Mädchen" arrives rosy-cheeked in E♭ and her lover appears "ihr voll Entzücken" in B♭. The listener then expects that the rest of the poem and musical setting will explain the interrelationships of the storm and the two lovers. The use of different harmonic regions for each stanza cleverly projects the confusion and tension of the "Begegnung." The duality of A♭ minor, for instance, underscores the confusion about the meaning of the storm to the lovers' meeting: Is this meeting a reunion after another meeting during the storm? Does the minor mode indicate some sort of danger or misfortune, either in the past or yet to come? The diverse connotations of E♭ maintain the suspense: What happened to the girl to redden her cheeks? Why is she wandering about? Further, the function of B♭ is twofold: (1) the boy comes to meet the girl; (2) his appearance clarifies hers—they are meeting as shy lovers after a stormy night. The harmony B♭ definitely functions as V of E♭, and the appearance of B♭ retrospectively clarifies the function of E♭ as tonic. However, as already stated, neither the appearance of the boy nor the harmony of B♭ clarifies A♭, for the meaning of the storm to the lovers remains a mystery.

On a simple level, Wolf's linking of different harmonic regions with different textual elements is a direct application of associative tonality. The shift from A♭ minor to E♭ major to B♭ major easily conveys the shift in storytelling from the raging storm to the entrances of the shy maiden and hopeful lover. On a deeper level, Wolf has demonstrated the various textual conflicts in purely musical terms. The poetic conflict between lovers and storm is transformed into a musical conflict between fundamental harmonic relationships. The subdominant threatens to usurp the function of the tonic-dominant axis, and the dominant assumes a compensatory role in clarifying the tensions of the plagal axis.

Plagal substitution. During the first half of the song, Wolf uses the transformation of tonic function to create the harmonic ambiguity that conveys the mystery of the poetic narrative. As the music comes to a half cadence at m. 32, the listener expects resolution of both poetic and musical conflicts. Wolf begins this resolution with the subtle device of plagal substitution. In mm. 33ff., the piano interlude shifts the tonal focus away from E♭, and the fourth stanza occurs in C minor. Wolf seems to have chosen C minor for several reasons. First, whereas the region of C minor is remote from that of A♭ minor, the use of minor mode in the fourth stanza clearly refers back to the song's minor opening, associating the regions of A♭ and C minor by modal affinity. This modal association in turn reinforces the use of plagal substitution. In the key of E♭ major, A♭ minor is IV♭ and C minor is VI. The region of C minor becomes a substitute for the opening IV♭ (A♭ minor), thereby carrying the opening storm imagery into the latter part of the song.

The choice of C minor is important in yet another way. C minor functions as part of a deceptive cadence in E♭, thus providing a musical vehicle for continuing the text. The text of this fourth stanza describes the boy questioning the girl. His seemingly simple question about fixing her hair includes a reference to the storm of the previous night and to the resulting disorder ("Unordnung") from the wind. Once again, this meeting seems to be about an earlier meeting that took place during the storm. In musical terms, the function of the deceptive cadence is traditional: first, it deters closure from an authentic cadence; and second, it sets up the expectation of a subsequent future closure. This double function of postponing one closure and preparing for another is, again, textually related. Communication between the lovers sets the stage for the expected clarification of the "Begegnung" which will, in turn, bring the poem and the song to a close.

In its modal association with A♭ minor and its role within the deceptive cadence, C minor serves to enhance musical continuity on several levels. It also serves as a musical reference to the temporal ambiguity of the poetry. If A♭ minor represents the storm of the previous night, then C minor may symbolize a recollection of the past during the present. The use of the C minor region as an oblique reference to the past is intensified by the use of modulatory piano interludes in mm. 33-36 and 45-48. These modulatory passages have two basic formal effects. First, they emphasize the special function of C minor by isolating that region from the rest of the song through the use of contrapuntal and harmonic progression rather than the previously used juxtaposition. Second, the Bᵇ leading tone to C minor, which is emphasized in these interludes, is an enharmonic associate to the Cᵇ of the Aᵇ minor region. Thus, an enharmonic link between the two plagal areas is created.

The punning of Bᵇ/Cᵇ is remarkable in view of the respective resolutions of Cᵇ and Bᵇ (see example 2-26). While Cᵇ functions as an upper neighbor to the *Kopfton* Bᵇ, Bᵇ functions in two different ways: (1) in mm. 34-35, Bᵇ is a chromatic pivot away from Aᵇ and toward Cᵇ; (2) conversely, in m. 48, Bᵇ functions as the pivot back to Bᵇ, where its reversal of harmonic orientation recalls its earlier "Cᵇ" role as upper neighbor to Bᵇ. Thus, while Bᵇ initially deflects away from the *Kopfton* Bᵇ, it ultimately corrects itself and returns to its initial function as the *Kopfton*'s upper neighbor in A minor. The association of Bᵇ and Cᵇ is a subtle but nonetheless important connection between the areas of Aᵇ and C minor, a link that also underscores the plagal substitution of VI for IVᵇ.

Ex. 2-26. "Begegnung": Relationship of C Minor to Aᵇ Minor; Overall Tonal Design

Dominant replacement. The use of C minor for the fourth stanza has yet another important meaning. Since the final stanza is in Eᵇ and there is no middleground dominant (the V in m. 48 is a foreground event), the large-scale VI-I progression (mm. 37ff.) can be heard as an example of dominant replacement. This replacement of a VI-I plagal cadence for the customary authentic cadence offers a musical analog to the complex ending of the poem. The final stanza of the poem is opaque: the poem's conclusion raises as many questions as it answers, as the boy stands transfixed in reverie and the girl "whisks around the corner." Questions about the meaning of the "Begegnung" reemerge as the listener wonders just where and when the "Begegnung" actually took place. The final stanza is depicted in Eᵇ. The Eᵇ region had been used earlier to depict the appearance of the girl. At that time, the function of Eᵇ was unclear; it was either a V to the storm key of A♭ or a I to the storm region of IV♭/ E♭. In either case, clarification of the relationship of the girl (E♭) to the storm (A♭) is only partially fulfilled by the entrance of the boy in B♭ as V/ E♭. The return of E♭ at the song's conclusion has a double effect. First, with the final foreground authentic cadence in this last stanza (mm. 55-56), E♭ reaffirms the presence of the boy as V/ E♭. Second, the foreground IV-I progressions in mm. 50-51 and 54 reinforce the plagal IV♭-I of the opening.

The dominant replacement occurring between the last two stanzas is vivid text depiction. The function of E♭ as the song's final tonic supports the interpretation that the poem suggests an illusory "Begegnung." If the storm is a fantasy, then A♭ minor is an illusory tonic. The association of E♭ major with the appearance of the girl is also delusive, since the girl exists only in the dream of the boy. The boy's harmony, V/ E♭, is resolved obliquely through VI, because his role of dreamer must be relayed through a plagal relationship. The use of dominant replacement is thus part of a replacement of the tonic-dominant axis (boy, reality) with the fantasy-associated plagal axis (girl, storm).

The linking of the boy—as representing reality—with the dominant function is subtle and ironic. Although the boy is the catalyst of the poem, it is his dream that is the poetic substance. Because Wolf associates dream imagery (storm, girl) with the plagal axis (A♭ minor, the initial E♭ minor, and C minor), the role of the dominant is relegated to an obscure relationship within E♭. The use of the dominant in mm. 23-32 is indirect; it does not resolve to E♭ and only relates retrospectively to the preceding E♭ section of mm. 13-22. In m. 48, the dominant is used more traditionally, but its foreground status keeps it outside the middleground plagal axis. Thus, although the song includes a half cadence (mm. 22-32), the overall harmonic design of the song is based on the relationship of the tonic to plagal elements (IV and VI), and the large-scale authentic cadence is replaced by a large-scale plagal cadence.

Overall formal design. The overall tonal design of "Begegnung" is offered in example 2-26. The *Kopfton* B♭ is embellished by its upper neighbors, C♭ and C♮. The underlying harmonic progression of the song—understood as IV♭-I-V-VI-I—may be divided into two parts: (1) the progression to V of E♭ (mm. 1-32) which is enriched by plagal ambiguity; and (2) the closing VI-I cadence, which is the aforementioned dominant replacement. The closing plagal cadence creates a symmetry with the opening IV-I progression, and the middleground dominant, B♭, becomes a harmonic fulcrum surrounded by two plagal axes. The centricity of B♭ is symbolic of the poetry, where the boy assumes the role of central and pivotal protagonist. Additional comments on the formal design of the plagal axis will be found on pages 55-57.

Before closing this discussion of "Begegnung," one other subtle aspect of Wolf's formal design in this song must be considered, i.e., his use of tessitura in the vocal line (see example 2-27). The beamed half notes in the treble clef demonstrate how Wolf utilizes the upper tessitura of the vocal line to reinforce the E♭ tonality and to emphasize metrically key words of text. In the second stanza in E♭, the voice sings high E♭ to the words "Mädchen," "schon," "Strassen," and "glüht," and this high E♭ is itself embellished by neighboring high F's. In the B♭ section that follows, the neighbor-note F becomes the main structural pitch and is sounded on the word "nahn." In the C minor section, E♭ regains its function as main high melodic pitch. This high E♭ then moves to D in preparation for a contrapuntal resolution to E♭ in the final stanza. In the C minor section, the high E♭-D motions occur first on the interrogative "ob...gemacht," and then on the reference to the storm: "offnen Stübchen...in Unordnung." Finally, the vocal line in the last section rearticulates the high E♭ on the words "Anmut" and "rauscht." While the registral emphasis of key words of text is certainly a characteristic device of *Lieder* in general, Wolf's systematic use of this high register creates a convincing melodic counterpoint to the harmonic progression in the bass. Interestingly, this upper tessitura does not begin until the key of E♭ is presented in the second stanza. The melodic high point of the first stanza is the C♭, which embellishes, in the middle register, the *Kopfton* B♭.

Ex. 2-27. "Begegnung": Formal Design and Text

Summary. The use of the plagal domain in "Begegnung" is effective. In a general sense, plagal elements represent the poetic imagery of mystery and fantasy, and the plagal axis depicts the opposition of fantasy to the reality that is represented by the tonic-dominant axis. The transformation of tonic function in the song's first half enables Wolf to portray the initial poetic ambiguity, and the lingering doubt between A♭ minor and E♭ major continues through the song's conclusion. This residual harmonic irresolution suggests that the poem's temporal and sexual confusion remains unresolved at the end of the poem. The additional techniques of plagal substitution and dominant replacement also contribute to textual depiction, and Wolf's use of C minor is especially powerful in enhancing the simultaneous textual aspects of confusion and continuity.

Conclusion

Dominant Replacement

In the foregoing analyses, dominant replacement occurs in varying degrees on both the foreground and middleground levels. Several general conclusions can be drawn. First, we have shown that plagal structures—the plagal cadence and the plagal axis—are inherently weaker than their dominant counterparts, and that subdominant replacement of the dominant (on any structural level) results in a loss of tonal clarity. The inherent weakness of plagal structures leads in turn to a second general conclusion: dominant replacement necessitates the use of an accompanying compensation to counterbalance the weak plagal structure and clarify the obscured tonal focus. In each of the Wolf songs examined, the compensation is accomplished first and foremost by foreground authentic cadences. In addition, the song "Sterb' ich," which incorporated a middleground plagal axis, used a bass pedal and an ostinato as compensatory elements. Finally, we have seen that with adequate compensation the subdominant can replace the dominant, and that the new tonal polarity (the plagal axis) exploits harmonic ambiguity to a degree unparalleled within the common-practice tonal system.

Structural Implications of the Plagal Middleground

Example 2-28 compares the tonic-dominant axis with the plagal axis. In example 2-28a, the tonic-dominant axis is depicted as the Schenkerian *Ursatz* in its simplest design, a 3̂-2̂-1̂ *Urlinie* descent. It clearly defines tonality in two ways: first, through the powerful fifth relation in the bass (I-V-I), and second, through the melodic stepwise descent to 1̂. In contrast, the fifth relation in the plagal axis (example 2-28b) has no clarifying melodic descent. Either the

Ex. 2-28.   Comparison of Authentic and Plagal Axes

   a. Tonic-dominant axis   b. Plagal axis

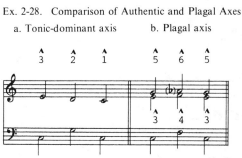

melodic motion is static, with Î as a pedal, or it is inconclusive, as 3̂ and 5̂ do not descend to Î. This paradigm is borne out in both Wolf songs that utilized plagal axes; in example 2-29, the middleground readings of "Sterb' ich" and "Begegnung" show that in both songs the *Kopfton* does not descend, but instead remains suspended above the tonic. As to be expected, foreground authentic cadences compensate for both the lack of *Kopfton* descent and the inherent plagal weakness in these songs. In both songs, the foreground authentic cadences are especially strong right before the final tonic: in "Sterb' ich," the return to I in mm. 13-14 is accompanied by chromatic elements within a dynamic swell; and in "Begegnung" the authentic cadence of m. 48 occurs with a crescendo to "forte" in the final piano interlude.

Ex. 2-29. Plagal Axes in "Sterb' ich" and "Begegnung"

The inconclusiveness of the plagal axis can also be obviated through the use of formal symmetry. The middleground tonic-dominant axis achieves closure when the *Urlinie* resolves 2̂-1̂ with the harmonic progression V-I in a contrapuntal affirmation of the tonic.[17] In the absence of such compelling contrapuntal closure in the plagal axis, the inherent harmonic symmetry becomes a basis for formal design. In example 2-30, the plagal axes of "Sterb' ich" and "Begegnung" are shown as symmetrical structures which begin and end on the same or equivalent structures. In "Sterb'ich," the *Kopfton* is 5̂ above

Ex. 2-30. Symmetry in the Plagal Axis

I, the two fifths surrounding a middleground tenth within the region of the subdominant. In "Begegnung," a more complex symmetry occurs, as the middleground IV♭-I opening progression is mirrored by a closing middleground VI-I progression, both involving neighbor notes to the *Kopfton* $\hat{5}$ above I. As already noted, the middleground dominant functions as a fulcrum surrounded by the symmetrical plagal structures. Harmonic symmetry is thus another compensation for the weakness of the plagal axis. In the absence of a compelling contrapuntal *Urlinie* descent, the plagal axis must rely upon a symmetrical return to the tonic to create unequivocal closure.

Limitations within the Plagal Domain

One final observation must be made with regard to Wolf's use of dominant replacement and the plagal axis. At the opening of this chapter, Wolf's exploration of the plagal domain was characterized as tentative and largely conservative. Indeed, of over two hundred and sixty songs, only a few utilize either dominant replacement or a middleground plagal axis. It is impossible to know whether Wolf's restricted exploration of dominant replacement and the plagal axis is due to a limited interest on the point of the composer, or to the constricting formal problems inherent in the new harmonic structures themselves. Nevertheless, however limited Wolf's exploration of dominant replacement and use of a plagal axis might have been, those songs that do utilize these plagal structures reflect remarkable harmonic innovation and expand upon what is clearly a rich and complex plagal domain.

Gesegnet sei das Grün

(How I love green, mm. 1-9)

Schlafendes Jesuskind
(Sleeping Christchild)

Hugo Wolf
(Original-Ausgabe)

19 wel - che Bil - der hin - ter die - ser Stir - ne, die - sen
    all ___ the won-drous vi - sions seen be - hind that brow, those

pp

21 zart
    schwar - zen Wim - pern, sich ___ in sanf - tem Wech - sel ma - - len!
    long dark lash - es, chang - - ing oft in sweet suc - ces - - sion.

pp   ppp

23.

pp

27. pp wie in tiefes Sinnen verloren
    Sohn der Jung - frau, Him - mels - kind! ___
    Blɛs - sèd Vir - gin's heav'n - ly child! ___

ppp   pppp

Wir haben beide lange Zeit geschwiegen

(We have both long been silent, mm. 6-10)

Gesang Weylas

(Weyla's song)

(Orig. Des-dur.)

Langsam und feierlich.

Du bist Orp-lid, mein Land! das
Hail sa - cred isle! dear land! far

fer - - - ne leuch - tet; vom Mee - re dam-pfet dein be -
dis - - - tant shin - ing! The mists, be-guil-ed by thy

sonn - - ter Strand den Ne - - - bel, so der Göt - ter Wan -
*sun - - ny strand_ from o - - - cean, chap-lets for the gods_*

Sterb' ich, so hüllt in Blumen meine Glieder
(Wrap me in flowers when my end doth come)

Harfenspieler I

Hugo Wolf.
(Original-Ausgabe).

Wer sich der Ein-sam-keit er- .gibt, ach! der ist bald al-lein; ein je-der lebt,— ein je-der liebt,— und lässt ihn— sei - ner Pein.

Begegnung
(The meeting)

Lebhaft bewegt.

5. Was doch heut Nacht ein Sturm ge-we - sen, bis erst der Mor- gen sich __ geregt!
What dreadful storm last night was rag - ing un - til the mor-ning-light __ ap-peared!

9. Wie hat der un - ge - be - tne Be-sen Ka - min und Gas - sen aus - ge-fegt!
The un-in-vi - ted broom was sweeping and soon the streets and chim-neys cleared!

13. Da kommt ein Mäd - chen schon die Stra - ssen,
Now down the street a maid comes wand'ring,

17. das halb verschüch - tert um sich sieht; wie Ro - sen, die der Wind zerbla - sen, so
glances a - round half tim - id - ly; like ro - ses, that the wind's been blowing thus

21. un - stet ihr Ge - sicht - chen glüht.
glow her cheeks so ten - der - ly.

25. Ein schöner Bursch tritt ihr ent - ge - gen, er will ihr voll Ent - zü - cken nahn:
With ra - pid steps a youth ad - van - ces, radiant with joy his love to greet,

29. wie sehn sich freu - dig und ver - legen die un - ge - wohn - ten Schel - me an!
with what em - barr - assed joy - ful glances the two young know - ing rogues do meet!

Er scheint zu fra - gen, ob das Lieb-chen die Zö - pfe schon zu - recht gemacht,
He seems to ask with voice so ten - der, if she's had time her hair to comb,

die heu - te Nacht im off - nen Stübchen ein Sturm in Un - ord - nung gebracht.
that last night got in sad dis - or. der when swept the storm - wind through her room.

Der
The

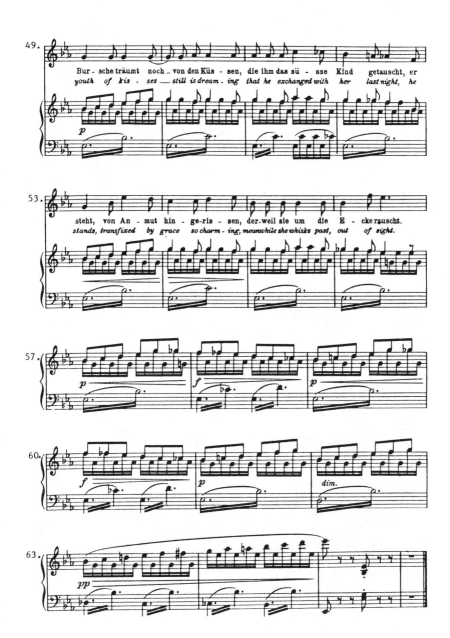

Bur - sche träumt noch _ von den Küs - sen, die ihm das sü - sse Kind getauscht, er
youth of kis - ses _ still is dream - ing that he exchanged with her last night, he

steht, von An - mut hin - ge-ris - sen, der-weil sie um die E - cke rauscht.
stands, transfixed by grace so charm - ing, meanwhile she whisks past, out of sight.

3

Third Relations

During the common-practice period, root movement by third was usually a simple harmonic progression (such as I to III or I to VI) whose function was auxiliary to a more overriding progression by fifth. The only exception occurred in the minor mode, where the structural polarity of the third relation, I to ♭III, replaced the usual fifth relation, I to V. This preference for I to ♭III in minor resulted not from the desire for a third relation *per se*, but from the special interrelationship between the relative major and minor regions. For the most part, third relations functioned either as part of a progression whose harmonic goal was V (as in the arpeggiation I-III-V) or else as part of an embellishment or prolongation of a member of the tonic-dominant axis (as in the neighbor-note motions I-VI-V or I-VI-IV to V). Theorists in the eighteenth and early nineteenth centuries noted that progression by third was less important and "weaker" than that by fifth, and most theoretical discussions of harmony focused upon the more important fifth relation.

By the later nineteenth century, composers began to explore new harmonic functions for third relations that were either unrelated to fifth relations or that actually replaced them. For example, Schubert and, later, Brahms used simple third relations such as I to III♯ or I to VI♯. For late nineteenth-century theorists, the task of conceptualizing the newly emerging third progressions was difficult and so it remains today. The present study of Wolf's use of third relations begins by tracing the theoretical views on both traditional (common-practice) and progressive (later nineteenth-century) third relations. The focus will then shift to how Schenker placed third relations within his analytical framework, and how his common-practice norm can be used, once again, as a gauge for determining the conformity or innovation of Wolf's musical structures. Where chromatic third relations do not fit comfortably into Schenker's analytical framework, alternative analyses will be introduced.

Third Relations in Historical Context

In the traditional comparison of progressions by third and fifth, the third relation always emerged as secondary. The predominant strength of the fifth progression was demonstrated through both mathematical formulations and the prominent position of the fifth in the overtone series. In *Le Istituzioni harmoniche* of 1558, Zarlino considered the fifth the most important interval after the octave within the *numero senario*.[1] In Rameau's ground-breaking studies of harmony, the importance of the fifth relation was stated first in *Traité* (1722) as a mathematical principle within a reinterpretation of Zarlino's *senario*, and later as an acoustical phenomenon in *Nouveau système* (1726) within an incorporation of the acoustical theories of Mersenne (*Harmonie Universelle*, 1636) and Sauveur (*Principes d'acoustique et de musique*, 1700).[2] Acoustical discussions of harmony continued in Helmholtz's *Die Lehre von den Tonempfindungen* (1863) and formed the basis of Riemann's important treatises *Die Natur der Harmonik* (1882) and *Vereinfachte Harmonielehre* (1893).[3]

No matter what their theoretical persuasion, all theorists after Rameau agreed upon the unparalleled strength of the fifth relation and the inferior status of progression by thirds. By the late nineteenth century, scientific proofs of the fifth's superiority were complemented by new analytical systems that demonstrated (within actual muscial compositions) both the superior fifth relation and the relatively weak and subordinate third relation. Hauptmann's dialectic understanding of Rameau's three pillars of harmony was offered in *The Nature of Harmony and Metre*.[4] In addition to his acoustical studies, Riemann systematically applied Rameau's harmonic concepts—including, of course, the importance of the fifth relation—to musical analysis and music instruction.[5] Riemann's understanding of third relations is particularly instructive. Whereas he acknowledges the emergence of new third relations in the late nineteenth century ("since Beethoven, Schubert and Liszt"), Riemann warns that the new harmonic relations resulting from some third relations are remote from the tonic and must be used sparingly and with care.[6]

Riemann's cautious acknowledgment of third relations is echoed and elaborated upon in the studies of Rudolf Louis and Ludwig Thuille, whose *Harmonielehre* of 1906 remains a popular harmony textbook in German-speaking countries.[7] Louis and Thuille state that third relations play either a subordinate or disruptive role within the tonal system, and they describe third relations as either functioning within a key ("innerhalb der Tonart") or within an abandonment of tonality ("die Tonart verlassend"). Third relations within a key are subordinate to the fifth relations and function primarily as harmonic substitutes for the three main harmonies, the tonic, dominant, and subdominant. Third relations that weaken or undermine (abandon) a tonality do so because an actual (or implied) fifth relation simply does not exist.[8] Thus, while contemporary theorists duly noted the emergence of new late-nineteenth-century third relations, this recognition included a reiteration of earlier theoretical concerns for the problematic nature of third relations.

Schenker and Third Relations

Schenker maintained the traditional view of the third relation: his *Ursatz* is predicated upon the unequivocal structural force of the fifth relation, and this in turn relegates the third relation to embellishing functions. As early as 1906, Schenker maintained in his *Harmonielehre* that the third relation was inferior to the fifth relation because of the overtone series.[9] Later, in *Free Composition* (1935), Schenker refined his view of third relations, stating that they were still inferior to fifth relations, but for a new reason: the third relation was subsumed by the fifth relation in the *Bassbrechung*. The progression I to III was part of a I-III-V arpeggiation; I to IV was part of either a I-VI-V embellishing progression or a I-VI-IV arpeggiation that ultimately progressed to V. For Schenker, third relations were called "dividers" within an arpeggiation (see example 3-1):

> the meaning of this third-divider (fig. 14) changes according to whether it remains within the first harmonic degree, as at (a), or whether it achieves the value of an independent root, especially when the third is raised (III♯) as at (b). However, in both instances the essential unity of the fifth-arpeggiation prevails over the third-divider.[10]

Ex. 3-1. Schenker, *Free Composition*, fig. 14

Schenker's assertion that third relations were subsidiary to those by fifth on both acoustical and (more importantly), analytical grounds is supported by a recent study of third relations in the early nineteenth century by Harold Krebs.[11] Krebs documents how third relations function as component parts of arpeggiations of the tonic triad. He cites numerous examples of third relations in Haydn, Mozart, and Beethoven where the tonic triad is prolonged by a bass arpeggiation unfolding over time, and where "passing" third progressions are prolongational. Krebs also discusses other third relations that are not part of an arpeggiation—those that function as auxiliary motions to or preparations of the dominant (e.g., by neighbor-note motion, VI-V). Later, Krebs takes the third relations outside the tonic-dominant axis and cites "circular" progressions (such as III-III/III-III or III-VI/III-III), where he again assigns the third related progressions to "embellishing" functions. Here, they serve to prolong a particular scale step; directed harmonic motion *per se* is negligible. Krebs states that third relations that are "independent of the tonic-dominant axis" place tonality in jeopardy since in the absence of the fifth relation the third relation "weakens" and obscures tonality. Krebs concludes that in some music of Schubert, Chopin, and Liszt, such formal elements as text and motivic design create formal coherence in the absence of a coherent harmonic design.

In his study, Krebs also concludes that Schenker's emphasis on the fifth relation limits the applicability of Schenkerian analysis to certain early nineteenth-century extended-tonal third relations. His study thus highlights the very crux of the problem in analyzing later nineteenth-century third relations: third relations seem to depend too much upon the tonality-defining fifth relation. Kreb's study raises, but does not necessarily answer, a number of critical questions: Does the inherent weakness of the third relation preclude an adequate definition of tonal focus? If it does, is that due to the lack of a fifth relation alone, or does it also involve some ambiguity inherent in third relations *per se*? And finally, are unity and coherence only achieved outside the bounds of tonal structure, and might such pieces involve double tonality, atonality, or some nontonal means of organization? The analyses that follow will address these questions and will demonstrate how both double tonality and motivic continuity assume the formal roles once confined solely to the tonic-dominant axis.

Wolf's Use of Third Relations

The beginnings of the use of chromatic third relations can be seen in the late works of Beethoven and in the works of Schubert and Brahms. Wolf contributed to this evolution of third relations in the 1880s and 1890s by composing songs that used third relations in a variety of contexts. Some of Wolf's songs use third relations within the tonic-dominant axis; others employ third relations that extend beyond a clear, singular tonality. The latter songs offer an opportunity to explore new functions of third relations and to attempt to answer the theoretical questions raised above.

Wolf's use of third relations falls into three basic categories. The first of these comprises all third relations used within a tonic-dominant axis in a more or less traditional fashion. The second consists of those nontraditional third relations that form more complex harmonic structures called "chains of thirds." While Wolf's chains of thirds ultimately fall within the purview of the tonic-dominant axis, the extensive use of chromaticism suggests the existence of a more complex tonal organization, including the possibility of a double tonal scheme. The third category comprises those third relations that occur unequivocally within a double tonal scheme (these will be presented in chapter 4). The song discussed in the section entitled "Third Relations and Poetic Metaphor" falls into the first category, but is given separate treatment because it demonstrates a particularly striking exploitation of third relations for unusual poetic depiction.

Third Relations within a Tonic-Dominant Axis: "Ach, des Knaben Augen" and "Wie lange schon war immer mein Verlangen"

Two Wolf songs demonstrate the more traditional role of the third relation within the governance of the tonic-dominant axis. These are "Ach, des knaben Augen" and "Wie lange schon war immer mein Verlangen."

"Ach, des Knaben Augen"

"Ach, des Knaben Augen," from the *Spanischesliederbuch* (21 December 1889), exemplifies two instances of embellishing third relations, one as a neighbor-note motion and the other as an oscillating progression. As shown in example 3-2, the tonality of F major is prolonged by the progression IV to VI;

Ex. 3-2. "Ach, des Knaben Augen": Middleground Reading

scale step VI is tonicized briefly (m. 4) and ultimately serves as a neighboring harmony to the dominant which occurs initially in m. 8 and more prominently in m. 9. The *Kopfton* is presented in the customary open-note notation, and the melodic line combines the vocal line (stems up) and RH piano part (stems down). On a foreground level, the harmony VI comes not as a third from I, but rather through IV. On a middleground level, however, VI relates as a prolongational third to I within the larger progression I to V. The important arrival upon VI in m. 4 is supported by the text "Und ein Etwas strahlt aus ihnen" (see example 3-3 and the text translation): the "forte" arrival upon VI on the mysterious word "Etwas" is reinforced by the vocal line arrival from the *Kopfton* C (5̂) on "Ach" in m. 1 to high F (8̂) on "Etwas" in m. 5. The resulting structure shows that the tonal vocal pitch (8̂) is supported not by I but by VI, or that the vocal "Etwas" is sung on the tonic pitch even though its harmonic support is not the tonic harmony. The lack of tonic support for the vocal "Etwas" suggests that the text expresses something special or unusual. When the text returns from the spiritual to the personal realm ("das mein ganzes Herz..."), the vocal line returns to 5̂ and the piano accompaniment returns to the tonic of F major.

Ex. 3-3. "Ach, des Knaben Augen": Third Relations and Text

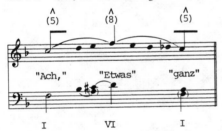

The second verse begins in m. 9, where the dominant is prolonged to four measures. During the ensuing mm. 16, a different third relation occurs, again in conjunction with a specific poetic idea. The key of A♭ is projected with barely a connective to the previous V/F; and the harmony A♭ is prolonged by its subdominant (D♭) in a transposed variant of the opening material. (Note how this section does not go analogously to VI, which would be a return to F.) As example 3-4a shows, the section in A♭ can be heard as a prolongation of C by its third, A♭, with the A♭ section being framed by C⁷ (V⁷/F). In another interpretation (ex. 3-4b), the A♭ section can be considered a component of an F *Bassbrechung*, with the A♭ as an element of modal mixture (♭3̂). Note that the excursion into A♭ was suggested in m. 6, where the B♮-A♭ of the piano part functioned with the vocal D♭ as an augmented sixth chord that emphasized the arrival upon the tonic in m. 7. In yet a third way, the harmonic area in A♭ also

Ex. 3-4. "Ach, des Knaben Augen": Interpretations of A♭ Section

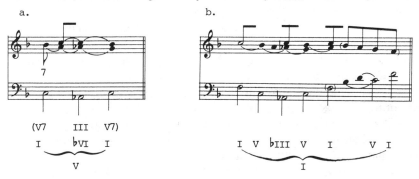

a.

(V7   III   V7)

I   ♭VI   I

V

b.

I   V   ♭III   V   I   V   I

I

can be considered a "third substitute" for F major—a substitution for the tonic that includes modal mixture.[12]

The three different interpretations of the A♭ section bring up a theoretical issue that is unique to this type of third relation: Does the A♭ section form a third relation with the tonic, F major, or with the dominant, C major? The answer is that it does both, and that it is precisely the ambiguity of this third relation that makes it so interesting and powerful. The preference for functional ambiguity of course contradicts Schenker's system, but it is adopted here because it conveys more about the text setting and about Wolf's concept of tonality.   •

Wolf returns to F in m. 16 through a traditional circle-of-fifths progression. Example 3-5 explores the subtle interrelationships among A♭, D♭, F, and C. The D♭ (IV/A♭) is reinterpreted as a ♭VI/C (♭VI/V/F) as well as a

Ex. 3-5. "Ach, des Knaben Augen": Tonal Interrelationships

♭III   IV/♭III♭III   (VI)   V/V   V
♭VI/V♭II/V   ♭VI/V♭II/V   V/V   V

third relation to F as ♭III.[13] Rather than choosing one reading over another, the "meaning" of the third relation might be the very richness of multiple associations and functions between F major, A♭ major, and C major.

The third relation of A♭ to F major and C major is thus clearly connected to the tonic-dominant axis of F. As the text translation shows, the text in mm.

13 ff., "Säh' er dann sein Bild darin, . . . " suggests, in two ways, a shift to an unusual harmony. First, the line preceding the A♭ section, "Blickt' er doch . . . hin," presents the subjunctive: if . . . . then; and second, the text includes the unusual image of the child viewing his own reflection. The beginning of the phrase is on V^7/F—a fitting musical metaphor for a subjunctive clause—and the A♭ section then depicts the child viewing his own image. If A♭ is a third substitution for F, then the key of A♭ major is a transformed "image" of F major. While in this way the text supports the reading of A♭ as a third substitute for F, the A♭ section also can be considered an embellishment to V^7/F (C^7), as the A♭-C third serves in an embellishing relationship within the entire second phrase:

"Blickt' er doch. . . Säh' er dann . . . Würd' er . . . grüssen."
C^7 A♭ C^7
(if only he would look, he would see . . . would greet.)

Text to "Ach, des Knaben Augen"
[*Spanischesliederbuch*, 21 December 1889]

Ach, des Knaben Augen sind	Ah, the boy's eyes seemed
Mir so schön und klar erschienen,	To me so beautiful and clear,
Und ein Etwas strahlt aus ihnen,	And from them something shines,
Das mein ganzes Herz gewinnt.	Which enchants my whole heart.
Blickt' er doch mit diesen süssen	If he would but turn
Augen nach den meinen hin!	Those sweet eyes toward mine!
Säh' er dann sein Bild darin,	Then would he see his image mirrored,
Würd' er wohl mich liebend grüssen.	And indeed might give me loving greeting.
Und so geb'ich ganz mich hin,	And so I give myself entirely,
Seinen Augen nur zu dienen,	To serve only those eyes,
Denn ein Etwas strahlt aus ihnen,	For something shines from them
Das mein ganzes Herz gewinnt.	Which enchants my whole heart.

The text thus supports the notion of an ambivalent function of A♭ within the two harmonic domains of F and C. The conditional mood of the text suggests a hope or yearning that the child greet the singer. It is not clear whether the child ever in fact does this, or, for that matter, if the child ever really sees his own reflection. The conditional mood of the text encourages several interpretations of the third relation in this song, including the possibility that the third relation depicts an ambiguous situation that is represented in a musical analog of harmonic ambivalence.

While Schenker's analytical system clearly depicted the harmonic progressions in "Ach, des Knaben Augen," Schenker's system was less useful for modeling the functional ambiguity accompanying the third relation. A Schenkerian reading does not readily depict the A♭ section as having several possible functions at one time.

"Wie lange schon war immer mein Verlangen"

"Wie lange schon war immer mein Verlangen" is a charming song from the *Italienischesliederbuch* (4 December 1891). The poem tells of a woman who has been yearning for a lover who is a musician ("Musikus"). The lord grants her wish and the lover-musician arrives and plays his violin. Wolf depicts the poetry with mock solemnity—he casts the song in the minor mode and fills it with a variety of musical puns and ambiguities. The result is a song of wit and humor.

One of the song's most dramatic structures is the third relation between the minor tonic (F minor) and its natural minor submediant (D minor). The ♭VI functions as the conventional upper neighbor to V, but the use of modal mixture (D minor instead of D♭ major) creates a sense of tonal flux within the embellishing I-VI-V progression. The section in D minor (mm. 14-22) diverges from F minor, and the neighboring function of ♮VI is only understood retrospectively, after the prolonged section on the dominant (mm. 23-37).

An expectation for a large-scale VI-V progression is suggested in the piano's introductory measures. There the melodic motive F-E♮-D♭ suggests an ultimate resolution of D♭ to C. The motion to D minor instead of D♭ major occurs through the transformation of that motive F-E-D♭ to F-E-C♯. The pitch D♭/C♯ (♭$\hat{6}$ in F minor) thus becomes both a pivotal pitch and a pitch of functional ambivalence as ♭$\hat{6}$ (D♭) in F minor becomes $\hat{7}$ (C♯) in D minor. The transposition of the motive in D minor to D-C♯-B♭ becomes transformed as well as in mm. 14-22: first to D-D♭-B♭, then to E♭♭-D♭-B♭, and finally back to D♮-D♭-B♭. The melodic vacillation between D♮ and D♭ reinforces the notion that, in the D minor section, the D♮ is a substitute for D♭.

The text suggests the use of double-entendre and irony. While the word "Musikus" means music-lover, it also denotes a musician who is a lover. The ironic use of the minor mode intensifies the confusion of this opening text, as does the incessant use of such melodic dissonances as the tritone and the augmented second. If the meaning of the first statement is vague, it becomes clearer on the word "gut" where the expected melodic resolution to A♭ is altered to A♮ and V⁷/F minor shifts chromatically to V⁷/D minor. Perhaps such yearning for a musician-lover does not bode well for the future, as the first phrase of text (lines 1 and 2) cadences deceptively on a dissonant harmony, V⁷/♮VI. This unexepected cadence in D minor contains another gesture of Wolfian wit: the vocal line ending of A♮ could have been a Picardy third if the piano part had resolved to F and not to D. In this characteristic separation of vocal and piano parts, Wolf suggests that the naive yearning of the singer may be undermined by forces she does not yet know.

Text to "Wie lange schon war immer mein Verlangen"
[*Italienischesliederbuch*, 4 December 1891]

Wie lange schon war immer mein
  Verlangen:
Ach, wäre doch ein Musikus mir gut!
Nun liess der Herr mich meinen Wunsch
  erlangen
Und schickt mir einen, ganz wie Milch
  und Blut.
Da kommt er eben her mit sanfter Miene,
Und senkt den Kopf und spielt die
  Violine.

How long has my yearning been:
Ah, would a musician be good for me!
Now the lord has granted me my wish
And sent me one, all peaches and cream.
Here he comes, with gentle mien,
and bows his head and plays the violin.

Phrase 2 begins in D minor and presents a transposed variant of phrase 1 in F minor, with A♮ functioning as a link between F minor (A♮ as the Picardy third) and D minor (A♮ as $\hat{5}$). The transposed melodic figure (F-E♮-D♭) now becomes D♮-C♯-B♭. The modal mixture ♮$\hat{6}$-♭$\hat{6}$ (D♮-D♭) is reiterated as the wished-for lover is described: "ganz wie Milch und Blut." Again, the music suggests ironic tension, as the vocal line remains all but fixated on B♭ and D♭. On the text "mich meinen Wunsch erlangen/Und schickt mir einen," B♭ is a common tone between F minor and D minor (♭$\hat{6}$ of the latter) and D♭ is the connecting musical pun (D♭ = $\hat{7}$/ D minor). Again melodic interruption implies a humorous treatment of the text. The melody that presents the descriptive terms "Milch und Blut" suggests a return to the *Kopfton* C, but this melodic motion is deferred. The pitch B♭ remains the dissonant melodic focus in m. 21 and becomes the seventh of V^7/ F minor in the third phrase. This recalls the aborted motion to A♭ in the first phrase, where the vocal line ended on A♮ instead of A♭ in m. 12. The connection between m. 12 and m. 21 is striking, for it suggests that the section begun in D minor (mm. 12-22) might be an interpolation that postpones the dominant prolongation. This could be text-related, with the last four lines of the poem representing a fantasy of the singer rather than a depiction of actual events. This is in keeping with Wolf's whimsical treatment of the poem and gives the section in D minor (and the function of the third relation) yet another meaning, namely, the depiction of fantasy in a more remotely related key. The third phrase depicts the arrival of the "Musikus," which might be only imaginary.

The entire third phrase is an extended prolongation of the dominant. Again, the description of the "Musikus" is rendered with the dissonant augmented second, E♮-D♭. The vocal line ends on the *Kopfton,* and Wolf once again conveys uncertainty, as a descent or resolution from C is not sung. The humorous piano coda (mm. 32-38), which depicts the inept violin-playing by the curious "Musikus," includes a descent from the *Kopfton* C and concludes the song—and possibly the fantasy—with unabashed caprice.

Motivic transformation and coherence. Example 3-6a shows a middleground sketch of the song. The D♮-C bass motion is a chromatically altered harmonic enlargement of the melodic motive (C-D♭;⌐♮) heard first in mm. 5-10 and later (in retrograde) in mm. 25-30. The C-D♭ motive recurs transposed in the D minor section (mm. 14-22) as A♮-B♭. Example 3-6b demonstrates how the underlying melodic motion creates an elegant symmetrical structure between C and A♮, with A♮ as the fulcrum. The bass motion F-D♮-C thus accompanies a carefully rendered melodic design, which projects the main melodic pitches C and A♮ with motivic neighbor notes. The contextually unusual thirds F to D♭ (or C to A♮) are softened by motivic connections (neighbor notes and augmented seconds), as Wolf relates two remote harmonies through motivic repetition.

Ex. 3-6. "Wie lange schon"

    a. Middleground Reading (descent in piano only)   b. Melodic Symmetry

F min:I V7   VI   V7   I II V   I
              V7/VI⌐_____⌐

As suggested earlier, the motive F-E♮-D♭ is transformed through enharmonic equivalence, the F-E♮-D♭ becoming F-E-C♯, which creates the shift to V^7/D minor. The transported motive within D minor itself is transformed in order to return to the original key of F minor: in m. 17, the C♯ becomes D♭ as the harmony is $G♭^7$ (+6/ V/ F); in m. 19, D♮ is respelled E♭♭ as an upper neighbor to D♭ above G♭6; and, finally, in mm. 21-22 the E♭♭ reverts back to D♮ and the motive D♮-D♭-B♭ assumes yet another meaning—D♮/ D♭ represents modal variants of $\hat{6}$ in F minor above V^7. With the arrival of the dominant seventh in mm. 23ff. (third line of text), the ambiguity of D♮/ D♭ has been exploited and then clarified, especially during the D minor section. Note that the section in D minor begins in m. 14 but remains in that key for only two measures. In m. 16, ♭VI/ D (B♭) functions as a common chord between D minor and F minor (♭VI/ D = IV♮/ F). From this point onward, the harmonic motion remains unstable until the arrival of V^7/ F in mm. 21ff.

Prolongation of dissonance. The figured bass symbols in example 3-6a reveal another important aspect of the song, namely, its extensive use of dissonance.

The only symbols of consonance are the 5's at mm. 5, 14, and 38 (the song's end). The extensive dissonance in this song is remarkable—as example 3-7 indicates, every harmony between mm. 5 and 14 and from m. 15 onward is some form of dissonance. In mm. 7, 10, and 16, the consonant harmonies are in $^6_4$ position; and with the exception of the $G\flat\,^6$ chord in m. 19, all other harmonies are either diminished triads, augmented sixth chords, or seventh chords. The degree of dissonance is important in this song because it creates a harmonic dissonance out of which the unusual form of modal mixture emerges. The dissonance of D minor within F minor is easily assimilated in m. 14 because it has been prepared by the dissonance preceding it. Measures 15ff. continue the level of dissonance through the third line of text, and the next consonant point of arrival is the final tonic in m. 38. (Again, the consonant harmonies in mm. 28, 32-33, and 35 are all embellishing passing harmonies.)

Ex. 3-7. "Wie lange schon": Chromatic Density

In depicting a poem of irony and humor, Wolf used a third relation in the guise of modal mixture to alter a normally commonplace embellishing motion, ♭VI to V. To accommodate the middleground chromatic alteration, Wolf creates a foreground of dissonance and chromaticism so extensive that the arrival on the altered VI is heard as consonant.[14] Wolf also creates overall coherence during the song by developing a melodic motive whose elements echo the semitonal shifting that is so much associated with modal mixture.

Schenkerian analysis. As example 3-6 suggests, it is altogether possible to offer a coherent Schenkerian reading of this song. The *Ursatz* remains intact and the altered VI, with its D♮ and A♮, are simply elements of modal mixture. Example 3-8a shows a more detailed Schenkerian reading of mm. 5-14, where the chromaticism is reduced to the cadential motion V^6_{5-I} in D minor. Prior to the cadence in D minor (with ♭VI substituting for I in m. 7), an F minor tonic arpeggiation prolongs that triad. In a more idiosyncratic reading, example 3-8b illustrates how, by retaining the chromatic density as a formal factor, the chromatic shift to D minor is anticipated in the texture, the harmonic syntax, and, most importantly, in the chromaticism of the preceding progression.

Ex. 3-8. "Wie lange schon"

a. Schenkerian Reduction, mm. 5-14   b. Chromaticism and Dissonance, mm. 5-14

Example 3-8b thus complements the Schenkerian reading by underscoring the chromatic derivation of the altered VI.

Third Relations within a Tonic-Dominant Axis that are Circular Progressions

In the category of simple third relations within a tonic-dominant axis, Schenker's system was limited only in the depiction of tonal ambiguity. In the category of circular third progressions, or a chain of major thirds, new analytical issues arise and the use of Schenkerian analysis becomes more problematical.

Wolf's use of circular progressions may be considered less innovative than that of other late-nineteenth-century composers in that his circular progressions are anchored to the tonic-dominant axis.[15] In order to fully understand why Wolf adopted a more conservative use of circular third progressions, we will begin by examining the circular third progression as a theoretical construct. As always, our discussion will include a careful consideration of how Schenker conceptualized this extended-tonal structure and how his system might accommodate it.

The progression by major third occurs in two separate musical contexts. First, the third chain by itself creates an underlying bass progression outlining an augmented triad: I-III♯-♭VI-I, a chromatic structure whose function is inherently unclear. Second, when the third chain is linked to a dominant (i.e., I-III♯-♭VI-V-I), the problematic augmented triad is subsumed by the tonic-dominant axis and the chromaticism of ♭VI assumes a more embellishing function as neighbor to V. In this instance, however, the chromatic third relation, I-III♯, remains problematic. In both cases, two fundamental questions arise: (1) whether the function of the circle of major thirds is that of progression or prolongation; and (2) at what structural level the chromatics of the third chain function, both within and outside the governance of the tonic-dominant axis. Considering first the third chain outside the tonic-dominant axis, the structure may be interpreted in several ways. In the progression I-III♯-♭VI-I, ♭VI may be replacing V in an altered tonic arpeggiation or ♭VI may function as an interruption or interpolation of an implied tonic arpeggiation: I-III♯-[♭VI]-(V)-I. If ♭VI is indeed a substitute for or replacement of V, does the resulting equal subdivision of the tonic octave result in a prolongation of I similar to that of the *Bassbrechung*? Concerning the existence of a third chain within a tonic-dominant axis, the essential question is how to adjust the chromaticism so that the melodic line does not undermine what otherwise is a diatonic tonic arpeggiation in the bass.

Applicability of Schenker

The answers to these questions will affect, of course, the applicability of Schenkerian analysis to pieces that use third-chain progressions. Fortunately, Schenker himself discussed some of the issues under examination here, and his consideration of the chromaticism of the third I-III♯ within the *Bassbrechung* will now be discussed.

In *Free Composition* (p. 91), Schenker says: "even so basic a degree-progression as I-III$^{♯3}$ ♮V in major, and the same progression in minor with III♮5 and V♯3, brings about a conflict of chromatic tones." He does not suggest that this "conflict" contradicts in any way his *Bassbrechung*, because the chromatics occur above the bass. Later (p. 135) in the same book, Schenker says of the problematic third relations in the major:

> when, in *major*, $\hat{5}$ is the primary tone, a progression to
>
> $$\begin{array}{c} 3 \\ III^{♯3} \end{array}$$
>
> creates difficulties; such a progression also requires a raising of the primary tone, and it must be approached logically through auxiliary harmonies, as in Beethoven's Op. 53, first movement, mm. 35-45.... measures 74ff, of course, supply g♯2, d♮2 and c♮2.[16]

See example 3-9. Schenker thus admits to a difficulty in the progression of I to III♯ in major, but he continues to suggest that through "auxiliary harmonies" the effect of "raising the primary tone" (i.e., to a tone outside the given tonality) will be mitigated. For the analogous situation in minor, Schenker suggests the

Ex. 3-9. Schenker, *Free Composition*, fig. 100/6

$$\hat{5}\text{————}♯\hat{5}\text{——}♯\hat{4}\text{——}\hat{3}$$
$$g^2 —(a^2)— g♯^2 — f♯^2 — e^2$$
$$\text{I} —(\quad)—\text{III————}$$

need for some sort of "correction" procedure: "it is then the task of the development to eliminate the chromatics."[17] Beethoven's Op. 57/I is

Schenker's example of the chromatic displacement in minor, where the *Kopfton* C over F becomes C♭ over A♭ (III♭).[18] Oster's commentary in *Free Composition* is instructive:

> Schenker mentions only briefly that Beethoven's *Waldstein Sonata* Op. 53 shows the bass progression I-III-V-I. This progression, so common in minor, was rather infrequently used in major before Beethoven's time. [Oster cites the tendency of II in minor to resolve to III]...thus the minor mode has an inherent tendency to move to III. As a consequence, the III in major has to be approached through auxiliary harmonies which carry with them further chromatics...for these reasons we rarely find I-III-V in major, particularly not in earlier composers.... Beethoven was the first to apply it to the fully developed sonata form...it is important to understand that the III is not just a "mediant" as it is usually described; its true significance is as a third-divider, a tone of arpeggiation of the way from I to V.[19]

Oster, then, reiterates Schenker's position. Neither theorist considers that chromatic variants undermine the basic tonality during the course of the *Bassbrechung*. The problems arising from the arpeggiation I-III♯-V were either mitigated by interpolated material or "corrected" over time.

Schenker also explored the third chain itself in *Free Composition*. In his figure 100/6, in fact, he presents the very structures in question, including one example from a Wolf song that will be analyzed later in this study. Example 3-10 reproduces Schenker's figure 100/6. The chains of major thirds arise in a

Ex. 3-10. Schenker, *Free Composition*, p. 135

Chopin, Étude op. 25 no. 11 (cf. Figs. 76,3; 100,2a and 107)

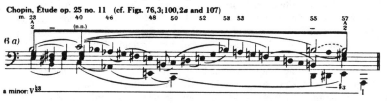

Figs. 100 [cont.]-102

Beethoven, Violin Sonata op. 24, 2nd mvt.

Hugo Wolf, "Das Ständchen" *(Gedichte von Eichendorff)*

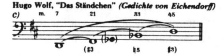

general discussion of *Bassbrechung* and Schenker comments: "here we have a descending register transfer by means of three major thirds. . . . "[20] Schenker's citation of third chains in figure 100/6 is curious in that he does not distinguish between structural levels. While in the Chopin *Etude* the chain of thirds occurs as prolongation of V and in the Beethoven *Sonata* the final tonic is preceded by its dominant, the Wolf song is presented without any clear indication of structural level. Schenker's apparent lack of concern for structural levels in figure 100/6 might have been inadvertent, or he may not have felt such a distinction applicable to the topic at hand. In any event, he cites a chain of major thirds in the Wolf example without reference to the overriding *Ursatz* (does he consider figure 100/6c a background?); and he seems to consider the *Bassbrechung* in "Das Ständchen" to be a long-range prolongation of a governing tonic harmony, even though the tonic is represented by an augmented triad (D-F♯-B♭-D).

Schenker's reticence on the augmented triad in figure 100/6 remains puzzling. Several later theorists have attempted to come to terms with the third chain unconnected to a tonic-dominant axis. In her 1967 doctoral dissertation, Sonia Slatin cites the provocative figure 100/6 and offers an eloquent query about the unanswered problems of the augmented-triad *Ursatz*:

> . . . several questions arise as a result of these examples. How is it that an arpeggiation that includes the replacement of a tone as vital to the meaning of the triad as the fifth can function on the same unifying level as the purely diatonic triad? How can the raised fifth—a product of counterpoint which is totally unrelated to the harmonic origins of the fifth indigenous to the diatonic triad—substitute for the true fifth, and join in the function of the large-scale arpeggiation as a source of unity on an ultimate level of meaning and perception? The illustrations, slurs and all, point to nothing else of significance in this connection but the "filling-in" of an octave span by means of successive major thirds. But the filled-in octave span, although it functions as a source of integration and coherence . . . is nonetheless secondary to that of broad triadic horizontalization as a means of achieving overall unity, according to Schenker's concepts. The problem presented by this kind of arpeggiation is not explained by the theorist. Perhaps these and similar analyses suggest a development of Schenker's ideas that, because of his death, he was unable to pursue.[21]

Over a decade later, Gregory Proctor's 1978 dissertation, *Technical Bases of Nineteenth-Century Tonality: A Study of Chromaticism*, reiterates Slatin's concern about the augmented triad and offers a new analytical solution—what Proctor calls a "transposition operation." With the transposition operation, Proctor maintains that the unique symmetrical structure that is obtained from the equal subdivision of an octave replaces the concept of *Bassbrechung*: "the concept of symmetrical division removes the question of arpeggiation as an observation of analytic force . . . where the arpeggiation of an augmented triad gives no contrapuntal information."[22] Proctor's concept of transposition is interesting in that it allows for the possibility of more than one tonality: a central harmony does not have to be prolonged, although he maintains that it might be. The harmonies involved might not be directly related, but, rather, might relate to one another as components of a transposition scheme. Whereas Proctor's theoretical method may be applicable to other nineteenth-century composers, it only applies to the present study of Wolf in its contention that within such harmonic structures as the arpeggiated augmented triad, more than one tonality may be operative. While both Slatin and Proctor acknowledge the difficulty in applying Schenkerian theory to the chain of thirds progression that has no anchoring V, Slatin does not offer any solution to the questions she raises and Proctor rejects Schenkerian analysis altogether. Because Wolf's third chains are for the most part bound to a tonic-dominant axis, Proctor's transposition operation is as inapplicable as Schenker's analytical framework. The following analyses will propose altogether different analytical ideas.

Songs with Chains of Thirds: "Das Ständchen," "In dem Schatten meiner Locken," and "Und steht Ihr früh"

Three songs exemplify Wolf's use of third chains. The songs "Das Ständchen" (Eichendorff text, 28 September 1888) and "In dem Schatten"(Spanish text, 17 November 1889) use third-chain progressions in remarkably similar ways and thus offer the opportunity for comparison. In a sense, they represent variants of the same harmonic procedure. The third song, "Und steht Ihr früh" (*Italienischesliederbuch*, 3-4 April 1896), demonstrates an altogether different type of third chain and will be examined separately.

Example 3-11 compares the use of the same third progression, I-III♯-♭VI-I by the two songs. They both include an abrupt juxtaposition of I and III♯: both begin with a complete phrase in a clearly defined tonality ("Das Ständchen" closing on a clear-cut V/D and "In dem Schatten" closing on an equally clear V/B♭), only to be followed by a repetition of the opening material on the level of III♯ without any suggestion of, or preparation for, a change in tonal focus. Both songs then present a retrospective harmonic connection for I and III♯. In "Das Ständchen," the material is repeated once again on the level of ♭VI; in "In dem Schatten," the material begun on III♯ concludes with a progression to ♭VI. The "retrospective" relationship of III♯ to I is made all the more intense by the juxtaposition, in both songs, of I and III♯ in the connection between either the first two phrases of text ("In dem Schatten") or the first two stanzas of text ("Das Ständchen"). In this way, the songs align unusual harmonic relations with opposing textual ideas.

Example 3-11 summarizes the harmonic language of the two songs. "Das Ständchen" represents a straightforward presentation of the harmonic relations in the chain-of-thirds progression. Each stanza is presented in a

Ex. 3-11. Comparison of "Das Ständchen" and "In dem Schatten"

a. "Das Ständchen"

b. "In dem Schatten"

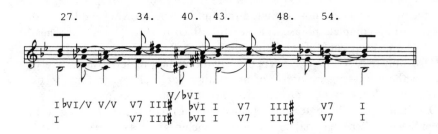

different harmonic region of the arpeggiation. A *Kopfton* is emphasized throughout and all third relations are cast within the tonic-dominant axis. In contrast, "In dem Schatten" is considerably more complex. Each stanza is represented by an entire harmonic progression—either an ascending or descending arpeggiation—involving I, III♯, V, and ♭VI in diverse orderings. "In dem Schatten" can be considered a virtual exploration of the diverse interrelationships between the various harmonies; III♯ does not always progress to ♭VI, just as ♭VI does not always resolve to V before proceeding to I. In comparison to "Das Ständchen," then, "In dem Schatten" is more harmonically progressive. The individual study of each song that follows will explore how the text and harmonic language relate, and how each song exemplifies unique uses of the chains of major thirds.

Before proceeding to individual analyses, a note of caution must be proffered regarding the use of text to "explain" the unusual thirds in circular progressions. While the text may enhance the understanding of the music, the harmonic structures must still be understood solely in musical terms. Because third chains have such elusive functions, the unusual third relations found in them are especially susceptible to misguided reliance on the text. Nevertheless, it must be emphasized that the text explains only the impetus for selecting unusual harmonies. It does not explain how an unusual harmony functions, or how it is to be understood as a discrete musical structure.

"Das Ständchen"

"Das Ständchen" sets a text by Eichendorff which depicts an aged minstrel hearing a young student serenading his lover. The atmosphere of splashing fountains and rustling trees reminds the minstrel of his past; in his youth, the minstrel had also sung to his love on summer evenings. Finally, the reverie is tinged with sadness as the minstrel recalls that his love of earlier times is gone and wistfully bids the younger singer to continue singing. Each stanza expresses a discrete portion of the minstrel's experience and is associated with a different tonality. The singing student is heard and the aged minstrel identifies with the young student in the key of D; contemplation of the sounds of the evening (fountain splashing, trees rustling) provokes a recollection of times past, which corresponds to music in the key of F♯; memories of the minstrel's own singing as a youth are evoked in B♭; and the minstrel recalls the death of his beloved, returns to the present, and bids his younger counterpart to continue singing in D major.

Text to "Das Ständchen"
[Eichendorff, 28 September 1888]

Auf die Dächer zwischen blassen	Between pale clouds
Wolken schaut der Mond herfür,	The moon peers on the rooftops,
Ein Student dort auf der Gassen	A student there in the street
Singt vor seiner Liebsten Tür.	Sings before his sweetheart's door.

Und die Brunnen rauschen wieder	And again the fountains rush
Durch die stille Einsamkeit,	Through the silent solitude,
Und der Wald vom Berge nieder,	And the trees of the mountains bend,
Wie in alter, schöner Zeit.	As in former, happy times.

So in meinen jungen Tagen	Just as in my young days
Hab' ich manche Sommernacht	Had I also many a summer night
Auch die Laute hier geschlagen	Plucked the lute here
Und manch lust'ges Lied erdacht.	And invented many a joyful song.

Aber von der stillen Schwelle	But from the silent threshold
Trugen sie mein Lieb zur Ruh',	Has my love been borne to her rest,
Und du, frölicher Geselle,	And you, merry youth,
Singe, sing' nur immer zu!	Sing on, sing on forever!

The use of more remote third relations is suggested by the shift in text from present to past, from active experience to pensive recollection. Wolf carefully prepares the listener for these various shifts in harmony. First, the piano introduction adumbrates the idea of tonal ambiguity by depicting the strumming of the serenader (see example 3-12). The open fifth (a) and the juxtaposed fifths (b) suggest the tonalities of G, D, or even A major.[23] After the first stanza has clearly been established in D (mm. 6-20), the shift to F♯ seems a dramatic contrast. In fact, this shift to F♯ was anticipated by subtle surface details in the first stanza: the A♯ of the F♯ section was suggested in m. 12 (where A♯ as B♭ was a modal variant of IV in D). Then in the second stanza, the B♭ (within IV♭/ D) becomes reinterpreted as A♯ over F♯; while at the same time the tonic D is carefully undermined by the prolonged use of a melodic neighbor note C✗ (mm. 23-24; 25; 29-30).

Ex. 3-12.   "Das Ständchen": Piano Introduction

The juxtaposition of the keys of D and F♯ is replaced by clear modulatory sections between stanzas two, three, and four. The change in procedure is once again prompted by the text: the second stanza ends with a reference to the past, "wie in alter, schöner Zeit," which leads to the key of the past, B♭. The means of modulation from F♯ to B♭ is consistent with the association of D to F♯; enharmonic pitches are transformed through reinterpretation from one key to another (see example 3-13). The modulation from F# to B♭ again occurs through the minor subdominant: the B major chord (IV/ F#) is reinterpreted as ♭II/ B♭ (C♭-E♭-G♭), which then proceeds to ♭VI/ B♭ (F#-A#-C# becoming G♭-B♭-D♭), which in turn resolves to V/ B♭.

Ex. 3-13. "Das Ständchen": Enharmonic Pitches in Modulation

The connection of the third and fourth stanzas is similar to that of stanzas two and three. As the reverie comes to a close, so the key of B♭ ends and the present returns in D major. The harmony IV/ B♭ becomes ♭II$_4^6$ in D, which resolves to V/ D in m. 43 (example 3-14). Note how the $^6_4$ position of ♭II keeps B♭ in the bass, so that the bass descent B♭-A corresponds to the melodic motive B♭-A (♭$\hat{6}$-$\hat{5}$ in m. 43 and incomplete neighbor in m. 44).

Ex. 3-14. "Das Ständchen": Common Chord Retransition, mm. 42- 43

Several aspects of the final stanza are noteworthy. First, Wolf sets this final stanza apart and reinforces the notion of reprise by adding in mm. 45-46 a literal repetition of the introductory bars that preceded the first stanza (mm. 7-8). Second, Wolf took a liberty with the text that was for him highly unusual: he repeated the final line of text in a six-bar coda. This coda creates a strong association between the first and last stanzas in an attempt to dispel any tonal ambiguity that might remain from the use of internal third relations.

Considered as a musical structure, the chain of thirds in "Das Ständchen" creates an augmented triad that does in fact resolve to a comprehensible tonic arpeggiation (see example 3-15). The augmented triad is not a replacement for the *Bassbrechung* (which is beamed), but instead serves to embellish that triad (note the flag on B♭). One function of this chain of thirds, then, is to extend the prolongation of the tonic (through ♭VI) or embellish the resolution to V (with ♭VI). Two analytical questions remain unanswered; (1) How does the ♯3 of III function in this song, and (2) how do we explain the chromatic alteration of the *Kopfton* F♯ to F♮ (over ♭VI)?

Ex. 3-15.   "Das Ständchen": Middleground *Bassbrechung*

    I   III♯ (♭VI)   V   I   V   I

The chromatic alterations in "Das Ständchen" are tenable within D major because both A♯ (as B♭) and F♮ can be understood as modal variants of 5̂ and 3̂. The voice leading in example 3-15 shows how A♯ functions as an upper neighbor (B♭) to A, while F♮ becomes a chromatic passing tone from *Kopfton* F♯ to lower neighbor E. The progression from III♯ to ♭VI clarifies the transformation of A♯ to B♭, and the 4̂6̂ suspension above V effects a smooth transition from ♭VI to V, with F♮ functioning as ♭3̂.

When viewed as modal mixtures and neighbor notes, the chromatic elements in "Das Ständchen" seem to enhance rather than to weaken the tonality of D, and the chromaticism does not in any way obfuscate the *Bassbrechung*. There is, however, another altogether different way to view the construct in example 3-15. Example 3-16 recasts the harmonic structures of example 3-15: the primary motion remains I to V, but the intervening harmonies III♯ and ♭VI do not prolong I, serving instead as harmonic interpolations between I and V—as motion within (but separate from) the progression from I to V. Rather than being prolongational, the progression to III♯ and ♭VI direct motion away from I—with ♭VI then returning to V. While the inherent ambiguity of third relations creates an illusion of closeness between I and III♯, the common tone F♯ is the only link between two otherwise remote harmonies. This reading takes into account the fact that the motion from A to A♯ is not heard as A to B♭ until m. 31. From m. 21 to m. 30 the 5̂ (A) is altered, not by a neighbor note, but by a chromatic displacement: A is not embellished by B♭ spelled as A♯; A is replaced by A♯. Likewise, the tonic is not prolonged by III♯, but is displaced by it. The harmony ♭VI, then, pivots back to D major through its dominant. In sum, the tonic is not expanded through arpeggiation, and III♯ does not "divide" the motion from I to V. The harmony III♯ displaces the tonic and the motion between I and V extends beyond the confines of the tonic and dominant.

By recasting the function of III♯ from "divider" to interrupter, the function of the chain of thirds is one of interpolation rather than prolongation.

The dotted lines between I and III♯ suggest the tenuousness of functional relationship between the two chords, and the beam between III♯ and ♭VI indicate that the two harmonies function as a pair outside the tonic-dominant axis. The flag on ♭VI then shows the subsequent function of ♭VI as upper neighbor to V—as an ultimate reconnector to the tonic-dominant axis. Example 3-16 thus suggests that while the chain of thirds functions in one sense within the tonic-dominant axis, it exists as well outside and separate from that axis. In this interpretation, since the third relations exist outside the *Bassbrechung*, the heretofore problematic chromatic alterations within arpeggiation are eliminated.

Ex. 3-16. "Das Ständchen": Alternative Reading

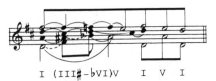

I (III♯-♭VI)V   I   V   I

When compared to the analysis in Example 3-16, Schenker's reading of a large-scale *Bassbrechung* for "Das Ständchen" (his figure 100/6(c), example 3-9) remains unclear. The song seems less about a *Bassbrechung* of D than about a shifting away from and subsequent return to D. Schenker's augmented triad *Bassbrechung* is furthermore curious, as his sketch does not show that the B♭ does resolve to A on a background level. What does seem clear here is that using the concept of *Bassbrechung* limits the functions of III♯ and ♭VI. These harmonies need not prolong I; instead, the third relations might be considered separate harmonic structures with independent functions and identities. This non-Schenkerian view of third relations incorporates a shift in stature for third relations from subsidiary and merely embellishing to structurally independent.

"In dem Schatten meiner Locken"

As noted earlier, the overall use of thirds in "In dem Schatten" is similar to that in "Das Ständchen." However, while both songs involve changes in time sequence or mood, the conflicts between past and present in "In dem Schatten" are combined with conflicts between and within the protagonists.

A young woman is sitting with her lover who has fallen asleep. She cannot decide whether or not to awaken him. This conflict reminds her of the frustration of combing her hair—she takes great care to comb her hair only to have the wind "ruffle" her locks. Recollection of that frustration leads her to think about her lover and her conflicts about him. He expresses anxiety to her about his yearnings for her; and while he calls her a snake (as though she endangers him), he falls asleep (as though he feels safe with her). Whereas in "Das Ständchen" Wolf conveys a tripartite series of states in the text with three distinct tonal areas, he depicts ambivalence or conflict in "In dem Schatten" by using two keys related to one another by one third and connected to one another by another third.

Text to "In dem Schatten meiner Locken"
[*Spanischesliederbuch*, 17 November 1889]

In dem Schatten meiner Locken,	In the shadow of my tresses,
Schlief mir mein Geliebter ein.	My beloved has fallen asleep.
Weck' ich ihn nun auf?—Ach nein!	Shall I awaken him now?—ah, no!
Sorglich strählt' ich meine Krausen	With care I comb my ruffled
Locken täglich in der Frühe,	Locks daily in early morning,
Doch umsonst ist meine Mühe,	Yet in vain is my trouble,
Weil die Winde sie zersausen.	For the winds dishevel them.
Lockenschatten, Windessausen	Shadows of curls, rushing of winds
Schäferten den Liebsten ein.	Have lulled my love to sleep.
Weck' ich ihn nun auf?—Ach nein!	Shall I awaken him now?—ah, no!
Hören muss ich, wie ihn gräme,	I must hear how it would grieve him,
Dass er schmachtet schon so lange,	That he yearned so long,
Dass ihm Leben geb' und nehme	That they give or take life,
Diese meine braune Wange.	These my brown cheeks.
Und er nennt mich seine Schlange,	And he calls me his serpent,
Und doch schlief er bei mir ein.	And yet he falls asleep beside me.
Weck' ich ihn nun auf?—Ach nein!	Shall I awaken him now?—ah, no!

The song begins in B♭ and the first phrase ends on V/B♭: the lover has fallen asleep in the shadow of her tresses. Her question "Weck' ich ihn nun auf?" is cast in D and her tentative answer in G♭ returns the song to the original key of B♭. Note that when Wolf juxtaposes the opposing tonalities of B♭ and D in mm. 1-8, he interrelates the two regions through thematic repetition. Although m. 5 is in the new region of D, the material presented in m. 5 is really a transposition of m. 1. This reprise of m. 1 is then interrupted by the sustained D major chord in m. 6, which functions more like a dominant than a tonic, as it is rhythmically analogous to the V/F of m. 4.[24] Example 3-11 (p. 92) demonstrates the interrelationships of the three main harmonies: D is ♭VI of G♭; G♭ is ♭VI of B♭. The function of D major is understood in retrospect, when the F♯ becomes G♭ and resolves to F as ♭VI to V in B♭. The second stanza also begins in B♭, as the girl thinks about the problems of combing her hair. The first four measures end on V/B♭ as in the first stanza, but the second phrase shifts to D, as the conflict emerges ("Weil die Winde sie zersausen"). The shift from B♭ to D occurs through a common chord: IV/B♭ becomes ♭II/D. The E♭ harmony can also be heard as an incomplete augmented sixth chord in the key of G minor, with D major functioning as V/G minor. This reiterates the notion that D major can function both as a dominant and a tonic, the D-as-dominant being first suggested by the sustained D chord of m. 6. The function of D as V/G minor is reiterated in m. 23, where the vocal line sings a C♮ above the piano's D major chord. The arrival upon D is prolonged through a descending chromatic passage, mm. 23-26, as the girl notes the various things that have lulled her lover to sleep ("Lockenschatten, Windessausen schlaferten den Liebsten ein"). The D tonality is then quickly replaced by B♭ again, mm. 27ff., B♭ now assuming the role of the disrupting tonality through which the girl wonders: "Weck' ich ihn nun auf?"[25] The predictable answer "Ach nein" is consequently recast into D♭, which becomes ♭VI of F, the dominant of B♭.

The third stanza begins on V⁷/B♭ and this stanza depicting the lovers' conflicts is portrayed by a appropriate dissonance: a vacillation between V⁷/B♭ and D (mm. 34-39). In this unstable section, the key of D may be considered a substitute for B♭—either as V or I. A partial synthesis of the conflict between B♭ and D finally occurs in m. 40, as the third relation F♯ major functions as ♭VI of B♭ and III♯ of D. The juxtaposition of (and conflict between) B♭ and D recurs in the final stanza: B♭ is the setting for "und er nennt mich seine Schlange, und doch schief er bei mir ein" and D is the tonality for the recurring question "Weck' ich ihn nun auf?" The answer "Ach nein" is once again in the intermediary harmony of G♭, which one last time functions as ♭VI to V of B♭, the key in which the song ends.

Harmonic relations. While it is easy to demonstrate that each musical gesture is reflective of the text, the various third relations in "In dem Schatten" must also be understood as musical structures in their own right. For instance, the ♭VI-I progression in mm. 40-43 can be understood as an elision of V for dramatic purposes. The text explains the lovers' ambivalence and the third relation depicts the conflict by juxtaposing ♭VI and I. The harmony ♭VI sets the text of agitation and confusion, while B♭ (I) depicts the return of the original sleeping state in the new context of the lovers' acknowledged ambivalence. By eliding a resolution to V, the song maintains a certain level of confusion even as it returns to the tonic and the problems of the sleeping lover. In solely musical terms, the elision of m. 42 allows for a reprise of the opening material in mm. 43ff., with the half cadence in m. 47 analogous to that of m. 4. While the elision of V results in the third progression ♭VI-I, example 3-17 shows how the ♭VI-I progression exists within a larger V⁷-I progression (mm. 35-43), with D major (III♯) a substitute for I. As its upper neighbor, ♭VI prolongs V and thus becomes an extension of V. A resolution to V is elided because it is unnecessary: ♭VI extends V and ♭VI-I substitutes for V-I. Thus, this third relation functions as a substitute for the fifth relation that it came to replace.[26]

Ex. 3-17. "In dem Schatten": ♭VI-I Progression, mm. 40-42

V7 III♯   ♭VI   I

The return of ♭VI to its former role as embellishment of V in mm. 52ff. is noteworthy. Again, the text offers an explanation: the return to the original poetic setting suggests a return to the original harmonic language and syntax: mm. 43-55 are essentially a reprise of mm. 1-12. In another sense, the return to the ♭VI-V function also reflects Wolf's basically conservative use of third relations. The substitution of ♭VI-I for V-I in mm. 43 is unusual for Wolf and its special function is underscored by the return to a more traditional use of thirds in mm. 52ff.

The third relation between I and III♯ is complicated. The retrospective connection of III♯ to I by ♭VI has already been discussed; and in other places III♯ has functioned as ♭VI/♭VI. The recurrence of III♯ is so persistent, however, that its function defies simple categorization. Throughout this song, III♯ (D) recurs in opposition to the tonic (B♭), and the musical structure suggested by this B♭-D oscillation in "In dem Schatten" is that of double tonality.

Double tonality. As discussed in chapter 1, double tonality generally suggests the existence of two distinct tonal domains (each with its own tonic-dominant axis, etc.) that coexist and compete for tonal supremacy. In "In dem Schatten," the third relation intensifies the double tonality: the common tone D functions both to connect the two tonalities and to amplify the ambiguity between them. The semitonal shifts (B♭-A, F-F♯) intensify the tonal ambiguity and lack of clear focus. The ambiguity is further enhanced by the reciprocal relationship of both tonalities to a third tonal area (♭VI): one tonality is a ♭VI of the ♭VI of the other. (This relation, III♯=♭VI/♭VI, emerges strongly at mm. 40-42.)

To summarize, the region of D major suggests double tonality because it extends beyond its local function of III♯/ B♭. At times, D major functions as III♯ en route to V; at other times, it is ♭VI/♭VI, or it is a substitute for V in B♭ (e.g., in mm. 5-8, 20-26, 36-39)). In either of the latter two cases, D major functions as a tonal opposition to B♭ major that is a replacement rather than a polarity. This use of double tonality is highly innovative for Wolf, though it is worth noting that the ultimate arbiter of this double tonal scheme is the traditional tonic-dominant axis, with B♭ functioning as the final tonic. Even though D major disrupts B♭ major, it never entirely usurps the role of B♭ as the primary tonic.

The most disruptive effect of D major is the ambiguity cast upon V/B♭ (F major) by ♯3 of III, F♯. Recalling Schenker's concern about the progression I-III♯ in major, one is reminded that Schenker would call the opposition of F♮ and F♯ in this song "a conflict of chromatic tones" that would have to be "corrected" over time. While the clear authentic cadence in B♭ certainly "corrects" the extensive earlier F♯ chromaticism, the double tonal reading of this song exploits the idea of chromatic displacement as a primary formal device. The double tonal scheme thus permits III♯ to function beyond its role as "divider," the ♯3 of III displacing 5̂ for a variety of formal effects.

Schenkerian reading by Felix Salzer. A reading of "In dem Schatten" by Felix Salzer offers us a Schenkerian interpretation of this song.[27] Salzer considers the motion I to ♭VI as the main progression of the first 12 measures of the song: the D is merely a "passing chord" between I and ♭VI (see example 3-18). Further, Salzer claims the F♯ in the D chord is due to "mixture," i.e., there is no tonality of D; the altered III passes to ♭VI, the latter being a neighbor to V. Salzer's reading causes various problems. He not only diminishes the importance of the section in D, but he also dismisses the first harmonic motion I to V in mm. 1-4:

> it is essential, in order to hear the whole motion as an organism, not to be unduly diverted by that prolongation [I-V], and to be able to hear the following D-major chord as a passing chord between the I and the VI which is preceded by its own applied dominant.

Salzer acknowledges that the "melodic events . . . present some problems" in his reading, but offers, nonetheless, the unfolding *Bassbrechung* as the overriding tonal structure. His reading does not acknowledge any conflict between the tonalities of B♭ and D, and it does not attempt to correlate the musical structure with poetic text.

Monotonality. The fundamental theoretical issue challenged by "In dem Schatten" is that of monotonality—the premise that one tonality, as expressed by one triad, is prolonged over the course of a given piece. Particular problems with monotonality arise with the third progression I-III♯-♭VI because the chromaticism of III♯ suggests a harmonic realm outside the governing tonality. The song "In dem Schatten" thus demonstrates how some third relations can lead to a double tonal framework. Rather than emphasizing the predominance of one tonality over the other, the harmonic events of such pieces trace the conflict between the two conflicting tonalities. For pieces that utilize third relations such as those found in third chain progressions, a double tonal reading may complement, or even be preferable, to a Schenkerian reading. While they are less systematic than Schenkerian analysis, such double tonal readings offer new vehicles for interpreting tonal ambiguity, especially the tonal conflicts that depict complex poetic tensions.[28]

Ex. 3-18. "In dem Schatten": Reading by Felix Salzer, *Structural Hearing,* fig. 382

"Und steht Ihr früh am Morgen"

"Das Ständchen" presented a clear example of a chain-of-thirds progression within the purview of the tonic-dominant axis. The chain-of-thirds progression was, depending on interpretation, either an embellishment of or an interpolation within a *Bassbrechung* (example 3-19a). "In dem Schatten" also demonstrated a chain of thirds within the governance of the tonic-dominant axis, but the complexity of the poem and its setting allowed for occasional use of third relations outside a tonic-dominant axis. Indeed, the vacillation from I to III♯ was so prominent in "In dem Schatten" that a double tonal reading was offered in example 3-19b.

The *Italienischesliederbuch* song "Und steht Ihr früh" (3-4 April 1896) exemplifies yet another use of a third chain. The tonic-dominant axis still functions as the underlying tonal framework for the song (mm. 29-30 and 37-38), but as example 3-19c shows, the progression I-III♯-♭VI-I occurs twice without any resolution of ♭VI to V. The song thus permits an exploration of the chain of thirds temporarily independent of a tonic-dominant axis.

Ex. 3-19. Third Relations and *Bassbrechung*

I III♯♭VI V I   C: I   ♭VI   V   I
             E: ♭VI I   V   III♯

Example 3-20 presents a summary sketch of "Und steht Ihr früh." The tonic-dominant axis is given a dotted beam; the augmented triad arpeggiation occurs twice in succession (mm. 1-24). Between mm. 24-30 the ♭VI-I motion is

Ex. 3-20. "Und steht Ihr früh": Middleground Reading

expanded: ♭VI eventually moves back to III♮ in m. 28 (i.e., ♭VI moves to III, which is for the first time not chromatically altered) and III♮ progresses to V (i.e., not to ♭VI) in m. 29, resolving to I in m. 30. The remainder of the song diverges from third relations altogether and presents a straightforward I-IV-V-I progression.

The third relations within the third chain and their interconnections are identified to one another. Each harmony, built upon the successive scale steps, is transformed, through the addition of a seventh, into a dissonance; each seventh is then reinterpreted as an augmented sixth chord (+6), whose resolution elides the usual authentic cadence (e.g., +6-V-I), and creates instead a cryptic +6-I cadence. The resulting third relations (i.e., I-III♯, III♯-♭VI, ♭VI-I) are therefore all products of a functional reinterpretation and elided resolution. In one sense, what has taken place has been a substitution of a third relation for the tonic-dominant axis; the augmented sixth chord literally replaces the V⁷ chord.

The aural effect of this chain of thirds is one of increasing instability.²⁹ In a structure analogous to that in "Das Ständchen" (see example 3-16, p. 97), the alteration of the diatonic *Bassbrechung* changes the function of that arpeggiation. The arpeggiation is less a prolongation and more a disruption; that is, the progression to III♯ and subsequently to ♭VI is harmonic motion away from—not prolonging—the tonic. Conceivably the progression could continue and establish a new tonal center on A♭ or C♮, for instance, rather than return to the initial tonic, E. The chain of thirds thus does not continue to tonal clarity but rather serves to undermine the original tonal focus.

Formal devices in "Und steht Ihr früh." Two procedures articulate form in this use of third chains: (1) repetition and transposition become complementary formal devices; and (2) functional ambiguity or lack of tonal clarity generates a new level of dissonance which, in turn, creates form in the emergence of a new type of resolution. While repetition—particularly of an entire segment—is usually formally unambiguous, a particular level of transposition can infuse tension into that normally stable context. In this song, the transposition of the repeated segment up a major third challenges the notion of reprise with the problem of aural ambiguity. The lack of tonal clarity that results from these third relations requires some type of clarification wherein the tonic, if not initially clear, can ultimately be apprehended. The repetition-transposition procedure functions in concert with the ambiguity principle described in chapter 1. The opening third chains of "Und steht Ihr früh" establish tonal ambiguity that must be clarified during the remainder of the song.

The text supports the use of both repetition schemes and the ambiguity principle. The religious love poem falls into three sections: (1) a description of the beloved going to mass; (2) a vision of the beloved in prayer; and (3) a response to the beauty of the beloved, a beauty that is a gift of god. The two chains of thirds represent the first third of the text, where the singer describes the beloved arising out of bed, dressing, and going to mass. The repetition depicts a series of events: "you arise, you dress, you go to mass." The tension created by the chain of thirds reflects the excitement that the singer bestows upon these seemingly simple events: the rising from bed clears the sky of clouds and causes the sun to appear; the act of dressing causes angels to rush about in eagerness to assist; and the walking to mass causes crowds to follow.

Text to "Und steht Ihr früh am Morgen"
[*Italienischesliederbuch*, 3-4 April 1896]

Und steht Ihr früh am Morgen auf vom Bette,	And you rise early in the morning from your bed,
Scheucht Ihr vom Himmel alle Wolken fort,	You drive the clouds from the heavens,
Die Sonne lockt Ihr auf die Berge dort,	You lure the sun to those hills,
Und Engelein erscheinen um die Wette,	And cherubim vie
Und bringen Schuh und Kleider Euch sofort.	To bring your shoes and clothing.
Dann, wenn Ihr ausgeht in die heil'ge Mette,	Then when you go to holy mass,
So zieht Ihr alle Menschen mit Euch fort,	All people are drawn to go with you,
Und wenn Ihr naht der benedeiten Stätte,	And when you approach the blessed shrines,
So zündet Euer Blick die Lampen an.	The lamps are kindled by your glance.
Weihwasser nehmt Ihr, macht des Kreuzes Zeichen	You take holy water, make the sign of the cross,
Und netzet Eure weisse Stirn sodann	And moisten your white brow,
Und neiget Euch und beugt die Knie ingleichen—	And bow and bend the knee—
O wie holdselig steht Euch alles an!	O how radiantly it all becomes you!
Wie hold und selig hat Euch Gott begabt,	How gracious and blessed has God given you,
Die Ihr der Schönheit Kron' empfangen habt!	The crown of beauty you have received!
Wie hold und selig wandelt Ihr im Leben;	How gracious and blessed you travel through life;
Der Schönheit Palme ward an Euch gegeben.	The palm of beauty having been given to you.

When the beloved arrives at church to the text "so zündet Euer Blick die Lampen an," the rhythm of the chain of thirds changes. Harmonic contraction occurs in mm. 18-21, wherein the four-bar phrase structure is interrupted by a two-bar phrase in A♭ (mm. 18-19) which leads (by the augmented sixth chord) to C, mm. 20ff. The foreshortening of phrase length and concomitant quickening of harmonic rhythm strongly suggest the beginning of a change in action (part two of the text) to the participation of the beloved in the mass. Note that the walk to mass—which connects the preparation for with the participation in mass—is described during mm. 14-17, where the return to E major both completes the first third chain and begins the second, abbreviated third chain. The ensuing description of the beloved in prayer is depicted in an altogether different harmonic language. The pedal points of part one are gone and the use of functional harmony begins to clarify the tonality with a motion to III♮/E (m. 28) and V/E (m. 29). The earlier tonal ambiguity that had described the beloved going to mass is gradually dispelled in the description of the experience of prayer.

The final third of the poem expresses the singer's reaction to the beloved in prayer. A reprise of the opening material in mm. 30ff. suggests a return to the earlier description since the harmonic progression in mm. 30-33 is in fact the same as that of mm. 2-4. But the tonal clarification continues, as the final verses of the poem are set not to third relations but, rather, to the most commonplace harmonic progression: I-IV-V-I. In m. 34, the ambiguous augmented sixth chord reverts back to the traditional dominant seventh (V^7/IV), which progresses to IV and then to V of E. The third relations of the first part of the song are thereby suggested but then replaced by a more conventional progression as the song concludes in the definitive tonality of E major.

Harmonic function of circular progressions. The reference to and transformation of the augmented sixth chord in m. 33 (to V^7/IV/IV) is instructive. It suggests that the chain of thirds resulting from the unusual resolution of augmented sixth chords might possibly be substitutes for the more commonplace I-IV-V-I progression. This recalls the earlier query about whether equal subdivision of an octave into major thirds in fact prolongs the tonic, in this case, by representing a cadential progression analogous to I-IV-V-I. It also raises the issue of whether the resolution of the V^7/IV-IV in m. 33 suggests that mm. 1-24 comprise repeated attempts to progress from I to IV that were never fully realized until m. 34.

At first it seems as if I-III#-♭VI-I does prolong I, since there is no actual progression to another tonality. But does the lack of directed motion to another tonality represent a prolongation of a given tonal center? The answer seems to lie in distinguishing between structural levels and defining the term "prolongation." Prolongation means that a harmony or pitch is sustained on one level while it is expressed by implication or inference on another level. For instance, in example 3-21a, a tonic triad is embellished by IV; the neighbor-note motion to IV is a middleground event and is considered a contrapuntal embellishment of I that prolongs I on a deeper structural level. One important distinction, then, in determining if prolongation is in effect is whether additional harmonies are embellishing (contrapuntal) or whether they represent harmonic progressions away from the original harmony. In example 3-21b, the harmonic relations I-III#-♭VI-I are presented in a potentially embellishing relationship. If I is embellished by III♯ or by ♭VI, or if these pairs of chords (I-III♯, ♭VI-I) form contrapuntal structures, then I is prolonged by III♯ and ♭VI.

Ex. 3-21. Harmonic Function in *Bassbrechung*

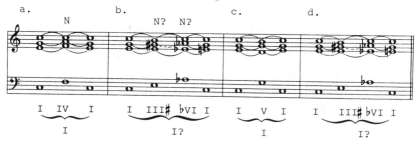

A second definition of prolongation is that a harmony is prolonged on a background level by a middleground harmonic progression that focuses upon or reinforces the prolonged harmony. In example 3-21c, the progression I-V-I reinforces the original tonic and thus prolongs that tonic. In example 3-21d, the progression I-III♯-♭VI-I is posited as a harmonic progression similar to I-V-I, rather than as a harmonic embellishment such as the neighbor motion I-IV-I. Does the progression I-III♯-♭VI-I reinforce I? In particular, does the progression ♭VI to I reinforce I, as does V to I? It would seem that ♭VI-I might well prolong the tonic, as ♭VI substitutes for V. The problem then arises in understanding the function of the progression to III♯. The progression I to III♯ does not embellish I (as IV might) and furthermore III♯ does not progress back to I (as IV or V might). Thus, because of III♯ the circular progression I-III♯-♭VI-I seems less a prolongation of I and more a harmonic structure that departs from I, progresses to ♭VI, and only then returns to I when ♭VI substitutes for V. The argument here is the same as that of the arpeggiation I-III♯-V not being a prolongation of I because of ♯3 of III. The tonality is undermined and thus cannot be prolonged by a III♯. As a result, circular progressions do not prolong I, but rather emphasize I by diverging from I (to III♯) and then returning to I (through ♭VI). The background structure, once again, does not cohere into a tonic prolongation: even though scale step III is in the bass, the chromaticism of ♯3 undermines tonal coherence and obscures tonal function.

Alternative reading for the chain of thirds. An alternative and radical interpretation of the third chain is that it is not a I-II♯-♭VI arpeggiation at all, but rather is a I-♭IV-♭VI plagal elaboration of the tonic (see example 3-22a).[30] Three factors support this reading. First, the foreground chromaticism of the opening suggests modal mixture (C♯-C♮, see example 3-22b). Second, the eventual progression to IV (A major) of m. 34 suggests that the progressions to A♭ major in mm. 6 and 18 were allusions to, or even initial attempts at the subdominant. Finally, the harmony that connects E major to A♭ major and A major is the same E^7 chord. This chord had earlier functioned as an augmented sixth in its resolution to A♭ major and functions now as an applied dominant that resolves to A major. The text also supports this reading, as the two sections in A♭ depict the religious powers of the beloved as she symbolically creates light ("die Sonne lockt Ihr" and "und wenn Ihr naht der benedeiten Stätte"), while the A major section (the real IV) describes how the beloved herself has been transformed ("wandelt") by the power of God.

Ex. 3-22.   "Und steht Ihr früh"

a. Alternative Reading

I   ♭IV   ♮VI   I

b. Foreground Chromaticism

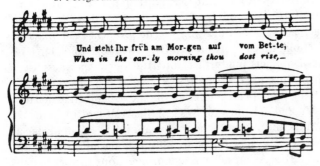

Und steht Ihr früh am Mor-gen auf   vom Bet-te,
When in the ear-ly morning thou   dost rise,—

   The interpretation of a I-IV-VI arpeggiation for the first half of "Und steht Ihr früh" has several implications. First, the problem of tonic prolongation through an altered *Bassbrechung* is eliminated altogether. As already discussed in relation to example 3-21, the prolongation of a harmony through its altered arpeggiation (example 3-21b and 3-21d) is different from a prolongation of that chord through embellishing harmonies (example 3-21a). Second, the I-IV-VI arpeggiation embellishes the tonic (IV and VI are neighboring harmonies to I and V), and the chromatic alteration of both IV and VI chromatically reinforce this embellishing function.

The logic of this unorthodox interpretation of "Und steht Ihr früh" is compelling. One last issue must be considered. If the section in A♭ is heard as an altered IV rather than an altered III, does this section remain a third relation at all? In terms of harmonic function, the relationship of E to A♭ could be I to ♭IV, the A♭ being a plagal relation rather than a third relation. This idea is certainly tenable in view of Wolf's experimentation with the plagal domain as discussed in chapter 2. The fact remains, however, that whether one labels the A♭/G♯ section a third relation or a plagal relation, the harmonic progression E to A♭/G♯ remains unstable and ambiguous and can be understood, at best, as a progression that relates to the tonic through temporary displacement.

Summary of Chains of Thirds

Several of the readings presented in this chapter have conflicted with Schenkerian principles, most notably his concept of diatonic monotonality. One might argue that I-III♯-♭VI-I is a harmonic progression altogether analogous to I to IV (motion away from I) to V to I (motion back to I), and in a sense, the two harmonic progressions are similar. The case against III♯ prolonging I rests on how one interprets the dissonance of ♯$\hat{3}$. A subordinate chord may progress away from a tonic, but it relates to I within a diatonic monotonal framework. An altered III may relate to a tonic by virtue of the shared scale step III, but the altered $\hat{3}$ of the mediant departs from the tonic domain. The chromatic alteration of the mediant was considered to be part of a double tonal scheme in "In dem Schatten," but was less disruptive in "Das Ständchen," where the altered III represented only a temporary displacement of tonal focus. The III♯ in the circular progressions in "Und steht ihr Früh" functions similarly to the III♯ in "Das Ständchen"—a temporary chromatic displacement of the tonality. Finally, in the absence of the tonic-dominant axis, the altered III in the circular third progressions intensifies the tonal displacement and creates a greater degree of tonal ambiguity. The subsequent recourse to traditional, unambiguous tonal progression in the latter part of "Und steht Ihr früh" further suggests that the tonal ambiguity created by the circular third progression was part of an extended-tonal ambiguity/clarification design in which the song's ambiguous opening was ultimately related to its conventional closing.

Third Relations and Poetic Metaphor: "Gesegnet sei das Grün"

The poem set by the *Italienischesliederbuch* song "Gesegnet sei das Grün" (13 April 1896) is an ingenious study of the metaphor, green. Green is a special color that symbolizes both the customary and the unusual. It is also the symbol of that which hunts and that which nourishes. Wolf uses one sonority, the

harmony C♯ major, as a musical counterpart to the poetic metaphor "green."
The harmony C♯ forms a third relationship with the tonic, A major, and Wolf
exploits the multiple associations of C♯ to A major in a brilliant musical analog
to the finesse of the poetry.

As a means of intensifying the multidimensional metaphor of green, the
poem exploits the rich symbolism of the word that characterizes that color: the
verb "kleiden" and its noun counterpart "Kleid." The poem is a veritable study
of the potential puns in the use of "kleiden" and "Kleid": as a transitive verb,
"kleiden" can mean "to clothe or dress"; as an intransitive verb, it can mean
"suit, become, look well on"; and as a reflexive verb, "sich kleiden" can mean
"to get dressed." The noun "Kleid" also expresses a variety of meanings:
"garment, habit, costume, dress." The poem is infused with images of green: a
green dress will be made, springtime is clad in green, my lover dresses in green,
the hunter habitually wears green, a green garment is worn by my lover, and
finally, green becomes all things and nurtures growing fruit.

Text to "Gesegnet sei das Grün"
[*Italienischesliederbuch*, 13 April 1896]

Gesegnet sei das Grün und wer es trägt!	Blessed be green and those who wear it!
Ein grünes Kleid will ich mir machen lassen.	I shall have a green dress made for me.
Ein grünes Kleid trägt auch die Frühlingsaue.	Spring meadows wear a green dress too,
Grün kleidet sich der Liebling meiner Augen.	The darling of my eyes wears green.
In Grün sich kleiden ist der Jäger Brauch,	To dress in green is the hunter's custom,
Ein grünes Kleid trägt mein Geliebter auch	My lover also wears green;
Das Grün steht allen Dingen lieblich an,	Green beautifies all things,
Aus Grün wächst jede schöne Frucht heran.	Every lovely fruit has grown out of green.

As the poet seems to delight in evoking the metaphor of green through the
use of the word "kleiden," so Wolf conveys these symbols through harmonic
manipulation. The two functions of C♯ that occur throughout the song (V/VI,
III♯) represent several of the levels of meaning bestowed upon green in the
poem. The progression I-V^7/VI-IV-V-VI sets the first line of text. The main
poetic theme (I love green and the wearing of it), is depicted in an
embellishment of a I to V progression that includes a secondary dominant
(C♯^{7}) and an irregular resolution.

The mobile character of C♯ major—which is first heard in m. 1, as a
secondary dominant seventh (V^7/VI)—resolves deceptively to D major
(VI/VI=IV) instead of F♯ minor (VI). The subsequent, also deceptive, arrival

of F♯ (VI) in m. 2 belatedly resolves the C♯^{7}, and IV and VI combine to embellish the dominant. The interchange between IV and VI is remarkable in view of the limited harmonic resources over the phrase as a whole: within the simple framework I-IV-V-VI, the C♯ harmony adds variety and chromatic embellishment. In a sense, the restriction in harmonic vocabulary is a musical equivalent to the laconic quality of the poetry: in few words—and few chords—the complexity of the metaphor green is given vivid portrayal.

The rest of the poem is a detailed description of how green is manifested, and the remainder of the song is an elaboration of the relationships between those chords that embellish the dominant—IV and VI—and the accompanying ambiguous C♯ harmony. The first phrase (mm. 1-2) has already been described as an enlarged I-V-VI progression. As the second line of poetry begins elaborating upon the appearances of green, the music correspondingly begins to explore aspects of the harmonic content of the opening phrase. The overall progression of phrase 1 (I-V^7/VI-IV-V-VI) is altered in phrase 2 (IV-V^7-V/VI-IV-+6-V). The third phrase is abbreviated to a repeated IV^6-V progression; the repetition in phrase 3 generates a rhythmic and harmonic tension and creates the impetus for greater harmonic activity in line 4. As the lover appears in the text of line 4, Wolf creates a musical climax by expanding the two-bar grouping of the first three lines into a 3-bar phrase. This metric expansion allows the fourth phrase to end on a strong half cadence in m. 9, where V is heard, for the first time, on the downbeat.

The first half of the song thus presents, somewhat as a series of harmonic variations, a group of brief progressions that encompasses a broad progression from the tonic of m. 1 to the dominant of m. 9. The expanded cadence of m. 9 creates the need for either harmonic closure or else a harmonic diversion away from the confined world of IV, VI, and V. The motion to C♯ major in m. 10 fulfills both these requisites. On the one hand, the C♯ of mm. 10ff. can be considered a third substitute for A major which at least partially satisfies the desire for closure. On the other hand, the key of C♯ major can be understood more simply as a tonal contrast to the key of A. For both interpretations, Wolf exploits the ambiguity of the augmented triad of m. 9 to ease the way from V^7/A to the key of C♯: the final eighth note of m. 9 is an altered V^7/A, E-G♯-B♯-D, where the augmented triad D-G♯-B♯ could be heard as an altered V of C♯ (G♯-B♯-D𝄪). The arrival on C♯ creates the large-scale progression I-VI-IV-V-III♯ (for I) and the subsequent cadence on V in mm. 17-18 renders the middleground of the entire work: I-VI-IV-V-III♯-V-I, where VI and IV embellish V, and III♯ either substitutes for I or participates as an altered mediant in a *Bassbrechung*.

The remainder of the song, mm. 12ff., returns to the tonic A through its V. A modified transposition in E of mm. 10-11 (in C♯) occurs in mm. 12-13, and m. 14 returns to the IV^6-V motion of mm. 5-6 for the song's second climax. The expansion of two bars into three, heard earlier in mm. 7-9, is now further augmented at mm. 14ff. to encompass four bars, and the song comes to a close.

While the second half of the text retains the descriptive quality of lines 2-4, the images of the final four lines of text become more entwined. Line 5 talks of the hunter habitually wearing green and the setting, phrase 5, is in C♯ major. The transposed sequence of this material in E depicts the lover wearing green and a symbolic connection is made: the singer is either hunting for or hunted by the lover in the combined traditions of the hunter's chase and the lover's courtship. The final two phrases of text continue to explore the imagery of love and conquest by invoking the sexual metaphor of fruit and nurturance. These final associations with green refer back to the opening lines (2-4) with the return to the IV^6-V progression in m. 14. The earlier description of green-clad things was part of a larger image of green: green is a symbol of a mating ritual, the stage is set with springtime and pretty dress, the hunting mate is in appropriate attire, and ultimately the sexual rite is expressed by the symbols of nurturing and fruit.

Schenkerian Analysis

Depicting this song in Schenkerian analysis is problematic only in terms of the ♯3 of III, which, again, creates chromatic displacement and might be interpreted as a third substitute for I in mm. 10ff. The problems of chromatic displacement with III♯ have already been discussed. Though the issue of third substitution was discussed earlier, in chapter 1, the idea warrants further exploration here because of specific textual references. If the section in C♯ is a third substitute for the tonic, then the arpeggiation, A-(C♯)-E is illusory, as III is appearing as a variant of I rather than a functioning "divider." This does not necessarily contradict the notion of prolongation through arpeggiation, for III♯ as a third substitute for I is, in fact, prolonging I (albeit in a special way). Both the functional ambiguity for III—mediant or tonic?—and the alternative representation of the tonic through the harmony C♯ exemplify Wolf's use of harmonic ambiguity to exploit poetic metaphor. Just as green is both a color and a symbol for various things, so C♯ is both a real and symbolic harmony. Example 3-23 shows a Schenkerian reading. The middleground bass structure is a *Bassbrechung*: I-(VI)-V-III♯-V-I, with VI embellishing V and III♯ substituting for I. Example 3-24 presents another sketch that attempts to incorporate some of the dynamism of the variation technique employed by Wolf. Dotted lines separate each of the six phrases. The initial motion to V by way of VI (mm. 1-4) is replaced by IV^6 (mm. 5-6) and the reiteration of patterns such as the repeated IV^6-V is shown. Motivic expansion is demonstrated in such details as the recurring D neighbor-note to the *Kopfton* C♯, an important melodic figure that reinforces the constant use of IV^6 in place of VI (where D is not a chord tone).

Ex. 3-23. "Gesegnet sei das Grün": Middleground Reading

Ex. 3-24. "Gesegnet sei das Grün": Rhythmic Variation

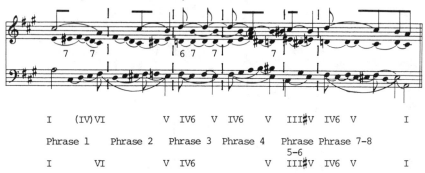

I	(IV)VI		V	IV6	V	IV6	V	III♯V	IV6	V		I
Phrase 1	Phrase 2		Phrase 3		Phrase 4		Phrase 5-6		Phrase 7-8			
I	VI		V	IV6			V	III♯V	IV6	V		I

Correspondence between Poetic and Harmonic Imagery

The functions of IV, VI, C♯, and C♯^{7} are all intimately connected to the development and manipulation of poetic imagery. As example 3-25 indicates, the functions of the three harmonies correspond to the changes in the text. In line/phrase 1, the three harmonies are introduced in the complex opening progression. The C♯^{7} chord is associated with the text "Gesegnet sei," IV with "Grün," and VI with "trägt." The pun on VI as "trägt" is obvious: the deceptive cadence carries the song forward. In line/phrase 2, the singer associates herself with IV as she will make a green dress, the crucial text "Kleid" being set to C♯^{7} (V^7/IV). Line/phrase 3 is developmental. The harmonic progression IV-V is repeated and IV, once again, is associated with green ("ein grünes Kleid"). The verb "trägt," then, becomes associated with IV rather than VI, suggesting a change in the function of the verb "tragen" from cadential to initiatory. The opening function of IV and its verbal associate "trägt," then, introduces an important new poetic element: line/phrase 4 mentions the lover, along with the lover's green garb, the text "sich kleiden" being set to the deceptive cadence V-VI. As the first half of the poem/song ends on a clear half cadence, the function

Ex. 3-25. "Gesegnet sei das Grün": Harmonic Function and Poetic Imagery

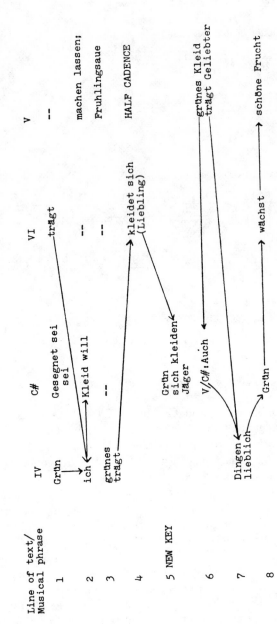

of the IV, VI, and C♯ harmonies have all undergone transformations: IV has been associated with the color green, with the singer, and with spring's greenness: VI has been associated with the verb "tragen" and has in turn carried the musical structure to various moments of relative repose; and C♯ and C♯^{7} have been associated with personal relationships to green: she blesses green and she will wear green.

The second half of the poem and song then develop the relationship between the metaphor of green and the lover. Line/phrase 5 presents the crucial concept of the green-clad hunter, and C♯ is tonicized in mm. 10-11. The connection between the hunter and the lover (line/phrase 6) then occurs through the transformation of the C♯ material (mm. 10-11) to E major (V/A major, mm. 12-13) and the juxtaposed harmonies C♯ and V/A are united by the crucial word "auch," which is set to the musical pun V/C♯. The return of IV for line/phrase 7 reasserts the original notion of "lieblich Dingen" being green, and the last line/phrase restates the initial harmonic relationships IV-V-C♯^{7}-VI within the sexual reference "aus Grün wächst...." The harmony IV remains associated with the loveliness of green, VI with verbs of action, and C♯^{7} with the concept of green as the generating poetic element.

Rhythmic Expansion

One final comment is in order regarding the rhythmic expansion of the repeated progressions involving IV, VI, and V. The expansion of the two-bar phrase of mm. 5-6 to a three-bar phrase in mm. 7-9 is only one of a series of rhythmic expansions that occur throughout the song as a musical corollary to the unfolding poetic imagery. The IV-V progression of m. 2 is expanded, in mm. 3-4 and mm. 7-8, to one and a half bars. The quarter-note IV-V progression of mm. 2-3 is augmented to half notes in mm. 5-7, and, as was mentioned earlier, the three-bar phrase of mm. 7-9 is an extended IV^6-V progression. The same is true for the extended four-bar phrase, mm. 14-17, which also depicts an elaborated IV^6-V progression.

Harmonic Simplicity and Extended Tonal Technique

Although "Gesegnet sei das Grün" uses such late-nineteenth century harmonic procedures as third substitution and a chromatic middleground third relation, the harmonic vocabulary of the song is relatively simple. This factor is noteworthy on two accounts. First, it is important to remember that the term "extended-tonal procedure" does not necessarily denote an excessive use of complex and unusual harmonies. Rather, the term may refer to an unusual application of relatively traditional harmonic relationships. In this song, Wolf interjects one unusual harmony (C♯ major) and one unusual harmonic progression (V^7/ VI-IV) into an almost commonplace series of repeated IV-V-VI progressions. This represents a more subtle type of extended-tonal procedure and demonstrates as well how late-nineteenth-century technique can occur with an economy of means.

The simplicity of harmonic means also suggests a second issue of note: the subtlety of Wolf's text depiction. Although this study has sought to explicate harmonic syntax without undue recourse to the text, the interrelation of text and harmonic design has been an ongoing feature in understanding late-nineteenth-century extended-tonal technique. In all of Wolf's songs, complex harmonic structures can be understood outside any reference to poetic content. However, the poetry always gives insight into why Wolf chose the musical elements he did. In the song "Gesegnet sei das Grün," for example, the subtle manipulation of seemingly simple harmonies can be considered a direct musical response to the textual development of symbol and metaphor. The intensity and complexity of an evolving musical structure to depict a complex poetic design is a different but equally innovative expression of extended-tonal technique. Thus, this song demonstrates in part how a formal design can be generated by subtle poetic objectives rather than by complex tonal issues. This type of extended-tonal technique is especially pertinent to Wolf's songs in general, for they depict poetic content to an extent unprecedented in the tradition of *Lieder* and perhaps equalled only by Wolf's beloved models, the operas of Wagner.

Conclusion

For the most part, Wolf's use of third relations may be characterized as conservative. Where he employed such chromatic third relations as I-III♯, he usually did so within a governing tonic-dominant axis, and the resulting structures often conformed to Schenker's *Ursatz*. This conservative use of third relations, then, exemplifies an expansion of common-practice tonality wherein a particular amount of chromaticism can be accommodated by the common-practice tonal framework.

Several of Wolf's outside third relations were more innovative. Where the chain of thirds remained outside a tonic-dominant axis in "Und steht Ihr früh," Wolf exploited the ambiguity inherent in such third chains and created harmonic motion with a barely established harmonic focus. Likewise, in "In dem Schatten," Wolf explored the harmonic ambiguity inherent in the third relations amongst I, III♯, and ♭VI, and created a complicated tonal language that suggested the need for a double tonal formal design. While Wolf's more innovative third relations never reached the advanced level of many other late-nineteenth-century pieces, his tentative expansion beyond the tonic-dominant axis and beyond the confines of monotonality surely anticipated the more radical use of third relations that was to occur in the music of his successors.

Finally, Wolf's use of third relations—no matter how conservative or daring—illustrates the compositional and analytical problems inherent in any use of nontraditional third relations. In the expanded use of third relations, even such a seemingly modest chromatic element as ♯$\hat{3}$ of III creates enormous challenges for both composer and analyst, as the introduction of one chromatic pitch in turn may suggest an entire network of chromatic and often remote ancillary harmonies. Some of the ramifications of Wolf's expanded use of third relations will be explored further in chapter 4 (Directional Tonality) and chapter 5 (Combinations of Extended-Tonal Techniques), where other extensions of third relations will result in harmonic structures altogether different from those of the common-practice period.

Ach, des Knaben Augen
(Ah, how fair that Infant's eyes)

Sanfte Bewegung

Ach, des Kna - ben Au - gen sind mir so schön und klar er -
Ah, how fair___ that In - fant's eyes, like twin stars in Heav - en

schie - nen, und ein Et - was strahlt aus ih - nen, das mein
beam - ing, and my soul en - rap - tured, dream - ing, soars to

gan - zes Herz ge - winnt.
realms beyond the skies.

Blickt' er doch mit die - sen sü - ssen
Soft his in - fant glanc - es, meet - ing

Au - gen nach den mei - nen hin! säh' er dann sein
moth - er's eyes, dis - pel her care: an he saw his

Wie lange schon war immer mein Verlangen
(How often have I prayed in fervent mood)

Liszt, Consolation #3

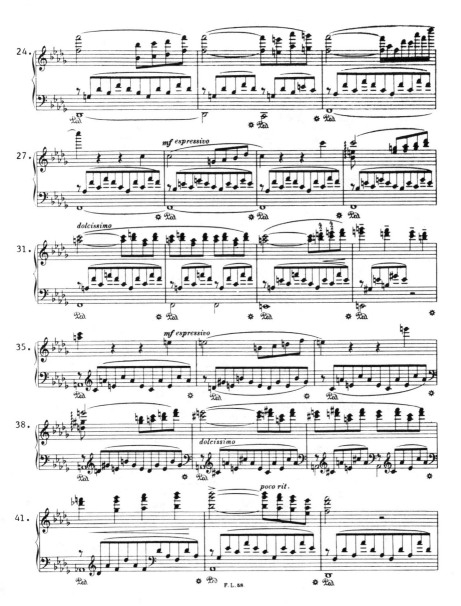

F. L. 58

Das Ständchen
(The aged minstrel)

Mässig.

Auf die Dä - - cher zwi-schen blas - - - sen
O'er the si - - lent vil-lage dream - - - ing,

Wol - - - - ken schaut der Mond____ her-für,
shines the moon from heav'n____ a - bove.

Begleitung immer pp

In dem Schatten meiner Locken
(In the shade of my tresses)

27.
Weck ich ihn nun auf?___
I'll not wake thee, love,___
Ach
sleep

a tempo

32.
nein!___
on!___
Hö - ren muß ich, wie ihn grä - me, daß er
And he tells me, fond - ly plead - ing, how his

36.
schmach - - tet schon so lan - ge, daß ihm Le - ben geb und
heart for me doth lan - guish, for me e - ver beat - - ing,

39.
neh - me die - se mei - ne brau - ne Wan - - - - ge.
bleed - ing, on my burn - ing kiss - es feed - - - ing.

Und er nennt mich sei - ne
Calls me "Vix - en" in his

Schlan - ge, und doch schlief er bei mir ein.
an - guish, and yet at my side he sleeps.

Weck ich ihn nun auf?_____ Ach nein!__
Fond love vig - il keeps,_____ and weeps!_

(John Bernhoff)

Und steht Ihr früh am Morgen auf vom Bette
(When in the early morning thou dost rise)

Und steht Ihr früh am Mor-gen auf vom Bet-te,
When in the ear-ly morning thou dost rise,___

scheucht Ihr___ vom Him-mel al - le Wol - - ken fort,
thy pre - - sence of all clouds doth clear___ the skies,

die Son-ne lockt Inr auf die Ber-ge dort, und En - ge-lein er-schei -
the sun is lured up - on the hills by thee, and cher-ubs all ap-pear___

9.
--nen um die Wet-te, und brin-gen Schuh__ und Klei--
__ most ea-ger-ly__ and bring thy morn__ing-rai--

11.
- der Euch so-fort.
- ment un-to thee.

mf

14.
Dann, wenn Ihr aus-geht in die heil'--ge Met-te,
Then when at ear-ly mass thou dost ap-pear,__

p

16.
so zieht Ihr al-le Men---schen mit Euch fort,
the peo-ple stop to gaze____ as thou draw'st near,

mf
f

28. o wie hold-se - lig steht Euch al - les an! Wie hold__ und se - lig
and ev'- ry movement shows thy beau-ty rare. What wond - rous gifts the

31. hat Euch Gott be-gabt, die Ihr der Schönheit Kron'__ em-pfan-gen habt!
Lord hath giv'n to thee, the crown of beau-ty was__ a-warded thee!

34. Wie hold und se-lig wan - - delt Ihr im Le - - ben; der Schön-heit Pal - me ward an
Thou'rt ve - ri - ly en - dow'd__ with ev'-ry charm,__ to thee be-longs most sure-ly

37. Euch ge-ge-ben.
beau-ty's palm.

Gesegnet sei das Grün
(How I love green)

4

Directional Tonality

The earlier chapters of this study have described various extended-tonal techniques that expanded upon normative, common-practice tonality. Common-practice tonality is predicated upon the concept known as "monotonality," the notion that all pitches within a tonal design create a pitch hierarchy based on one central "tonic" pitch.[1] This chapter will explore how Wolf extended the norm of monotonality by replacing it with a form of double tonality, one of Wolf's most dramatic harmonic resources for conveying poetic text. The songs that involve a double tonal focus are some of Wolf's most poignant and expressive works.

Wolf's Concept of Tonality in Historical Context

The underlying assumption of monotonality is that any digression or "modulation" outside the tonic is related back to and ultimately subsumed by that tonic. This concept is implied by Rameau in his *Traité,* where he discusses the role of the tonic in defining a key, shows numerous examples of modulatory progressions that begin and end on a tonic note, and describes the deliberate choice of a tonic to begin and end a piece.[2] Monotonality is described more precisely in C.P.E. Bach's *Versuch über die wahre Art das Clavier zu spielen* of 1762, where the author advocates a monotonal scheme in his discussion of the most innovative harmonic form of the Baroque, the "Free Fantasia." Bach describes in considerable detail the possibilities for modulation, which "may be made to closely related, remote, and all other keys." However, he also cautions that the fantasia must begin and end in one key and that this one key must be both adequately established at the beginning and amply restated at the end.[3]

The formal constraints of monotonality were recommended as well by later theorists such as Kirnberger, Koch, and Riemann. According to Kirnberger, modulation reflected the hierarchical relationships of various scale steps to the tonic, with modulation to closely related keys occuring more often and lasting longer.[4] Koch considered modulation a means of achieving variety in a piece where unity and coherence were established by the retention of one tonal center,[5] and Riemann believed that modulation within monotonality was a means of creating structural dissonance: "Thus the fundamental laws of chord succession, as well as of the succession of keys (modulation) may be deduced directly from the extension of these simplest musical conceptions of consonance and dissonance."[6] Mickelsen amplifies Riemann's statement as follows: "Modulation for Riemann does not signify a change of tonic but only a more distant removal from it. . . . The unrest felt in movement away from the tonic is a sense of dissonance, while the return is a return to consonance."[7]

Both C.P.E. Bach's and Kirnberger's views of monotonality may be considered precursors to that of Schenker, whose system depicted for the first time how subordination to a governing tonic occurs simultaneously on different structural levels. Schenker's view of modulation was refined over the course of his work and became clarified through his concepts of structural levels and scale-step *Auskomponierung*. What Schenker called "modulation" in his *Harmonielehre* of 1911, he later designated "illusory" events on the foreground in *Free Composition* of 1935. In his discussion of the *Ursatz* in *Free Composition*, Schenker characterizes the relationship of the diatonic background to "tonality" as follows:

> I call the content of the fundamental line, counterpointed by the bass arpeggiation, *diatony (Diatonie)*. . . . This is the fundamental, determinate melodic succession, the primal design of melodic content. In contrast, *tonality*, in the foreground, represents the sum of all occurrences, from the smallest to the most comprehensive—including illusory keys and all the various musical forms.[8]

Later in *Free Composition*, Schenker again discusses "illusory keys at the foreground level."

> The coherence of the whole, which is guaranteed by the fundamental structure, reveals the development of one single chord into a work of art. Thus, the tonality of this chord alone is present, and whatever else we may regard as a key at the foreground level can only be an illusory one.[9]

Schenker's refined view of monotonality thus incorporates two theoretical assumptions: first, monotonality occurs within a diatonic background. While chromatic elements may enliven the fore- and middleground, they cannot disturb the contrapuntal unfolding of the fundamental structure on the deepest structural level. Second, tonal progression on the middleground is an expression of the *Bassbrechung*. In contrast to the structural arpeggiation of III and V, tonicizations of other scale steps have only subsidiary, contrapuntal functions. The harmony VI, for instance, is understood as a neighbor to V, IV as a prolongation of I or, with II, as a preparation to V.[10]

Both the background diatonicism and the hierarchy of structural function found in Schenker's theory aptly reflect the musical language of the common-practice period. When innovative composers such as Beethoven (in his late works), Schubert, and Brahms began to infuse common-practice tonality with more structural chromaticism, what had been subsidiary or remote harmonies began to asume greater structural weight. Wolf's harmonic language emerged out of this innovative impulse, and he continued to move beyond the limitations of a structurally diatonic tonality. Wolf's extended concept of monotonality is perhaps most similar to that of Schoenberg, which the latter describes in connection with harmonic "regions":

> The concept of regions is a logical consequence of the principle of monotonality. According to this principle, every digression from the tonic is considered to be still within the tonality, whether directly or indirectly, closely or remotely related. In other words, there is only one tonality in a piece, and every segment formerly considered as another tonality is only a region, a harmonic contrast within that tonality.[11]

Schoenberg's is a more progressive view of monotonality. While his predecessors considered remote modulations as, at best, permissible exceptions to the limited rules of modulatory relations, Schoenberg encouraged a full exploitation of all potential harmonic relations. Schoenberg's more encompassing tonal concept clearly depicts the harmonic language of late-nineteenth-century music, including his own early extended-tonal works. These late-nineteenth-century pieces manifest progressive elements such as chromatic or enharmonic modulations to remote keys, including chromatic third relations.

The gradual but steady absorption of chromatic elements into monotonal middlegrounds resulted in much tonal extension by Wolf and his contemporaries. Although most of Wolf's songs are monotonal, a significant number do abandon the confines of monotonality and embrace a late-nineteenth-century alternative: a tonal scheme involving two different tonalities that coexist within one piece of music. This scheme will be called "directional tonality."[12]

Directional Tonality

Directional tonality uses two different keys in the following way. One key functions as an opening tonality; and after the first key is clearly established as a tonic, a transformation occurs whereby the initial tonic becomes a nontonic function within a second tonality. The piece then concludes in the second key. The ultimate effect of directional tonality is twofold: first, the original tonality loses its identity as a tonal focus in deference to the second tonality; and second, the piece is heard as beginning and ending in two different keys.

The difference between pieces that use directional tonality and simple monotonal pieces that begin in nontonic harmonies lies in the retrospective interpretation of the opening tonality at the end of the composition (i.e., in real-time listening): Did the piece begin on a nontonic harmony whose relationship to the real tonic eventually became clarified, or did the piece begin on a tonic whose function as tonic was contextually established and then altered during the course of the piece? Two other questions arise: first, did the opening harmony sound like a tonic by default (i.e., in an initial absence of any other functioning tonic) and only become more clearly understood when the real tonic appeared? Second, does a transformation occur so that a harmony that functioned clearly as a tonic initially becomes reinterpreted later as a nontonic harmony? Because the differentiation between directional tonality and certain monotonal pieces is dependent upon subtle interpretations, the following criteria will assist us in evaluating an opening tonality:

(1) the opening tonality must be adequately defined as a tonic (e.g., through a clear harmonic progression and/or authentic cadences over sufficient duration)

(2) if there is tonal ambiguity at the opening of a piece, there must be adequate evidence that the potential opening tonality differs from the closing tonality and is transformed into a nontonic harmony within the closing tonality

(3) the functional transformation itself must involve a change from tonic to nontonic, to distinguish that process from simple reinterpretation, where the function of a harmony is merely reconsidered.

In example 4-1a, the C major harmony changes function from a tonic to a subdominant of G major; in example 4-1b, the C major harmony loses any identity as tonic and is simply understood as IV/G.

Ex. 4-1.   Transformational Process in Directional Tonality vs.
Simple Reinterpretation in Monotonality

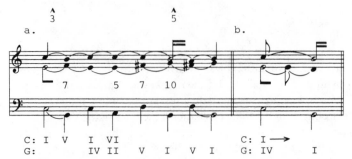

C: I   V   I   VI   C: I ⟶
G: IV II   V   I   V   I   G: IV   I

While the above distinctions may be subtle at times, the overriding factor is the coexistence in directional tonality of two equally weighted tonal centers within one musical work. The concept of directional tonality is particularly useful in depicting a lack of correspondence between openings and closings of pieces such as opera or *Lieder*, where such a tonal shift may depict a textual change in or transformation of feelings, ideas, or scenes.[13]

Applicability of Schenker

Even though Schenker's concept of monotonality is replaced by directional tonality, other Schenkerian precepts still apply. Indeed, the disparity between directional tonality and Schenker's monotonality is not as great as might be expected. Although it is clear from some of Schenker's own sketches of pieces with unusual openings that he did not use a double tonal scheme, this study will deliberately incorporate some of his analytical ideas into what otherwise would be a non-Schenkerian analytical framework.[14] This retention of some Schenkerian elements in sketches of directional tonal pieces emphasizes the fact that the present work is modifying or extending Schenker's method, not totally departing from it. The application of Schenkerian concepts to directional tonal pieces is, in effect, an attempt to reconcile the two different concepts of tonality.

Schenker's monotonality differs from directional tonality in that the former affirms coherence through the prolongation of one tonic triad, while the latter emphasizes a dynamic shift in tonal focus. In this context, the difference between Schenkerian and directional tonal readings lies in the distinction between Schenker's concept of retrospective understanding of a piece and the temporally dynamic nature of directional tonal listening in real time. Schenkerian analysis is predicated upon a distillation of musical events into an organic whole that is fully formed at the end of the work. The orientation of directional tonality, on the other hand, is the reverse: what is interesting about such a piece is the very process of transformation—how an opening is heard as expressing one tonality, how the function of that opening harmony changes, and how the opening ultimately yields to the closing tonality. While both interpretations of formal design emphasize the role of formal closure, the two differ dramatically in their interest in the formal opening. In Schenkerian analysis the opening is ultimately subsumed by the closing, while in directional tonal analysis the opening remains a dynamic contrast to the closing.

At times, some of Schenker's ideas will be adapted idiosyncratically. For example, a *Kopfton* may be designated that does not descend, even though Schenker clearly disapproved of such an idea.[15] However, though directional tonal readings may alter some of Schenker's analytical ideas, the use of Schenkerian analysis within the interpretation of directional tonality will—

because of the analytical conflicts that result—help us gauge the innovation of Wolf's directional tonal pieces.

One of the most important Schenkerian elements that is retained in this discussion is the *Kopfton* designation. The function of the *Kopfton* in the context of directional tonality is dramatically altered. Just as a directional tonal piece involves a transformation of tonal focus, so, too, does such a piece include a transformation of what we might call a modified Kopfton* function.[16] The pitch designated as a Kopfton* in the original key will function differently in the second key. This can happen in several ways. For instance, the Kopfton* may continue its function as such for the entire work, but its relationship to the bass is altered (e.g., $\hat{5}$ of the opening key becomes $\hat{3}$ of the closing key); or, the Kopfton* of the first tonality may be replaced by a new Kopfton* within the second tonality. Example 4-2a shows how a transformation of key and Kopfton* might be depicted in a piece beginning in C major and closing in G major. The Kopfton* changes from $\hat{3}$ in C (E) to $\hat{3}$ in G (B). In this example, and throughout the rest of this chapter, the second Kopfton* will be designated by a double incomplete beam in order to distinguish it from the first Kopfton*, which is given the customary single incomplete bean. Example 4-2b offers a "background" reading of such a piece: the main melodic pitches retain their positions, but the first tonal center becomes understood as IV of the second. The flags on the melodic C and E indicate that the first tonality yields to the second.

Ex. 4-2.   Directional Tonality: Change of Key and *Kopfton*

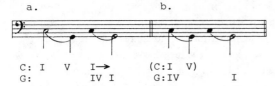

Comparison of Schenkerian and Directional Tonal Readings

An example of a nineteenth-century piece having an unusual opening will help us illustrate the difference between a strict Schenkerian and a directional tonal reading. The piece chosen for this comparison is the well-known Chopin *Prelude,* Op. 28/2, the score of which appears as figure 4-1 opposite.

In example 4-3a, Schenker interprets the E minor opening tonality as minor V of the closing key of A minor.[17] The G major cadence of m. 6 is heard only as part of an unfolding progression from E minor to V_4^6 in m. 15. According to Schenker's view of "mixture," the modal inflection of the minor V/A minor is corrected in m. 21, and the piece concludes unequivocally in A

Fig. 4-1. Chopin's *Prelude*, Op. 28/2

minor.[18] In contrast, the directional tonal reading in example 4-3b considers the opening from a different point of view. The opening is considered ambiguous: the piece begins in either E minor and/or G major, and this tonal ambiguity continues through the B minor section of mm. 8ff.[19] The ambiguity of E minor/G major and the subsequent move to B minor are both suggested in

Ex. 4-3.   Chopin *Prelude*, Op. 28/2: Schenker vs. Transformational Tonality

Ex. 4-3a.   Schenker's Reading [*Free Composition*, fig. 110/3(a)]

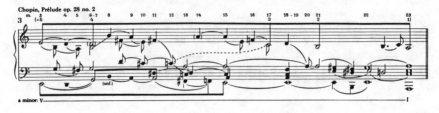

Ex. 4-3b. Directional Tonal Reading

the figuration of the opening measure, where the B-A♯-B-G motive points toward B minor and the bass oscillation E to G can be heard in either key. The section in B minor—so dramatically separated by rests and textural thinning—functions both as a pivotal harmony between the opening tonality of E minor/G major and the closing tonality of A minor. B minor functions also as an agent of transformation: when B minor loses its function as V♮/E minor and/or III/G major, it becomes II♯5/A minor and thereby initiates the shift to that closing key. Once again, the difference between the Schenkerian reading and the directional tonal reading is that while both agree that the opening E minor can be understood retrospectively as a minor V, the directional tonal reading does not define the initial function of E minor as that of dominant. While Schenker's interpretation of the opening is reasonable, it does not explore the extensive ambiguity and harmonic fluctuation that is heard over the course of the piece, and it does not depict how the cadence in G major and the section in B minor divert the ear away from E minor as V and A minor as I. The directional tonal reading, on the other hand, underscores the harmonic instability of the piece and thereby offers a different understanding of this complicated nineteenth-century work.[20]

Directional tonality differs from monotonality in two ways: there are two functioning tonics of equal status, and modulation or tonal shift occurs on the middleground level. Directional tonality helps to understand a variety of late-nineteenth-century harmonic techniques. For example, with its premise of double tonality, directional tonality can explicate extensive chromaticism: what seems to be chromatic displacement in one key might readily be understood as diatonicism in a second key.[21] In a different and more important way, directional tonality denotes a concept of tonality altogether different from that of monotonality because the musical structure is based not upon an axis or polarity of two different *harmonies* (i.e., the tonic-dominant axis), but rather upon an axis or polarity of two different *tonalities*. In this context, it is harmonic polarity that is extended; and form-giving tension between opposing harmonies is replaced by an analogous tension between opposing tonal systems.

Directional Tonality and Third Relations: "Der Mond hat eine schwere Klag' erhoben"

A directional tonal song that uses third relations is "Der Mond hat eine schwere Klag' erhoben" (*Italienischesliederbuch*, 13 November 1890). The song seems to begin in E♭ minor and, after a section in G♭ minor (spelled enharmonically as F♯ minor) and G♭ major, ends unequivocally in C♭ major. The tonal design of this song incorporates a closing tonic-dominant axis, making "Der Mond" especially useful for comparing a directional tonal with a Schenkerian reading.

Middleground Structure

Example 4-4 offers a complete middleground sketch of "Der Mond." The opening key of E♭ minor is established clearly by an ostinato figure that reiterates a I-V progression. The vocal line contains a clear Kopfton* (B♭ $\hat{5}$),

Ex. 4-4. "Der Mond": Middleground Reading

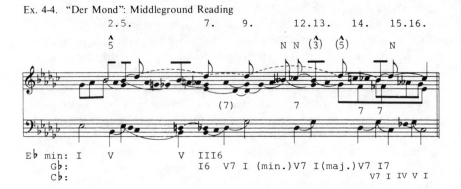

and the prevailing melodic motion in the vocal line (above the ostinato) is a motion toward $\hat{3}$, which is repeatedly interrupted on $\hat{4}$. In m. 6, a chromatic motion A♭-G♮-G♭ in the voice signals chromaticism in the piano part, and a modulation to G♭ minor ends on V/G♭ minor in m. 8. Beginning in m. 9, the piano reasserts the ostinato figure in the key of G♭ minor (spelled F♯ minor presumably for ease in reading) and the vocal line prolongs the Kopfton* B♭ through its upper and lower neighbors, A♮ (B♭♭) and B♮ (C♭). In m. 13, the song shifts to G♭ major and the Kopfton*, now $\hat{3}$ in G♭, begins to lose its prominence to the scale step $\hat{5}$, D♭. (The D♭ was alluded to earlier in mm. 5, 7, and 9, as is indicated in the graph by dotted slurs.) In m. 14, a second chromatic motion in the vocal line signals another modulation in the accompaniment, this time to C♭ major. The D♭ melodic note begins to function as an upper neighbor to the new tonic C♭, and the piece ends in C♭ major. In summary, there were two distinct shifts in tonal focus, E♭ minor to G♭ minor and then G♭ major to C♭ major. In both instances, the relationship of the new key to the original key of E♭ minor was by third (see ex. 4-5).

Ex. 4-5. "Der Mond": Third Relations and Bass Progression

Modulations

The two modulations in this song are similar in that both employ common chords and both are introduced by chromatic motion that intensifies the tonal shift. In mm. 6-8 (see ex. 4-6a), the V/E♭ minor becomes chromatically altered, D♮ to D♭, a chromatic shift that was anticipated by the chromatic vocal line filling in of the A♭-G♭ and B♭-A♭ neighbor-note figures. The first inversion G♭ major harmony of m. 7 then becomes the pivot chord III⁶/E♭ minor →I⁶/G♭ major. The resolution of V⁷/G♭ is heightened and emphasized by the E♭♭ neighbor, a final echo of the vocal line's initial chromatic motions. The opening of modulatory space also occurs in the vocal line (m. 7): the voice emphasizes D♭ (as opposed to the Kopfton* B♭) and its dramatic leap down a seventh has a cadential function (see the seventh leap, m. 4).

Ex. 4-6. "Der Mond": Modulations

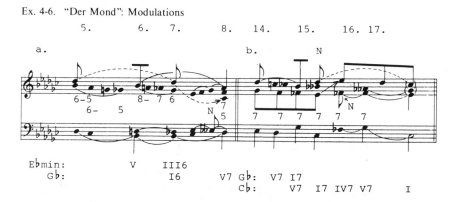

The second modulation, from G♭ to C♭, is also heralded by chromatic inflection in the voice; the D♭-C♮-C♭ of m. 14 is an exact transposition of the B♭-A♮-A♭ of m. 6. Chromatic neighbor notes again intensify the melodic motion to C♭ major. The interweaving of vocal and piano parts is especially powerful in mm. 16-17, as the piano literally ends the vocal phrase while the voice expresses the text "verblendet" (meaning "blinded," "dazzled," or "beguiled"). This second modulation (mm. 15-16) is motivically related to the first (mm. 7-8) by a repetition of the seventh D♭-E♭ (m. 15), a motive that is recalled when the B♭♭-A♭♭ echoes the earlier B♭-A♭. In m. 16, the idea of "verblendet" is associated with F♭ in the voice: F♭ is the final pitch alteration needed in the modulation to C♭.

Example 4-6b illustrates the modulation to C♭. The Kopfton* B♭ shifts to its upper third, D♭, which is in turn reinterpreted as an upper neighbor to C♭. This corresponds to a general use of overlapping thirds within the modulations of this song. The third that connects the closing D♭ to C♭ (E♭, D♭, C♭), is somewhat concealed in the RH piano part in mm. 16ff. This was anticipated by a third, D♭-B♭, in the vocal line of mm. 14-15, and is echoed in the lowest voice of the final RH piano gesture, B♭-A♭♭-G♭. The entire modulation to G♭ major is reinforced by a 5-*Zug*, G♭-C♭ (beamed in ex. 4-6b).

One final reading, example 4-7, summarizes the piece. The large-scale bass motion spans the third from E♭ to C♭. (The flag on G♭ accents the common tone association of that pitch with E♭ and C♭.) The pitch motion around Kopfton* B♭ is straightforward, despite the complex chromaticism and modulation. The B♭ in the voice rises from G♭, and the vocal B♭-A♭ motion continues to refer back to that G♭ in unfolding descending thirds that elide phrases. The vocal A♮ and B♮ of mm. 11-12 (spelled B♭♭ and C♭ in the graph) are chromatic neighbors around the Kopfton* B♭ which ultimately descends back, in an inner voice, to G♭ at the end of the piece. The vocal D♭ is a third associated with B♭ that functions somewhat analogously to the opening third, G♭-B♭. This D♭ becomes increasingly important through the two modulations: in contrast to G♭, which is all but a pedal throughout the song and functions as a common pitch to all three key areas (E♭, G♭, and C♭), D♭ is a volatile pitch that is continuously reinterpreted throughout the song.

Ex. 4-7. "Der Mond": Summary Sketch

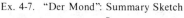

The depiction of the poetry in "Der Mond" is both clever and beautiful. In the first three phrases, mm. 1-6, it is not altogether clear to whom the poet-as-singer describes the moon and the moon's complaint. While the singer narrates the poetry in the characteristic Wolfian *parlando* style, the reiterated piano ostinato (in characteristic incomplete triads) depicts the issue of the moon's complaint that something is missing. The subtle interweaving of vocal line and accompaniment creates a continuous elision of phrases (B♭-A♭ in the voice to G♭ in the piano) and this creates a poignant musical expression of the central textual problem of incompletion.

Text to "Der Mond hat eine schwere Klag' erhoben"
[*Italienischesliederbuch,* 13 November 1890]

Der Mond hat eine schwere Klag' erhoben	The moon has raised a weighty complaint
Und vor dem Herrn die Sache kund gemacht:	And announced before the Lord That he no longer wants to remain in the sky;
Er wolle nicht mehr stehn am Himmel droben,	You have robbed him of his splendor.
Du habest ihn um seinen Glanz gebracht.	When he last counted the host of stars,
Als er zuletzt das Sternenheer gezählt,	Something was missing from the full number,
Da hab'es an der vollen Zahl gefehlt;	Two of the most beautiful you have stolen:
Zwei von den schönsten habest du entwendet:	The two eyes that have blinded me.
Die beiden Augen dort, die mich verblendet.	

The alteration of pitch focus from B♭ to D♭ in m. 7 coincides with a change in poetic subject. As the D♭ assumes more importance within the modulation, it becomes associated with the object of the singer's discourse (the lover). The melodic D♭ descends to E♭ over the C♭ harmony in m. 7, and the phrase ends in the new key of G♭. These pitch associations recur in m. 15, where the second modulation takes place: on the text "Augen," the lover's eyes, D♭ shifts again down to E♭ over the C♭ harmony, and the new and final tonic is established. Modulation in this song thus expresses the nature of the changing subject of the text—the changing references from "der Mond" to "du" (the lover) to, ultimately, "die beiden Augen."

The chromaticism used to initiate and enhance the modulations in this song suggests the textual idea of potential motion. The moon threatens to leave the heavens (A♭-G♮-G♭) and the word "droben" dramatizes the descending moon with the falling B♭-A♮-A♭. In addition, there is a musical pun on the word "entwendet," where the chromaticism depicts the notion of stealing.

The use of the minor mode in mm. 9-12 is prompted by both the text and the music. The tone of the text changes slightly, becoming more conversational or explanatory than accusatory. And, perhaps more important, the use of F#-G♭ minor generates the melodic pitches B♭♭ and C♭, which become upper and lower chromatic neighbors to the Kopfton* B♭ in the new key of G♭. The text in the middle (G♭ minor) section is an emphatic commentary on the moon's concern about the stars as the vocal line becomes more active and the harmonic motion more dramatic. The strong arrival on the dominant (V⁷/G♭, m. 12) creates maximum suspense before the final resolution of both text and song. The last phrase of text reveals the real meaning of the situation: the missing stars are the eyes of the singer's beloved. The key of C♭ is obtained by the addition of F♭—on the word "die" which refers to "die Augen." Thus, what is ultimately stolen is the F♭—in order to establish the new key of C♭.

This wonderful song develops an elaborate metaphor of transformation: the stars become transformed into the eyes of the lover and the key of E♭ minor becomes transformed into the key of C♭ major. The textual agent of this transformation is the lover ("Du"), who is associated with a pitch reference, D♭. The key of G♭ becomes the harmonic agent of transformation—the modulatory key—and the melodic D♭ serves as final melodic agent of modulation and transformation. The singer is too dazzled to speak further and the piano ostinato concludes the song: the mystery is solved and the new key is established.

Thirds and the Tonic-Dominant Axis

The third relations that create the shift in tonal focus in "Der Mond" are reinforced on the deepest structural level by the tonality-defining tonic-dominant axis. The long-range third-progression from E♭ minor to C♭ major is achieved by the internal third progression E♭ minor to G♭ major, after which G♭ becomes V in the overall progression to C♭ major. Other thirds in this piece both support the main harmonic progressions and, at the same time, amplify the tonal ambiguity that is so often associated with third relations. In particular, a special type of third-related pitch ambiguity is exploited here: vertical thirds function as "common" thirds throughout, allowing the tonal shifts to be related by common-tone dyads. In the modulation from E♭ minor to G♭ minor, the common dyad is G♭-B♭; in the modulation from G♭ to C♭, there is no common dyad, but the common pitch G♭ is reinterpreted and the original dyad E♭-G♭ of E♭ minor returns to connect the song's opening with its conclusion.

Comparison of Schenkerian and Directional Tonal Readings

While the change in "Der Mond's" tonal focus has been demonstrated easily, the sketches in ex. 4-6 and ex. 4-7 do not interpret the relationship between E♭ minor and C♭ major. Does the piece begin in one key, E♭, and end in another, C♭, or does the initial key of E♭ represent III of C♭? Whether the song is heard as being in one or several keys is less important than allowing for the possibility that the song may be interpreted in several different ways. On the one hand, the text suggests that there is an initial problem of two missing stars whose mystery is solved at the poem's conclusion, represented musically by a change in key (E♭ → C♭ = question→answer, problem→solution). On the other hand, the solution to the poem's mystery is a symbolic one, and thus E♭ might be considered a symbol for the actual tonality of C♭.

Example 4-8a and example 4-8b compare directional tonal and Schenkerian readings of "Der Mond." Both readings explain the opening tonality differently. In example 4-8a, the directional tonal reading shows an opening in E♭ minor with $\hat{5}$ (B♭) as Kopfton*. The modulation to G♭ begins in m. 6 and the new key of G♭ is attained by m. 9. The opening Kopfton* B♭ is now undermined by its melodic counterpart D♭ ($\hat{5}$ in G♭), which is emphasized by its lower tessitura. From m. 9 on, the two Kopftöne*, B♭ ($\hat{3}$ in G♭) and D♭ ($\hat{5}$ in G♭), compete for the role of main melodic pitch as both become pivotal pitches in the transformation of G♭-as-I to G♭-as V. With the modulation to C♭ major, both B♭ and D♭ become dissonant melodic pitches that resolve to pitches of the C♭ major tonic triads (B♭ resolves through A♭♭ to G♭—recall that G♭ was the melodic origin of B♭ in mm. 1-2—and D♭ resolves as a neighbor note to C♭). Within the context of directional tonality, the song may be understood in two ways. First, it may be viewed as a piece that incorporates two transformations, the first (E♭ minor to G♭ minor) involving a change of Kopfton* and the second (G♭ major to C♭ major) involving a resolution of the Kopfton* in lieu of a Kopfton* descent. Second, the song may be understood as a piece that begins in E♭ minor and ends in C♭ major and where G♭ is a large-scale pivot whose

Ex. 4-8. "Der Mond": Comparison of Directional Tonal and
          Schenkerian Readings

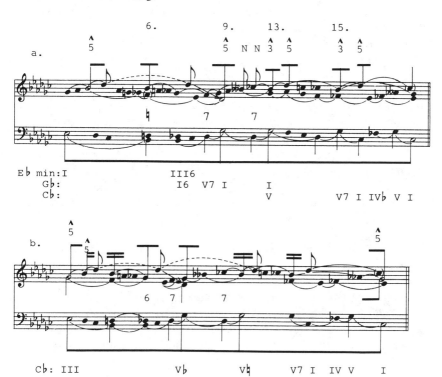

function changes from III/E♭ minor to V/C♭ major. Both interpretations involve a transformation of Kopfton* (from B♭ to D♭) as well as a change from opening to closing tonalities.

The directional tonal reading is encouraged by the piano accompaniment. The piano ostinato establishes unequivocally the key of E♭ minor in the opening four measures. There is no reason for the listener to think the opening E♭ minor harmony is anything but a tonic, E♭ being clearly defined as such by its dominant in mm. 2 and 4. When the piece closes in C♭ major, the opening in E♭ minor remains an opening key that differs from the closing key.

The Schenkerian reading in example 4-8b is also persuasive. The opening key of E♭ minor and the middle key of G♭ minor/major are understood as arpeggiations of the C♭ tonic triad that closes the song and these tonal shifts comprise the Schenkerian *Bassbrechung*. The *Urlinie*, however, is somewhat problematic. The vocal pitch B♭ cannot function as a *Kopfton* in C♭ major, even though B♭ recurs as a significant melodic pitch throughout mm. 2-16. In example 4-8b, B♭ is given a double incomplete beam to illustrate its prevalence as a melodic pitch whose important role is not otherwise adequately notated. If the vocal pitch B♭ cannot function as *Kopfton*, then the piano ostinato pitch G♭ can. The G♭ *Kopfton* ($\hat{5}$) is idiosyncratic, however, for it does not descend at the song's conclusion. The Schenkerian reading also does not accommodate a clear understanding of the function of the melodic pitch D♭, which occurs as a dissonant pitch as early as m. 5 within III/C♭ major.

Whereas the *Bassbrechung* of the reading in example 4-8b thus encourages a Schenkerian reading, the *Urlinie* problems undermine the use of Schenkerian analysis as the sole interpretation of this complicated song. The directional tonal reading addresses those issues not easily interpreted by Schenker's system and offers an alternative view of the tonal shift during the course of the song. The directional tonal reading does not claim that at some level E♭ is not heard as III, nor G♭ as V, of C♭ major. Rather, the directional tonal reading asserts that the opening tonality of E♭ minor is heard as a tonic first, and is later reinterpreted as III/C♭ major. Further, the close in C♭ major does not fully negate the earlier perception of E♭ minor as a tonic in its own right.

Directional Tonality and Plagal Relations in "Mir ward gesagt" and "Lebewohl"

Two songs combine directional tonality and plagal relations. These are the *Italienischesliederbuch* song "Mir ward gesagt," and the Mörike song "Lebewohl." Both songs use extensive amounts of chromaticism and ambiguity to destabilize the opening tonality and prepare for the shift to the closing tonality.

"Mir ward gesagt, du reisest in die Ferne"

"Mir ward gesagt" (25 September 1890) exemplifies three extended-tonal techniques. Through various harmonic, rhythmic, and textural factors, the song represents a vivid example of the ambiguity principle defined in chapter 1. Further, with its large-scale IV-I structure, the song depicts both the use of the middleground plagal axis and the use of directional tonality.

The ambiguity principle. Two plagal elements contribute to the ambiguity in this song: first, the opening tonality occurs in the region of the subdominant, and second, plagal substitution intensifies the ambiguity within the plagal axis.

The ambiguity principle is strongly suggested by the text. The singer is distraught at hearing that her lover is going away "in die Ferne." Initially, her reaction is one of intense anxiety; she queries: "Ach, wohin?" and "Den Tag?", and her anxious despair consumes the first half of the poem. Eventually, the singer's anxiety turns to sadness. Her tears will accompany her lover and she beseeches him to remember her. The anxious questions of the first half are replaced in the second half, initially by sadness and then by hopeful acceptance, as the singer finally requests "Gedenk' an mich, vergiss es nicht." Wolf divides his setting of this poem into two distinct sections. Section 1, the ambiguity phase, sets lines 1-4 in mm. 1-8 (with a half-bar introduction); and section 2, the clarification phase, sets lines 5-8 in mm. 10-20, (with a three-bar piano postlude). The two sections are connected by a two-beat piano interlude in m. 9.

Text to "Mir ward gesagt, du reisest in die Ferne"
[*Italienischesliederbuch,* 25 September 1890]

Mir ward gesagt, du reisest in die Ferne.	I was told you were traveling afar.
Ach, wohin gehst du, mein geliebtes Leben?	Ah, were are you going, my dearest life?
Den Tag, an dem du scheidest, wüsst' ich gerne	The day you depart, I would like to know.
Mit Tränen will ich das Geleit dir geben.	With tears I will moisten your path.
Mit Tränen will ich deinen Weg befeuchten—	Think of me, and hope will shine from me!
Gedenk' an mich, und Hoffnung wird mir leuchten!	With tears I am with you, everywhere—
Mit Tränen bin ich bei dir allerwarts—	Think of me, do not forget, my heart!
Gedenk' an mich, vergiss es nicht, mein Herz!	

Wolf's depiction of the singer's initial confusion and anxiety exploits four different forms of musical ambiguity. First, the song opens with characteristic incomplete triads in the RH that create immediate tonal ambiguity: Does the piece begin in E minor or G major? Second, the use of foreground chromaticism in both hands of the accompaniment, especially in the LH, creates a density of dissonant nonharmonic tones that obscures harmonic meaning and inhibits resolution patterns. Third, Wolf creates what might be called a "staggered resolution" technique where resolution of melodic patterns does not coincide with resolution of harmonic patterns. Fourth, Wolf begins his song on an incomplete measure (to be called "m. 0") and infuses the first half of the song with unusual rhythmic tensions that include truncated three-beat phrases in mm. 5-6. When combined, the various kinds of ambiguity create a dissonant, equivocal musical structure that requires further definition and resolution—all of which occur in the "clarification" phase of the song's second half. Each form of ambiguity will now be discussed in turn.

Tonal ambiguity. The lack of tonal focus at the beginning of the song continues in varying degrees almost to the song's end. The song clearly ends in D major, but the song's opening can be understood in either G major or E minor (see example 4-9). The ensuing tonal shifts intensify the dual reading; the key of A minor (mm. 2-3), for instance, can be heard as a plagal component of either opening key (IV/ E minor or II/ G major); the key of B minor (mm. 5 and 8) can be heard easily as III/ G major or as V♭/ E minor. To make the issue even more complicated, the predominance of B minor throughout this song strongly suggests that B minor might be a third potential opening tonality, especially since B minor supports the Kopfton*, D, in mm. 3, 5, and 10. An interpretation of B minor as opening tonality would invoke the transformation of tonic function, with I-V in E minor becoming IV-I in B minor and the song's opening (mm. 0-1) would be heard as IV/ B minor rather than I/ E minor.[22]

Ex. 4-9.   "Mir ward gesagt": Tonal Ambiguity

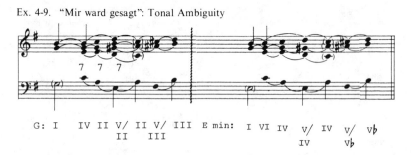

In order to simplify the discussion of tonal relations in this song, one of the three possible tonalities will be chosen as the tonal focus of mm. 1-8, while continuing tonal ambiguity will be designated by the symbol [e/ G/ b].[23] The rationales for choosing one key over another are illustrated in example 4-10, where compelling cases can be made for any one of the three keys. In all cases, the potential opening key is related to the clear closing key of D major, and the interior region of F# minor (mm. 10ff.) is related to either the opening or closing tonality. In example 4-10a, a reading in G major shows how mm. 10ff. can be heard as A major, with the resulting large-scale structure being IV-V-I in D major. In example 4-10b, an equally plausible case is made for B minor as tonic, understanding mm. 10ff. to be in F# minor, which creates a large-scale structure in D: VI-III-VI-V-I. Several factors support the reading in example 4-10c, where E minor is the opening tonality. First, mm. 10ff. are again heard as F# minor and the resulting large-scale structure in D is: II-III-VI-V-I. Second, E is heard as the root of the G-B third in beat 2 of m. 1, especially in light of the fact that the G major triad of m. 1 beat 3 is in $^6_4$ position.

While in some of the discussion that follows the opening tonality is labelled E minor, the real meaning of the opening eight measures is a lack of tonal focus, or a confusion of tonal meaning (hence, [e/G/b]). Although the closing tonality of D major is unequivocal, the relationship of the opening tonality to the closing tonality of D major remains unclear as well. What makes the confusion tenable is the concept of plagal substitution, for all three keys in question can represent a basic plagal function in the subsequent key of D major: E minor = II/D; G major = IV/D; and B minor = VI/D.

Chromaticism. Wolf uses both obvious and subtle forms of chromaticism in "Mir ward gesagt." His use of chromatic passing tones in the foreground is an obvious means of creating both local harmonic ambiguity and a general texture of foreground dissonance. The surface chromaticism is subtle as well in that it foreshadows later chromaticism at the middleground level, where tonal shifts occur through chromatic inflection. Chromatic elements that are not part of the piano ostinato are introduced carefully in the vocal line, where they facilitate the long-range tonal transformation. Example 4-11 outlines the main harmonic motion of the song. Ambiguity continues through m. 13, at which point the clarification begins.

The first chromatic pitch to be sung, C# (m. 4), is structurally the most important. It is followed one bar later (m. 5) by G#, which plays both a structural and a motivic role throughout the rest of the song. The E# of m. 8 and D# of m. 13 participate to a lesser degree in the tonal transformation and will be discussed accordingly. In a general sense, the relationship of large-scale chromaticism to the ambiguity principle is one of structural function: what functioned as chromatic embellishments (neighbor notes) in the ambiguity phase become structural in the clarification phase.

As already stated, C# is the most important chromatic pitch of the song. Not only is C# the first altered vocal pitch in m. 4, but it recurs in the voice twice, in mm. 6-7 and mm. 10-11. The vocal C# is introduced in the

Ex. 4-10. "Mir ward gesagt": Alternate Interpretation of Tonal Design

a.

<table>
<tr><td>G: I</td><td>III</td><td>V/V</td><td></td><td></td><td></td><td>V</td></tr>
</table>

$$
\begin{array}{c|c|c|c|c}
7\ 7 & 6 & 6 \\
& 4 & 4
\end{array}
$$

D: IV   VI   V   VI   V/V   IV$^6_4$ V   I

b.

B min: IV   I   V/V   V♭   I

D: VI   V/III   III   VI   V/V   V   I

c.

E min: I   IV   V♭   V/II   II

D: II   VI   III   VI   V/V   IV   V   I

Ex. 4-11. "Mir ward gesagt": Chromaticism

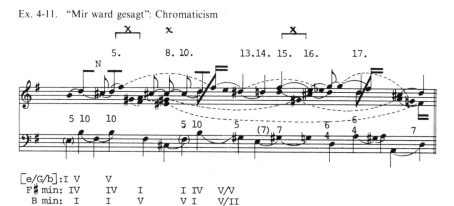

intermediary harmonic regions of B minor and F♯ minor, and thus it participates in the tonal transition from [e/G/b] to D major. The chromatic pitch C♯ as a lower neighbor to the Kopfton* D (flagged in example 4-11) anticipates the imminent structural relationship of these two pitches: C♯ will become the leading tone to D, which will become the closing tonic. The functional shift of D from Kopfton* to tonic is itself anticipated in m. 13, where D♯ temporarily displaces D♮ to create a V⁷/C♯ chord. The chromatic shift from V⁷/C♯ (m. 13) to V⁷/A (V⁷/V/D, m. 14) is the crucial step toward defining D major as a tonic. The ambiguous minor subdominant areas (E minor, B minor) are replaced by the more definitive major dominant regions (E major, A major), and the voice intensifies the chromatic shift as it sings F♯-E-D♯ in m. 13 and then an abrupt D♮ in m. 14. (Note that the introduction of D♯ in m. 13 is parallel to the introduction of C♯ in m. 4, and that the D♯ functions as a neighbor note to D♮ in a subtle analog to the earlier C♯ function as neighbor to D.)

Let us now trace the role of D♮ from m. 14 to the song's conclusion. The effect of the vocal D♮ in m. 14 is one of displacement: it becomes a dissonant seventh of the E-seventh chord, and its destabilization coincides with the loss of its Kopfton* function during the subsequent tonal shift to the key of D. The pitch D♮ is never heard again as a vocal consonance, and its altered status is reiterated once more in m. 16 as the D♯ (respelled E♭) functions clearly as an upper neighbor to D, the D occurring as a dissonant fourth within a ⁶₄ chord. The chromatic embellishments of D (C♯, D♯/E♭) thus reinforce its various functions and the C♯ becomes a middleground element within the tonal transformation.

The chromatic pitch G♯ is less structurally important than C♯. It does, however, fulfill an important role as a recurring pitch of tonal transition that is nested within a three-note motive, D-F♯-G♯ (motive X). (The various occurrences of G♯ are linked by dotted lines in example 4-11.) The pitch G♯ is first heard in the RH piano part in m. 2, where E minor becomes V^7/IV in the first harmonic shift to arise from chromatic alteration. The first vocal G♯ occurs as part of motive X in m. 5, where the motive is sung in B minor and the G♯ displaces A in the abbreviated phrases of mm. 5-6. Motive X recurs in the voice in m. 8 as part of the pivotal C♯^{7} chord that connects the ambiguous first half of the song to the clarifying second. The final recurrence of motive X is in the crucial mm. 15-16, where the G♯ of the voice is negated by a G♮ in the bass (m. 16) and the key of D major is finally established. In general, the vocal G♯ (and motive X) have functioned as a connector between the pivotal harmonic areas of B minor (V♭/E minor, VI/D major), F♯ minor (II/E minor, II/D major) and D major itself, as the G♯ initially resolves to A on a local level and ultimately becomes the leading tone to V/D in the crucial E^7 chord of m. 14.

Staggered resolution technique. The most vivid ambiguity in this song results from what will be called a staggered resolution or overlap technique. In this overlap technique, linear pitch structures do not coincide with harmonic ones and resolution patterns become contrapuntally staggered. Example 4-12 demonstrates the resulting dissonance. The melodic D of m. 2 occurs over an E^7 chord, but does not initially function like a seventh. The pitch D moves up to E in m. 4, deferring the resolution as D-as-seventh to the last beat of the measure (notated by an arrow). Meanwhile, the harmonic motion of mm. 2-3 (V^7 to I of A minor) is projected in the bass, but not in the upper parts (piano or voice), and the result is a "$^4_2$" dissonance above the bass that resolves idiosyncratically with continuing upward movement of the upper parts. The overall effect of this technique is a discontinuity between treble and bass, in which the clearest harmonic progression is undermined by melodic dissonance and the melodic motion is often disconnected from its expected harmonic support. As a result, the vocal line often sounds unstable and unfocused, and this aptly mirrors the anxiety and confusion of the text.

Ex. 4-12. "Mir ward gesagt": Staggered Resolution Technique

As might be expected, this staggered resolution technique continues in mm. 10-13 where the opening material is repeated in F# minor until the clarification begins in mm. 14ff. Simpler dissonance—predominantly the $^6_4$ position—replaces the opening's dissonances discussed above and the treble and bass parts are no longer out of phase.

Rhythmic ambiguity. Tonal ambiguity, chromatic displacement, and staggered resolution are all reinforced by a subtle rhythmic imbalance that permeates the song's first half. Rhythmic ambiguity begins at the very outset: the opening half measure ("m. 0") is either an upbeat to m. 1 (as it is written), or a first measure that is truncated by a misplaced bar line. The tension caused by the two-beat "m. 0" is enhanced by the dissonances on the downbeats of the measures that follow: in m. 1, the F# bass is an accented neighbor note (to E or G), as is the bass B of m. 2; the bass A of m. 3 has been noted as a dissonance resulting from the staggered resolution technique and the bass C of m. 4 is dissonant because of the lingering alto G#. In mm. 5-6, the rhythmic imbalance is intensified by the two disruptive three-beat phrases that lead to the C#-seventh chord of m. 8. The imbalance ultimately is rectified by the two-beat measure 9, but not until the rhythmic tension of mm. 1-8 has contributed substantially to the general tension of the song's first half.

One interpretation of the rhythmic ambiguity is that the first half of the vocal line is misbarred (see example 4-13). A rebarring of example 4-12, allowing the initial melodic gesture of the voice to imitate the opening piano upbeat, "corrects" much of the metric ambiguity in the actual setting, and certain vocal gestures are strengthened by the metric change. The eighth-note figure of the opening recurs consistently as an anacrusis, except for m. "h", where the vocal line is complicated by the *accelerando* to the cadential C#-seventh chord of m. "i". The resolution of D to C# is strengthened by being in the first half of m. "e", just as the dramatic sixth D-B is emphasized by being on the downbeat of m. "g". Finally, the arrival of the vocal line above the C#-seventh chord is underscored by its occurrence on the downbeat of m. "i", and the two-beat rest that follows is recast into a weaker metric position than the actual $^2_4$ bar of m. 9.

Ex. 4-13. "Mir ward gesagt": Vocal Lined Rebarred (mm. 1-10)

Directional tonality. The ambiguity principle just described creates a remarkable musical counterpart to the tensions of the poetic text. While the transformation of tonal focus has already been discussed to some extent, the following analysis will trace the tonal transformation in greater detail. This discussion will also examine how certain pitch/text associations contribute to the overall tonal shift. See example 4-14.

Ex. 4-14. "Mir ward gesagt": Directional Tonality

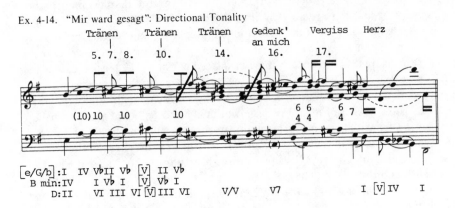

As described earlier (pp. 143-45) the concept of directional tonality involves both a shift in tonal focus and a concomitant change in Kopfton*. Although the complexity of the opening tonality, [e/G/b], has already been discussed, the problem in choosing D as a Kopfton* (m. 5) needs to be explored further. The difficulty in determining the Kopfton* in this song suggests that the already impressive amount of ambiguity occurs in yet one more guise, namely confusion of melodic focus. The central problem with assigning D as Kopfton* is that it does not align with the potential opening tonality of E minor. The Kopfton* can perhaps best be understood as emerging from the melodic pitch B in E minor and attaining the status of Kopfton* within the ancillary key of B minor, where D is a tenth above B in mm. 5 and 8. A rationale for the function of B minor as harmonic support for the Kopfton* D may be considered as follows: since the various opening keys of [e/G/b] all interrelate as some form of plagal harmony in D major, B minor can be considered both an extension of E minor and/or a potential opening tonality in its own right. Whether B minor is heard as the actual opening tonality or as an intermediary harmony—or perhaps indeed just because it can have these several different harmonic functions—B minor becomes a logical tonality to carry the main melodic event of the song's first half.

Along with the use of the pivotal harmonic region of B minor, Wolf also associates the Kopfton* with a textual reference, the word "Tränen." The first occurrence of "Tränen" is in m. 7, where the word is connected to the lower neighbor C♯. This crucial pitch/text relationship signals the beginning of the departure from the opening subdominant regions of E minor, G major, and B minor, and it initiates, within the region of F♯ minor, a movement towards the dominant, A major. The association of the melodic C♯ neighbor to the harmonic region F♯ minor occurs on the word "Tränen" in m. 10, where F♯ minor is both II/E minor and III/D major. The motion toward D major is anticipated when the Kopfton* D is undermined the favor of the new Kopfton* F♯ (denoted by a double incomplete beam.) The melodic F♯ of mm. 12-13 assumes the position originally held by the Kopfton* D in mm. 3-4; and the transformation of Kopfton* from D to F♯ is heightened by its association with the word "Tränen" in m. 14.

The second tonality, D major, arrives with the G♮/C♯ tritone of m. 16 when the original Kopfton* (D) now functions as the new tonic. In m. 16, Wolf cleverly reminds the listener of the earlier D Kopfton* function with the text "Gedenk' an mich." The arrival of the new Kopfton* then is emphasized by the marvelous pun "Vergiss es nicht" on the vocal pitches D-F♯-A (m. 17). The new Kopfton*, F♯, is in the middle of an arpeggiated cadential $^6_4$ chord, and the old Kopfton* is a dissonant fourth. The dominant pitch A, meanwhile, leads down a third to the lower F♯ on the words "mein Herz." The new Kopfton*, F♯, becomes associated with the text "Herz" as the singer's tears are transformed by resignation and love.

The extremely ambiguous opening of "Mir ward gesagt" makes the song a complicated example of directional tonality. With three different tonalities competing as opening key, tracing the actual tonal transformation is indeed difficult. As mentioned earlier, the invocation of plagal substitution makes it possible to consider that the first half of this song becomes some sort of plagal element within the second tonality. The actual moment of transformation is not precise, but two different interpretations are feasible. First, the shift in tonal focus involves a gradual progression from [e/G/b] to F♯ minor to D major. The initial tonality of [e/G/b] is definitely supplanted in m. 10 by F♯ minor, which becomes III of D major and/or might be considered a substitute for A major (V/D). It is furthermore possible to consider F♯ minor as a pivot between E minor and D major, where II/E minor becomes VI/V/D which progresses to V⁷/V/D at m. 14. In this interpretation, the tonal transformation involves two regions, [e/G/b] and F♯ minor, both of which are understood first within [e/G/b]: the composite tonality [e/G/b] as I, F♯ minor as II; and then in D major: [e/G/b] becomes some form of subdominant; F♯ becomes III, or a substitute for V, or VI/V/D.

Transformation of tonic function. A second reading of tonal transformation focuses on the plagal transformation of tonic function (see ex. 4-15). With the use of this procedure, the shift in tonal focus can be linked to the middleground chromatic inflection mentioned earlier, and "Mir ward gesagt" becomes an elegant plagal structure.

Ex. 4-15. "Mir ward gesagt": Directional Tonality and
Transformation of Tonic Function

E min: I   V♭   II
B min: IV   I   V♭
    D: II   VI   VI/V V/V V   I

As already suggested, the transformation of tonic function occurs when the piece begins not in E minor but, rather, in IV/ B minor: the song begins in B minor, and the opening (mm. 0-5) is a plagal IV-I progression. As in the first interpretation, F♯ minor becomes the pivot between the opening and closing tonalities as VI/ V progresses to V^7/ V/ D (the crucial E^7 chord of m. 14). The E^7 leads eventually to V^7/D and the piece closes clearly in D major. The prominence of E minor over B minor at the opening contributes to the song's overall initial ambiguity. Also, the opening E minor is the crucial connector to the closing key, D major. The E minor opening, IV/ B (mm. 0-1), becomes transformed in m. 14 into a V^7/ V.

While this second reading may seem unduly complex, it does interrelate several particularly complicated harmonic structures. First, hearing the opening E minor as IV of B minor explains both the inability of E minor to support the Kopfton*, and the use of B minor as the Kopfton* support. Second, this reading also connects the opening E minor to the pivotal E^7 chord of m. 14, and thereby relates two of the song's important structural points of articulation. Finally, this connection between the opening E minor and the E^7 chord of m. 14 enables the transformation of tonal focus to be achieved not just by common chords (i.e., B minor and F♯ minor), but also by large-scale chromatic inflection: the functional changes of chromatic pitches C♯ and, in this context, G♯ become transforming agents in the tonal shift from [e/ G/ b] to D major.

Large-scale plagal structure. The concept of directional tonality involves two seemingly contradictory issues of large-scale structure. While the opening tonality might be understood as ultimately functioning within the closing tonality, the initial function of the opening tonality as tonic must be retained in the overall tonal design. In order to simplify the discussion that follows, we will consider the composite tonality, [e/ G/ b], to be the opening tonality, denoting it through a bass E. The B minor that supports the Kopfton* D will function as a second tonality within that composite opening. In ex. 4-15, accordingly, both bass notes E and B are notated (along with the closing D) in structurally weighted half notes. Example 4-16a focuses upon the song's tonal axis. Even though D major is articulated by its own dominant, the overall formal design incorporates the tonic-dominant axis within a more inclusive plagal axis. Although A major is a middleground V of D major, the harmony A major does not have a dominant function within the opening [e/ G/ b] tonality, and at best can be understood as having a subdominant function in E minor. The large-scale relationship of [e/ G/ b] to D major must be viewed independently from the tonic-dominant axis because that tonic-dominant axis does not function as such within the opening key. The plagal axis thus remains the overriding large-scale structure, and the composite opening tonality has a subdominant function within the second tonality, with bass E resolving by step to bass D (ex. 4-16b).

Two details of this directional reading are especially noteworthy. First, in example 4-15, the use of the downward circle of fifths to define and resolve D major (E to A to D) mirrors the upward circle of fifths (E to B to F♯ to C♯) that opened the song. The two distinctly different halves of the songs are thus joined by a subtle but nonetheless powerful balance of the most traditional harmonic motion: progression by fifth.

Second, in example 4-60c, when the plagal progression is expanded to incorporate B minor and the dominant of D, the fifth relation between E minor and B minor is heard as a fifth progression in the opening tonality that is symmetrical to the closing authentic cadence in D major. Once again Wolf compensates for the weakness of the large-scale plagal axis with the use of the dominant and with formal symmetry.

Ex. 4-16. "Mir ward gesagt": Large-Scale Plagal Structure

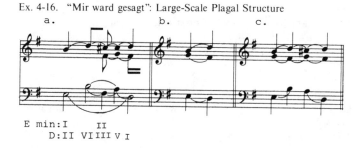

E min:I   II
  D:II VI III V I

The use of directional tonality in "Mir ward gesagt" has shown how a seemingly simple progression in D major (II-VI-III-V-I) can be understood as a complex tonal structure where the emphatic tonic-dominant axis functions within an overriding plagal axis. Furthermore, the shift in tonal focus that results from this subdominant emphasis exemplifies a new concept of tonality where two equal tonal centers coexist within one short musical work. Although the key of D major is in no way expected at the outset of the song, the function of the composite opening key [e/G/b] still lingers at the song's conclusion. This is a wonderful musical analog to the poetry, as the hopeful entreaties of the closing lines do not entirely eradicate the anxious queries of the opening.

"Lebewohl"

"Lebewohl" is one of Wolf's better-known Mörike songs (31 March 1888). With its dense chromaticism, despondent mood, and dramatic interplay of piano and vocal parts, it represents the quintessence of Wolf's *Lied* style. "Lebewohl" also exemplifies some of the more complex aspects of Wolf's musical language: it incorporates directional tonality within a large-scale plagal axis and utilizes linear and harmonic chromaticism within the characteristic ambiguity principle. In addition, the song also demonstrates how Wolf foreshadows important middleground events with subtle foreground detail.

The eight terse lines of "Lebewohl" depict the grief of someone rejected by an uncaring lover. The poem is neither a story nor a statement, but rather a reflection about the complex nature of lost love. Accordingly, both the poem and the musical setting are complicated structures whose internal relationships are often opaque. Wolf's setting of this poem—extraordinary in its subtlety and elegance—conveys a profound understanding of the complicated feelings of lost love.

The poem divides into two parts. The first half presents a curious portrait of the rejecting lover, whose seeming indifference ("mit getrostem Angesicht sagtest du's und leichtem Herzen") intensifies the pain of loss. In the poem's second half, the poet continues to dwell in sorrow: a "nimmersatter Qual" is overwhelming, and over and over again the poet's heart is broken.

Text to "Lebewohl"
[Mörike, 31 March 1888]

"Lebewohl"—Du fühlest nicht,	"Farewell" You feel not
Was es heisst, dies Wort der Schmerzen;	What it means, this word of pains;
Mit getrostem Angesicht	With benign expression
Sagtest du's und leichtem Herzen.	And light heart you said it.
Lebewohl!—Ach tausendmal	"Farewell" Oh, a thousand times
Hab' ich mir es vorgesprochen,	Have I said it to myself,
Und in nimmersatter Qual	And in insatiable torment
Mir das Herz damit gebrochen!	Broken my heart with it.

Wolf depicts the complexity of the text through several extended-tonal procedures. His use of directional tonality underscores the transformation of the singer's emotional state from ironic conflict (portrayed in G♭) to resigned sorrow (depicted in D♭). Wolf further interprets the subtlety of the poem by having the piano, not the voice, end the song in D♭. In m. 16, the singer alludes to the new key on the word "gebrochen," but only the piano postlude clarifies the new key, as it reiterates the "Lebewohl" motive in a haunting reminder of the lost love—and, perhaps, as the lost key.

By giving the singer a qualified relationship to the new key, Wolf conveys a basic ambiguity of the poetry: whether the singer is, in fact, not resigned to the loss (and thus to the new key of D♭) and therefore moves only tentatively out of G♭, the key of conflict. In addition, the change of key and the singer's inability to participate fully in D♭ reflect the irony of the conflict: How does one accept the loss of an unreciprocating lover? The piano alone—assuming a *persona* separate from that of the singer—is able to resolve the conflicts of G♭ by moving decisively into D♭.

In addition to using directional tonality, Wolf also employs an extensive amount of chromaticism to convey textual complexities. Ambiguous sonorities convey the singer's torment, and the resulting vocal line is unusually disjunct and expressive. Wolf's use of directional tonality and the ambiguity principle suggests not only the obsessive pain of the text, but also the transformation of emotion that occurs over the course of the poem. The change in tonal focus and the clarification of chromatic ambiguities thus become musical analogs to the nuances of the textual conflicts.

Directional tonality and plagal structure. In contrast to the complexity and ambiguity of "Mir ward gesagt," the use of directional tonality and the plagal axis in "Lebewohl" is unproblematic. Example 4-17 presents a middleground reading of "Lebewohl," with the chromatics eliminated in order to reveal the underlying diatonic structure. The opening tonality of G♭ major is clearly

Ex. 4-17. "Lebewohl": Directional Tonality

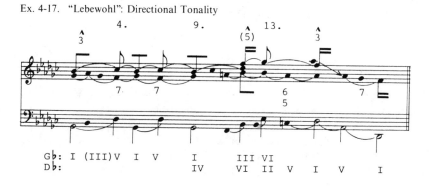

articulated by decisive half cadences in mm. 4 and 8. The tonal shift to D♭ can be traced through a circle-of-fifths progression in mm. 11ff., where III-VI/ G♭ becomes reinterpreted as VI-II/ D♭. The common-chord fifth-progression B♭ to E♭ emphasizes E♭, which becomes the actual pivot chord: VI/G♭ becomes dominant preparation (II) in D♭. The progression then continues by fifth to the authentic cadence in D♭. As in all directional tonal pieces, the opening tonality may ultimately be reinterpreted in the closing tonality (in this case, G♭ becomes IV in the closing tonality of D♭). Both tonalities are reinforced by authentic cadences, and as shown in example 4-18, a large-scale plagal axis emerges.

Ex. 4-18. "Lebewohl": The Plagal Middleground

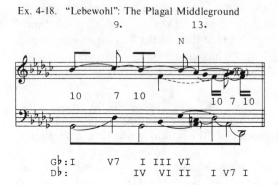

The actual moment of tonal shift occurs in mm. 13-14. There, the leading tone C♮ in the bass literally underscores the shift to D♭; and this arrival upon the new tonal center is emphasized by a climax in the vocal line in m. 14, where the voice sings the poignant text "nimmersatter Qual" on *fortissimo* A♭. The vocal climax on A♭ is actually part of a more elaborate climax in mm. 13-14. The high vocal A♭ of m. 14 echoes the prior appearance of that pitch in the RH piano part in m. 13, which sounds above the pivotal bass C♮. When the vocal line reiterates the high A♭ in m. 14, the RH counters with a descent, G♭ to F, and the key of D♭ is reinforced by the tritone resolution

$$G♭\text{-}F$$
$$C\text{-}D♭$$

in the accompaniment. Rather than continue to imitate the RH, the vocal line dramatically shifts from the high A♭ down an octave, regaining the middle register in which the song began and in which the song will now end. The key of D♭ is then reinforced by the piano postlude.

The assigning of a Kopfton* and the tracing of a coherent melodic line in "Lebewohl" are difficult because of Wolf's dramatic use of tessitura in both the vocal and the RH piano parts. The two Kopftöne* cited in example 4-18 show that in "Lebewohl" Wolf changed the actual Kopfton* pitch in order to preserve the Kopfton* interval of a tenth above the bass. The shift in melodic emphasis occurs in m. 11, where the vocal line stresses F in anticipation of the new Kopfton*. Then, in mm. 13-14, the B♭ Kopfton* loses its prominent melodic function and becomes a neighbor to A♭ within the progression E♭ to A♭.

The resultant plagal structure is similar to that of "Mir ward gesagt." Both songs begin in an opening key that ultimately is understood as a plagal harmony in the closing key: in "Mir ward gesagt" the opening tonality becomes II; in "Lebewohl," it becomes IV. Furthermore, since both songs contain a clear-cut tonic-dominant axis in the second key, the Schenkerian reading of "Lebewohl" (a IV-V-I progression in D♭) is as feasible as was the II-VI-III-V— I/D reading of "Mir ward gesagt." Nonetheless, the directional tonal reading remains preferable because it conveys more about the listener's experience of the song and of Wolf's depiction of the poetry. Through directional tonality, Wolf conveys the shift from poetic confusion in G♭ to poetic resignation in D♭. When G♭ loses its function as tonic and is replaced by D♭ (mm. 13ff.), the poetic conflict merges with the act of resignation, the conflict (G♭) internalized along with the pain of lost love.

Examples 4-19a and 4-19b offer middleground readings of "Lebewohl." Example 4-19a shows the weak plagal structure where, in the absence of the dominant, the ambiguous relationship between the closing tonic and its subdominant can be understood as a I to V progression in G♭. Example 4-19b fills in the common chords B♭ minor and E♭ minor, and adds the requisite dominant to confirm D♭ as the closing tonality. Several factors are worth noting. The pitch D♭, while not a Kopfton* generating melodic activity, does function as a cohesive pitch between the two tonalities and helps emphasize the shift to the key D♭. Also, the dominant (A♭), while necessary to clarify harmonic function within a plagal structure, is chromatically displaced within the opening key of G♭ major. The closing dominant of D♭ thus functions on a lower structural level than the framing tonalities of the song (in open-note notation in example 4-19b).

Ex. 4-19. "Lebewohl": Ambiguity of the Plagal Axis

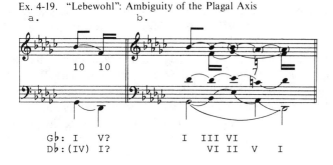

G♭: I   V?   I   III VI
D♭: (IV) I?   VI   II   V   I

Chromaticism. One of the most remarkable aspects of "Lebewohl" is that the song bespeaks pain and anguish within the context of the major mode. Wolf's compensation for a lack of the rich harmonic resources of the minor mode is the use of extensive linear and harmonic chromaticism. Linear chromaticism infuses simple harmonic progressions with dissonance, and expressive nineteenth-century sonorities (e.g., augmented triads, augmented sixth chords, irregularly resolving dominant seventh chords, and diminished seventh chords) create sections of harmonic ambiguity and unexpected resolution patterns.

Wolf also compensates for setting the song in the major mode by exploiting those elements of the plagal domain that are minor, e.g., II and VI. Where initially the chromaticism in "Lebewohl" creates dissonance and ambiguity (as it does in "Mir ward gesagt"), the role of chromaticism eventually changes as the music shifts toward clarification. During the ambiguity phase, chromaticism expands upon a repetitive diatonic progression, while during the clarification phase it produces the shift in tonal focus.

Chromaticism as expansion and continuity. Examples 4-20a and b sketch "Lebewohl" on the foreground and middleground, with all chromatic passing tones deleted to demonstrate the underlying harmonic progressions. As the Roman numerals below sketch b indicate, mm. 1-8 can be heard as variations upon the progression I-II-V, a varied repetition scheme wherein Wolf conveys the obsession in the poetry through harmonic reiteration. Note how the initial I-II-V progression, mm. 1-2, is frustrated by a rhythmic syncopation of II and then by a third substitution of $\text{III}_\natural^{\cdot 7}$ for V in m. 2. The rhythm of mm. 1-2 can be indicated:

$$\text{I} \quad \text{II} \ \big| \ (\text{IV}) \quad [\text{V}] \quad \text{III}$$

where the II chord (the IV of m. 2 substitutes for II) is held over the bar line and thereby expanded to three beats. This expansion of the dominant preparation harmony destabilizes the meter of the I-II-V progression and creates a rhythmic tension similar to that of "Mir ward gesagt." The substitution of III for V in m. 2 is a clever ploy: the progression to V is postponed for 2 bars and the listener's expectation is momentarily thwarted. This coincides with the text where the singer interrupts the reflection about "Lebewohl"—the reflection depicted by a linear descent from the Kopfton* $B\flat$—to interject anger at the lover. The text "Du fühlest nicht" is sung above the altered III chord. The $\text{III}_\natural^{\cdot 7}$ chord not only delays the arrival of V, but also anticipates the important structural role of III later in the song (cf. mm. 11ff.). It is indeed a credit to Wolf's genius that he is able to coordinate two unusual harmonic devices in the song's opening: a circumvention of harmonic progression and an anticipation

Ex. 4-20a. "Lebewohl": Chromatic Expansion

Ex. 4-20b. "Lebewohl": Chromatic Expansion (cont.)

of later harmonic events. The progression from II to V continues in the piano part of mm. 3-4, while the singer's rage and despair continues in a complex counterpoint above.[24]

As example 4-20b indicates, the arrival on V of m. 4 signals a close of the first musical phrase and the first line of text. The chromaticism of phrase one is presented in example 4-21, which shows the two functions of linear chromaticism within the entire song: (1) chromatic passing tones expand the musical space within the underlying progression I-II-V; and (2) the resultant descending chromatic lines create a linear continuity that spans the interpolated harmonic progression. The chromatic passing notes create illusory motion where harmonic progression is severely limited or disrupted. These chromatic elements propel the music forward even though the harmonic progression itself is static or repetitive. This is remarkable in view of Wolf's textual depiction: he is conveying an emotional fixation with a form of harmonic stasis, while at the same time conveying a sense of the distraction and conflict being experienced by the singer.

Ex. 4-21. "Lebewohl": Linear Chromaticism in mm. 1-4

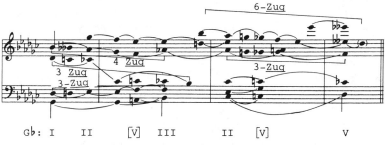

The descending chromatic lines have another remarkable effect: they create what will be called extended-tonal *Züge*. The Kopfton* B♭ generates a 4-*Zug*, B♭-F, (mm. 1-2), and this line is imitated and expanded into a 6-*Zug*, B♭-D♭, in the treble voice of mm. 2-4. This is accompanied in mm. 1-2 by a pair of 3-*Züge* in the alto (D♭-B♭) and tenor (D♭-F) and an additional 3-*Zug*, G♭-E♭, in the top voice. While most of the chromatic lines reach temporary closure with the arrival of V in m. 4, the 6-*Zug* (B♭-D♭) of the top voice and the 3-*Zug*, A♭-F, of the original Kopfton* voice, continue to propel linear motion through the cadence and beyond.

The use of continuously unfolding chromatic lines to impel harmonic motion is an extension of Schenker's diatonic *Züge*. Schenker's *Züge* prolong harmonies on the middleground level by defining specific large-scale harmonic areas. In contrast, Wolf's chromatic lines have a dramatically different effect; even within the prolongation, the harmony is disrupted and destabilized. The ultimate consequence of expanding the function of *Züge* is that of altering the very nature of tonal syntax: harmonic progression becomes obscured and harmonic relations become unstable.

Example 4-22 traces the chromaticism of the song's second phrase (mm. 5-8). This phrase is the most complex of the song and may exemplify a level of complexity and ambiguity that is unparalleled in Wolf's *œuvre*. The harmonic ambiguity is prompted by the text: the poet talks of the confusing attitude of the lover, and Wolf uses every ambiguous sonority possible to convey that poetic conflict. The first two beats of m. 5 contain augmented triads (denoted by + signs) and these are followed by two beats of unresolved dominant seventh and/or augmented sixth (denoted by +6 signs) chords. The ambiguous V^7/+6 chords recur in beats 2 through 4, and are in turn followed by a series of diminished seventh chords in m. 7. As sketch b of example 4-20 already indicated, this phrase develops important third motives: X (D♭-C-B♮) and Y (F-G-A♭), and expands upon two important harmonic areas, B♭ minor (III/G♭; VI/D♭) and C minor (altered VII/D♭). In one way, this second phrase can be heard as a variant of the first, where the I-II-III-II-V progression is expanded upon to include a lengthy prolongation of III and an interpolation of a section in the remote key of C minor. The instability of the phrase is further enhanced by the lack of correspondence between the vocal line and accompaniment, a discontinuity emphasized by the two and one-half-beat rest in the vocal line and by the dramatic shift in tessitura in the RH piano part. As the vocal line describes the lover's "getrostem Angesicht...und leichtem Herzen," the accompaniment's wanderings suggest either a Greek chorus commentary upon the singer's words or, perhaps, the voice of the singer's subconscious.

Chromaticism as part of the modulation. As the second half of the song begins, the chromaticism changes with the onset of the tonal shift. The accompaniment repeats the opening "Lebewohl" motive in m. 9, but the singer modifies the motive in m. 10 (B♭-B♮-A♭ becomes C-B♭-A♮). This signals a departure from both G♭ and the chromaticism associated with that key of conflict. The chromaticism of m. 11 involves a V^7/C, which is both an allusion back to m. 7 and a reference forward to the new leading tone C that occurs in the bass in m. 13. The chromatically altered chords of mm. 14-15 (♭VI/V and ♭II) anticipate the new tonality of D♭, as do the accented neighboring tones of m. 16. The piano postlude repeats the chromaticism of the opening, both as a means of reinforcing the new key and as a way of linking, through motivic reiteration, the opening and closing tonalities.

Foreground preparation for tonal shift. One final aspect of "Lebewohl" warrants further discussion, namely Wolf's use of motivic parallelism. The preparation for later middleground events in earlier foreground detail is

Ex. 4-22. "Lebewohl": Chromatic Ambiguity in mm. 5-8

another way that Wolf expands upon his tonal heritage; and what is especially remarkable is that Wolf foreshadows middleground structures within the context of directional tonality.[25]

In one sense, the tonal shift in "Lebewohl" involves a reinterpretation of common chord function. Part of what encourages the listener to accept this change in tonal orientation is Wolf's careful preparation, beginning in m. 2, for tonal transformation. The pivotal fifth progression B♭-E♭-A♭ is first suggested in m. 2, where a B♭^{7} chord (III♮$^{-7}$) ends the first subphrase. The potential resolution to E♭ is unfulfilled: B♭^{4} resolves in a deceptive cadence (using plagal substitution) to A♭ minor, IV♭/E♭ substituting for ♭VI/E♭. The interrelationships among B♭, E♭, and A♭ remain uncertain, as B♭ alludes to E♭ but resolves to A♭. In m. 4, a second reference to this harmonic family occurs in the piano part of the measure's second half. The V^7/G♭ moves to a B♭ half-diminished seventh chord, which moves to E♭$^4_2$, which in turn resolves to A♭ minor in m. 5 (the G♮ is a chromatic displacement of A♭ on the first beat of m. 5). The progression B♭-E♭-A♭ is now refocused: the E♭$^4_2$ is not elided, but rather intensifies the progression to A♭ minor by functioning as an applied dominant to II/G♭. The foreground use of the circle-of-fifths progression in mm. 2-3 thus anticipates the large-scale modulatory progression of mm. 11ff. Conversely, the arrival on B♭ minor in m. 11, and its subsequent progression to E♭ minor in m. 13, can be understood as a realization of the harmonic relationship originally suggested by the B♭^{7} chord of m. 2. Using both transformation of tonal function and plagal substitution in this climatic section, B♭ minor first progresses to V^7/II (C minor) in m. 11 and then arrives upon V^7/IV in m. 12. The ensuing progression of E♭ to A♭ in m. 13 is now almost predictable. The change in the mode of A♭ from minor to major effects the tonal transformation to D♭ major, and the tonal shift has been reinforced by the clarifying recurrence of the fifth progression B♭-E♭-A♭. The foreshadowing of important middleground events thus combines the two main extended-tonal procedures of this song: the change in tonal focus and the ambiguity principle. The fifth progression B♭-E♭-A♭ first occurs during the ambiguity phase as an initial obfuscation of harmonic function, but it becomes refocused during the clarification phase as it participates in the modulation to D♭ (see example 4-23).

Ex. 4-23. "Lebewohl": Foreground Detail to Middleground
Structure: Circle of Fifths

Another motivic parallelism occurs within the ambiguity between B♭ minor and D♭ major (see example 4-24). Whereas D♭ functioned initially as V/G♭ of a *Bassbrechung* in mm. 1-4, the alteration of B♭ (III) in m. 2 momentarily undermines the function of that arpeggiation. The actual shift to

B♭ in mm. 11-12 (III→V/VI) thus becomes a realization of a harmonic shift that was suggested in m. 2. The tension between D♭ major and B♭ major and minor (altered III and V of G♭, respectively) is transformed within the tonality of D♭ major. While B♭ major had functioned earlier as a dominant to II/D♭ (m. 12), in D♭—the new tonic—B♭ minor functions as a simple plagal element (VI, m. 13) that leads to the authentic cadence.

Ex. 4-24. "Lebewohl": Foreground Detail to Middleground
Structure: Relationship of B♭ Major to D♭ Major

Conclusion

Wolf's use of directional tonality involves two opposing but complementary compositional techniques that are evidenced by the songs analyzed here: the exploitation of some form of harmonic ambiguity, and the utilization of some sort of repetition scheme. The use of harmonic ambiguity is essential in directional tonality, as it prepares for the functional transformation of the opening key. This was especially vivid in "Mir ward gesagt," where no single opening tonality could really be determined. In both "Der Mond" and "Lebewohl," the openings were clearly in a particular key, but that key was gradually undermined by chromaticism and modulation. In both songs, modulation led to harmonic areas which, in turn, became pivotal harmonies en route to the closing tonality; and in both songs the modulations involved tonal destabilization through use of chromaticism.

Partly as compensation for the tonal instability inherent in directional tonality, the three songs analyzed above also utilize extensive repetition schemes. Both "Der Mond" and "Mir ward gesagt" use a recurring ostinato in the piano accompaniment and a repeated melodic idea in the vocal line. "Lebewohl" uses both a reiterated melodic motive (motive X) and a repetition of the dramatic opening measure at the beginning of the second half and in the closing piano postlude. The use of repetition to counterbalance harmonic instability also has a second, crucial function of creating inner coherence and continuity within a piece whose formal design is predicated upon tonal disorientation.

The shifting of tonal focus within directional tonality is one of the great innovations of late-nineteenth-century romantic music. Whereas the impulse toward directional tonality might result from textual demands, it also can be understood simply as another means of expanding common-practice tonality, one that stretched the tonal fabric beyond the limitations of monotonality. While it is beyond the scope of this study to analyze Wolf's purely instrumental music, it is interesting to note that Wolf did not use directional tonality in either his *D Minor String Quartet* of 1878-84, his symphonic poem, *Penthesilea* of 1883-85, or his most mature and successful instrumental work, *Italienische Serenade* of 1887.[26] While it is impossible to know why Wolf did not use directional tonality in his instrumental works, there is no reason to assume that he considered the form of double tonality to be either inappropriate or unworkable in untexted musical genres. One might speculate that Wolf's conventional monotonal designs for instrumental works were, more than anything else, a reflection of his relative inexperience in composing music of either large temporal scope or employing large orchestral resources. This is another instance where one wonders if a composer's untimely death prevented the realization of far greater musical potential.

The issue of whether or not directional tonal pieces cohere as well as their monotonal counterparts is subjective at best. What is evident from the Wolf songs studied in this chapter is that pieces that incorporate a shift in tonal focus can be both dramatic and comprehensible, and that such pieces assume an important position amongst the most highly expressive and beautiful music of the late nineteenth century.

Der Mond
(The moon)

Mir ward gesagt
(They tell me)

Lebe wohl
(Farewell)

8. leich - - tem Her - zen.
leave, with glad-ness.

Le - be wohl!
Fare thee well!

11. *f immer gesteigerter*
Ach tau - send - mal hab' ich mir es vor - ge - spro - chen,
Oh times a - gain to my - self that word I've spok - en,

13. *nachlassend*
und in nim - mer - sat - ter Qual mir das Herz da - mit ge -
thirs - ting e - ver more for pain till at length my heart is

16. bro - - chen!
brok - - en!

5

Combinations of Extended-Tonal Techniques

While preceding chapters have focused on a single type of extended-tonal procedure, we will now explore the way in which several different techniques combine within a song to create a musical structure of uncommon complexity and ingenuity. The combination of extended-tonal techniques exemplifies the ultimate in tonal expansion: predictable common-practice relations no longer necessarily exist but are instead replaced by new relations of undetermined strengths and formal effects.

Our examination of extended-tonal techniques will begin with "Wir haben beide lange Zeit geschwiegen," a song whose plagal elements were studied in chapter 2. The song unites the plagal domain with a large-scale third relation, ♭III-I. The remainder of the chapter will explore two additional songs: "In der Frühe," which combines several extended-tonal procedures within a framework of ambiguity; and "An den Schlaf," which combines plagal elements, third relations, and directional tonality. While "Wir haben beide" combines extended-tonal techniques in a relatively straighforward manner, both "In der Frühe" and "An den Schlaf" show tonal expansion at a higher level of complexity. All three songs are consummate examples of Wolf's extended tonality.

This chapter also highlights a particularly interesting historical factor about Wolf's musical language. While all three songs evince combined tonal extensions of impressive complexity, the dates of the songs do not indicate that combining extended-tonal procedures was an evolutionary phenomenon in Wolf's career.[1] Rather, he seems to have merged various compositional resources in his early Mörike settings of 1888, and then continued the practice through the last Michaelangelo songs of 1897.

Transformation of Tonic Function and Third Relations: "Wir haben beide lange Zeit geschwiegen"

"Wir haben beide" begins with five ambiguous introductory measures which are followed by two different extended-tonal techniques: the transformation of tonic function (mm. 6-10), and a large-scale third relation $\flat$III-I (mm. 10-13).

The text of the song expresses two basic ideas: two lovers had been silent in anger, but thanks to God they are now able to love and communicate once again. The seemingly simple poem presented Wolf with several formal problems. First, the sudden change from silent animosity to loving communication occurs within the first two lines of text. Second, the remaining six lines are really a threefold repetition of the same idea. Wolf's solution is to first convey the sudden shift of feelings through clarification of an ambiguous opening and then to vary the recurring idea of peaceful love through plagal transformation and a chromatic third relation. In both cases, Wolf ameliorates the potential tedium of a repetitious text by casting a reiterated musical phrase in an unusual and ambiguous harmonic context. The listener is so surprised by the harmonic twists that the musical repetition is a welcomed stabilizing factor.

Text to "Wir haben beide lange Zeit geschwiegen"
[*Italienischesliederbuch,* 16 December 1891]

Wir haben beide lange Zeit geschwiegen,
Auf einmal kam uns nun die Sprache
  wieder.
Die Engel, die herab vom Himmel fliegen,
Sie brachten nach dem Krieg den
  Frieden wieder.
Die Engel Gottes sind herabgeflogen,
Mit ihnen ist der Frieden eingezogen.
Die Liebesengel kamen über Nacht
Und haben Frieden meiner Brust
  gebracht.

We have both long been silent,
Suddenly speech returned to us again.
Angels, who fly down from heaven,
Bring peace again after war.
God's angels have flown down
bringing with them peace.
The angels of love came by night
and have brought peace to my breast.

Opening Ambiguity

Example 5-1 shows the voice leading of mm. 1-5. The harmonic function of these introductory measures is elusive: only mm. 4-5 are clear ($V^7/D\flat$), and only because of the resolution in m. 6. As already suggested, the lack of functional clarity in mm. 1-5 is related to the text, with the tonal confusion representing the repressive silence experienced by the angry lovers. Wolf further conveys the tension by outlining a diminished triad, B-D-F, in the accompaniment of m. 1 below a sustained F in the vocal line. The tension of ambiguous function and unresolving dissonance decreases in m. 3, as the voice sings F♯, a perfect fifth rather than a tritone. The sudden return of speech ("auf einmal") is depicted by a less ambiguous harmonic progression: the fifth B-F♯ moves to an augmented sixth chord that resolves to V⁷/D♭. The relationship of B to D♭ remains unclear, and presumably the opening sonorities will be clarified over the course of the song. The stems in example 5-1 highlight the parallel—and nonfunctional—motion between voice and accompaniment which expresses the lovers' tension and conflict. With the return of speech and the vocal F♯ (the original neighbor note G♭ is respelled) above bass B, the two parts now coalesce through conventional voice leading toward a resolution of the V⁷ chord.

Ex. 5-1. "Wir haben beide": Ambiguity of mm. 1-5

Transformation of Tonic Function

As already stated, the remainder of the text—and hence the rest of the song—repeats statements about the lovers' reconciliation. The first two such statements occur in mm. 6-10, where D♭-as-I becomes transformed to D♭-as-V/G♭ in a vivid transformation of tonic function. This procedure was discussed fully in chapter 2 (pp. 21-38), and the example from that chapter (ex. 2-5) is reproduced here as example 5-2. The functional transformation allows for the

Ex. 5-2. "Wir haben beide": Transformation of Tonic Function

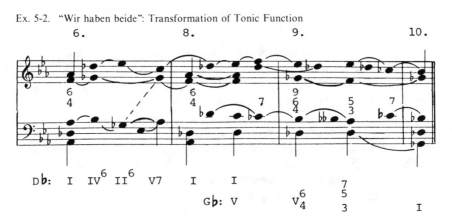

textual repetition: the music of D♭-as-I must recur within the new context of G♭-as-I. Thus, while the music echoes the restatement of text, the musical repetition is actually necessitated by the shift of tonal function.

Third Relations

Wolf sets the last textual repetition through the use of a third relation. Example 5-3a shows how the section in G♭ major ultimately is understood not as a tonic but as ♭III of the final tonic, E♭ major. Recalling the distinction made in chapter 3 between traditional common-practice third relations (embedded within a more structurally prominent tonic-dominant axis), and the more innovative late-nineteenth-century third relations (existing outside the purview of a governing fifth relation), the third relation in "Wir haben beide" must be assessed by determining whether or not it exists within a more important structural fifth relation. In example 5-3b the ♭III and I are connected by a V_3^4 (the last eighth note of the fourth beat of m. 13), but this fleeting V_3^4 is a foreground event. The third relation of mediant to tonic can only be considered a middleground harmonic structure that is indeed independent of a middleground tonic-dominant axis.

Ex. 5-3.   "Wir haben beide": Third Relations

As we have seen in chapter 3, the middleground third relation is a less stable structure than its traditional fifth-relation counterpart. A compelling interpretation of this middleground ♭III-I is that it functions as a third substitute for V-I, ♭III replacing the powerful V within a weaker third relation. This replacement of ♭III for V corresponds to the text; the section in E♭ is at once a change from and a repetition of the section in G♭. This adds a new dimension to the concept of varied repetition in tonal music: where the dominant traditionally functioned both as a contrast to and a strong progression to I, the third relation offers the contrast to I without the force of strong harmonic resolution. The "progression" ♭III to I is heard as a change in harmony but not as a resolution to I from ♭III. The resulting weakness of harmonic relationship undermines a sense of harmonic shift, a deemphasis that is desirable due to the static nature of the text. In a profound sense, the inherent weakness of the third relation allows Wolf to convey repetitive text without having to resort to a completely static, inert harmonic syntax.

Overall Structure with Combined Techniques

While it is helpful to consider Wolf's use of several extended-tonal techniques as being prompted by unusual text repetition, it is also necessary to evaluate the combination of extended-tonal procedures solely in musical terms. Both the transformation of tonic function and the third relation allows for both text and music to be repeated in different harmonic regions so that different lines of text are presented as both new and reiterated poetic ideas. Traditional harmonic progression is almost avoided: the sections in G♭ and E♭ sound more like components of a complex, nearly static harmonic structure rather than clear-cut points of arrival within a well-defined harmonic continuum.

Example 5-4a offers a middleground reading of "Wir haben beide." The opening on F is retrospectively heard as II, and the B chord in m. 4 as ♯VI in E♭ major. The section in D♭ is V/♭III and the section in G♭ is ♭III. The parenthesis surrounding the dominant of m. 13 emphasizes its foreground status. The melodic content of this song is as complicated as the harmonic relationships. The opening vocal pitch F eventually connects with the song's final F-E♭ descent ($\hat{2}$-$\hat{1}$; it is given a dotted line). The remainder of the vocal melodic line is a series of embedded neighbor-note motions. The main melodic pitch, A♭, of mm. 6ff. ultimately becomes an upper neighbor to the final G♭ of the vocal and piano parts, a resolution that does not occur until after the A♭ has been embellished by B♭ in the G♭ section (B♭ is given two flags to denote its neighbor-note function to A♭).

Ex. 5-4. "Wir haben beide": Middleground Readings

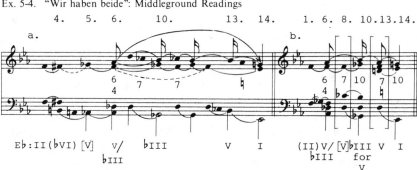

The Middleground Structure

Any interpretation of this song's middleground structure must take into account both the complexity of the plagal transformation of function and the inherent weakness of the third relation (♭III-I). Example 5-4b refines the middleground reading to the most essential structural components. It is a most revealing sketch, for if the foreground dominants to ♭III and I were omitted (mm. 8 and 13; in example 5-4b, they are inserted in brackets), the song would present an incomprehensible tonal structure. The unintelligibility of this song's middleground harmonic relations underscores several important recurring issues of this study. First, the expansion of tonality can create weak and idiosyncratic harmonic syntax; and second, the traditional criteria for understanding tonal structure, as explained by Schenker, often cannot be used to appraise these unusual structures.

Inapplicability of Schenker

Even though the analysis of this song asserts a monotonal reading, the song's eccentric harmonic relations and extensive chromaticism nearly preclude Schenker's analytical system. As a result, the readings of example 5-4a and b do not use Schenkerian notation. The transformation of tonic function defies Schenkerian analysis when it reverses the tonal progression in mm. 6-10; and the third relation replaces the tonic-dominant axis upon which Schenker's *Ursatz* is based. Furthermore, the chromaticism that results in the shift from D♭/G♭ to E♭ undermines the Schenkerian notion of tonal coherence through harmonic prolongation and negates the Schenkerian concept of a background structure expressing the tonic harmony.

Coherence through Foreground Dominants and Motivic Repetition

Since Schenker's analytical assumptions do not accommodate a transformation of tonic function or a ♭III-I third relation in major, "Wir haben beide" must be considered an anomalous tonal structure predicated upon unique formal devices. One such formal device is the use of compensatory foreground dominants to clarify ambiguous middleground harmonic relations.[2] The $V^7/G♭$ in mm. 8-9 is a crucial element in the transformation of tonic function, as the ♭7 above the D♭ harmony changes that chord's function from I/D♭ to $V^7/G♭$. Meanwhile, the V/E♭ in m. 13 can be understood as a compensating factor in the weak third relation. If one were to omit V/E♭, even taking into account its foreground status, the arrival on E♭ as tonic in m. 14 would remain unclear. Wolf further strengthens the arrival on E♭-as-I (mm. 14ff.) in two ways: he maintains a bass pedal (E♭) for most of the remaining eight measures; and, where the pedal is omitted temporarily in mm. 16-17, a progression I-V^7/IV-IV-$_\flat$III-I in E$\flat$ reinforces the tonic in another expanded use of the plagal domain. One last factor of coherence is continuous motivic repetition. In this case, the complete harmonic phrase that begins in the RH piano part in mm. 6 continues through the song's piano postlude. While each harmonic region repeats the harmonic progression within a new harmonic context, the recurring progression is itself a source of continuity and interconnection.

"Wir haben beide" reverses several traditional concepts of tonal coherence and exemplifies a tonal structure comprehensible through nontraditional factors. All three tonal areas, D$\flat$, G$\flat$, and E$\flat$, are understood only through use of foreground dominants, and the overall formal structure of the song is heard as one of emerging rather than sustained tonal focus. In this sense, this song exemplifies the ambiguity principle described in chapter 1: tonal focus is suppressed (like the lovers' speech) through extended-tonal ambiguity, and clarification comes through the eventual compensatory tonal definition of E$\flat$ major.

Plagal Ambiguity, Dominant Replacement, and Third Relations: "In der Frühe"

"In der Frühe" is from the Mörike collection (5 May 1888).[3] A complicated song, it combines the plagal domain, third relations, and a vivid example of the Wolfian ambiguity principle.

The text depicts the early morning confusion of someone who has suffered through an anxious, frightful night. The poem describes that curious predawn moment when the human spirit is besieged with doubts and fears as it tentatively struggles to look ahead to the emerging day. The poem, and thus the song, is concerned with the shifting of mood from painful despondency to joyful optimism.

Text to "In der Frühe"
[Mörike, 5 May 1888]

Kein Schlaf noch kühlt das Auge mir,	No sleep has cooled my vision,
Dort gehet schon der Tag herfür	Already the day begins
An meinem Kammerfenster.	At my bedroom window.
Es wühlet mein verstörter Sinn	My tortured mind thrashes about
Noch zwischen Zweifeln her und hin	To and fro amongst doubts
Und schaffet Nachtgespenster.	And creates nightly apparitions.
Angst'ge, quäle	Fear, agonize no longer my soul!
Dich nicht länger, meine Seele!	Be joyful. Already here and there
Freu' dich! schon sind da und dorten	Morning bells have (become) awakened.
Morgenglocken wach geworden.	

On a simple level, Wolf depicts the song's emotional transformation through shift in mode and change in tessitura. The first half of the song is in the minor mode and in the dark, low ranges of both voice and accompaniment. Extensive use of the plagal contributes to this despondent mood, and in lieu of the traditional polarity of major mediant or major dominant, the minor subdominant is the main harmonic contrast to the minor tonic. On a more complicated level, Wolf expresses the textual anxiety and confusion through several types of harmonic ambiguity, including tonal ambiguity within the ambiguity principle, exploration of plagal ambiguity, and special treatment of the dominant function.

The Ambiguity Principle

As we often have seen, Wolf conveys the textual confusion of "In der Frühe" with a complex version of the ambiguity principle. In mm. 1-10, the singer expresses anxiety and confusion through a musical setting of immense harmonic ambiguity. When, in mm. 11-22, the singer's thoughts begin to change from despair to hope, the harmonic relationships are simplified and harmonic function is clarified.

The ambiguity phase. One of the song's most obvious and powerful forms of harmonic ambiguity is the virtual lack of any real tonal focus up to the final arrival on D major in m. 18. This tonal ambiguity results from a lack of clear harmonic function for either individual sonorities or entire sections. In addition, harmonic function changes on a local level as chords are reinterpreted within new harmonic contexts. The opening three couplets of text are given a different harmonic region (D minor, A minor, and E minor, respectively). However, the interrelationship of ine three harmonic centers remains unclear. For example, does A minor (m. 6) function as V$_\flat$ of D minor (mm. 1-2) or is D minor IV of A minor? The opening tonality of D minor is immediately undermined by the shift to a B-major chord. This seems to function as a dominant in mm. 3-5, and this unresolved dominant is juxtaposed to a new section in A minor (m. 6). The new potential tonic, A minor, is in turn weakened, when E minor functions as either tonic or minor dominant in mm. 8-10. The functional confusion of D minor (mm. 1-2), A minor (mm. 6-7), and E minor (mm. 8-10) is never completely resolved. This lack of tonal clarity may be understood as text depiction, but it may also be considered a musical exploration of functional ambiguity for its own sake. The creation of musical tension and ambiguity as a formal device presumes a balancing section of resolution and clarification. In the "resolution" section that indeed follows, tonal focus and harmonic clarity are achieved within a new harmonic context.

Tonal discrepancy between voice and piano part. The ambiguity of the song's opening is most vividly dramatized in the disparity of tonal focus between the vocal line and piano accompaniment. As example 5-5 shows, the vocal line suggests A minor in mm. 1-2 and E minor in mm. 3-10. The shift from A minor to E minor may be understood as a progression in E minor: IV (m. 1) to V (mm. 3-4) to I (mm. 6-10). In contrast to the relative clarity of the vocal line, the piano accompaniment of mm. 1-10 offers a different degree of tonal confusion and perhaps a different tonal focus altogether. When the piano's opening D minor harmony of mm. 1-2 is impaired by the V/E in mm. 3-5, how do we relate D minor to the implied E tonality? Is the opening D minor a IV of A minor with the dominant triad on B being a V/V? Example 5-5 offers three possible harmonic readings of the piano part in mm. 1-10, although no one key seems sufficient to explain the various harmonic relations that occur, nor does a single key coincide convincingly with the vocal line. Furthermore, while the opening vocal line suggests A minor, the key signature of the song indicates D minor. On the other hand, the reading in E minor easily accommodates the harmonic relations in mm. 3-10 but does not easily account for the opening of the accompaniment in D minor.

Ex. 5-5. "In der Frühe": Ambiguity Principle: Harmonic Disparity
        between Vocal Line and Piano Accompaniment

The tonal discrepancy between vocal line and accompaniment is clearly related to the inherent textual conflict. The text bespeaks a dichotomy between despairing night and hopeful day, and the song exemplifies that textual conflict in a musical polarity of conflicting tonalities. If the piano accompaniment represents the frightful world of night and despair, then the tonal conflict between voice and accompaniment symbolizes the conflict between the poet and the anguish of the night. As the singer struggles to overcome fear and despair, the piano accompaniment (signifying in part the despondent night) produces tension and confusion through tonal ambiguity. This tension of a double-tonal focus between vocal line and piano part will be clarified in the song's second half, as—in the wake of day—the vocal line and accompaniment merge into a singular tonal framework.

The clarification phase. Harmonic clarification of the song begins in m. 11, after the tonality of E minor/major has been reinforced by the augmented sixth chord of m. 10. The sequential third-chain progression, E major-G major-B♭ major-D major, replaces the ambiguous harmonic relationships of the first half. The chain of thirds is not a traditional, clear tonal progression; yet, the systematic transposition of the material up a third in two-bar sequences directs the listener's attention toward an imminent and ultimately recognizable harmonic goal. In addition, Wolf's use of a transposition scheme by a third chain is a variant of the song's opening use of transposition by fourth to create functional ambiguity.

When the D major tonic is reached in m. 18, it is recognized because the transposition chain is broken in two subtle but convincing ways. First, the shift in tessitura from a high F♯ (RH, m. 18) to the lower F♯ (m. 19) alters the repetition pattern and suggests a registral connection between the final D major iteration in m. 18 and the initiating E major version of m. 11. Second, certain rhythmic changes—a truncation of motive and a change in phrasal rhythm—alter the transposition chain. The motive of the song's second half may be divided into two parts: the repeated four-beat motive (X) of mm. 11-12 (ex. 5-6a) is a neighbor-note figure (Y) followed by a rising third (Z); Y is then eliminated and Z recurs twice (m. 13) (ex. 5-6b). The transpositions in G major

Ex. 5-6. "In der Frühe": Motivic Repetition in the Third Chain

and B♭ major reiterate only motive X of mm. 11-12 and thus contract a three-bar phrase into two measures. The pair of two-bar phrases in mm. 14-17 represents a rhythmic acceleration within the transposition scheme that deemphasizes the potential for G major and B♭ major to be tonicized and gives them instead a passing function. When the D major section reintroduces the third bar of the initial three-bar phrase, it disrupts the rhythmic acceleration and creates an arrival upon D as the rhythmic and harmonic goal of the third chain. While the RH piano part in mm. 18ff. is an octave higher than the opening D minor section, the LH piano part and the vocal line retain their original tessituras and the song closes in its original register.

If the ambiguity phase includes a series of obscurely related transpositions of the opening D minor material, then the clarification phase may be considered a revised use of transposition wherein the successive components of the third chain contribute to a continuously emerging—and ultimately clear—tonal goal. The two parts of the ambiguity principle are thus related both by their common use of harmonic transposition (in lieu of harmonic progression) and by their respective uses of motivic repetition.

Motivic repetition. Motivic repetition is an important element of continuity throughout "In der Frühe." As example 5-7a shows, the various tonal regions are linked not by harmonic progression or voice leading, but by the cohesive power of motivic connection. Measures 6 and 8 are transpositions of m. 1 (m. 8 with a slight variation), and this motivic correspondence establishes continuity throughout the song's ambiguous opening. As the clarification phase begins in mm. 11ff., the listener hears the motivic repetition continue even as the harmonic focus becomes obvious. Example 5-7b demonstrates the difference. The melodic motive of mm. 1-10 recurs in mm. 11-22; however, the contrapuntal relationship of the melodic motive to the bass is altered. Rather than spanning a dissonant seventh above the bass, the altered motive now spans a consonant fifth. Thus, while the repeated motive continues, its function changes from being an element of tonal dissonance and ambiguity to a factor of consonance and clarification.

Ex. 5-7. "In der Frühe": Motivic Continuity and Contrast

Use of the Plagal Domain

"In der Frühe" explores the plagal domain in two different ways. During the first half of the song, confusion of harmonic function creates a functional ambiguity between tonic and subdominant harmonies. In the course of the second part of the work, a form of dominant replacement occurs: a prolonged dominant ($V_\flat^9$) of D major is replaced by a plagal progression II♯-IV-♭VI. The latter use of plagal elements to replace the dominant is also an extended-tonal use of third relations.

Plagal Ambiguity

The tonal ambiguity of mm. 1-10 was examined in example 5-5. Looking again at that example, we recall the difficulty in determining the opening tonality or even the initial D minor harmony's function. Many questions arise regarding tonal function and the use of the subdominant: If the vocal line sings in A minor, does the accompanimental D minor function as IV/A minor? If the first half of the song is in E minor, strongly suggested by the V chord on B in mm. 3-5, is the A minor harmony of mm. 6-7 IV/E minor? Further, is the opening D minor harmony some sort of IV/IV/E minor? And, equally puzzling, why is the key signature—a reliable indication of key identity with Wolf—D minor and not, say, A minor or E minor?

Example 5-8 shows how Wolf associates different harmonies with different textual elements. The A minor/D minor harmonies are connected to the distress of the singer: the opening Kopfton* A depicts the verb "kühlt," as the singer expresses need for relief from the night's anguish. The idea of disturbance and despair recurs again in mm. 6ff., where A minor is the supporting harmony for the text "(es) wühlet verstörter Sinn." The connection between the opening state of distress (mm. 1-2) in D minor and the later anxiety (mm. 6-7) in A minor is plagal: D minor is the subdominant of A minor. The harmonic shift from D minor to A minor reflects a continuation of the singer's

Ex. 5-8. "In der Frühe": Text, Transposition, and Plagal
         Ambiguity

distress; however, while the transposition scheme suggests a potential harmonic connection between mm. 1-2 and mm. 6-7, the plagal relationship weakens that connection and undermines the arrival upon A minor. As the singer continues describing the troublesome night, the tonal ambiguity of the progression D minor to A minor continues to another key, E minor. In a second plagal connection, A minor resolves to E minor. A plagal transposition scheme emerges: Wolf conveys a confused mental state through the evolution of weak harmonic structures that evade tonal focus. Such harmonic progression without definition would be virtually impossible when using the dominant relation. The listener is left with a sense of harmonic movement (harmonic tension=poetic confusion) without yet knowing the song's tonality.

The Dominant within Plagal Ambiguity

Wolf thus has exploited the weak plagal domain to convey textual confusion. Contrasting to the anxiety-depicting, weak plagal relationships of mm. 1-2 and 6-10 is the dominant harmony in mm. 3-5, which foreshadows the resolution of nocturnal conflicts through the dominant-associated emergence of day (ex. 5-8b). This dominant association of hope is continued in the song's second half by the chain-of-thirds progression, which, like the V of mm. 2-3, points toward and resolves to a real tonal center. The interpolation of the dominant within the plagal first half (mm. 2-3) is text-related: the semicadence on B occurs as the singer declaims, "Dort gehet schon der Tag herfür." Although the hint of a new day seems lost within the plagal relationships of the song's first half, a tonal connection between the V/E of mm. 2-3 and the E major section of the second half is established. The dominant of B, with its textual reference to "Tag," thus becomes a subtle harmonic link between the opening plagal chain (D minor-A minor-E minor) and the cadential third chain (E major-G major-B♭ major-D major). The dominant expresses hope for an end to despair and for an end to tonal confusion.

Special Usage of the Dominant

The dominant is used in two unusual ways: in the interruptive V on B (mm. 3-5), and in the dominant replacement resulting from the third chain of mm. 11-22. The harmonic function of the B dominant in mm. 3-5 is obfuscated by the surrounding tonal ambiguity and the dominant is imbibed with a curious somberness. This dominant does not resolve. Rather, it is left suspended as the song continues within the undefined region of A minor. Example 5-8b suggests that the B dominant resolves obliquely in mm. 11-13, where E major becomes a temporary structural goal. This, once again, corresponds to the text: the emergence, "dort . . . herfür," is linked to the effects of the new day: "Angst' ge, quäle/Dich nicht länger. . . ."

The dominant's function in mm. 3-5 is thus an allusion to a later E major section (mm. 11ff.), and the lack of immediate resolution casts the tonality-defining dominant into a role of deterring tonal definition. The suspended dominant function in the first half contributes to the prevailing tonal flux even as it suggests an ultimate tonal clarification in the poem's second half. The poignancy of this curious dominant is especially strong in m. 5, where the ambiguous authentic cadence in B (B=V or I?) emphasizes both the tonal instability of the preceding and succeeding sections. The ambiguous authentic cadence's irony is intensified by its isolation in the keyboard's low register, and the displacement of the authentic cadence is a musical counterpart to the alienation of the poet/singer, who remains silent during the cadence in m. 5.

Dominant Replacement and Third Relations

The most extraordinary form of dominant replacement in this song is the chain-of-third substitution for the traditional authentic cadence. Example 5-9 shows each successive link in the third chain adding a new plagal element (II♯-IV-♭VI) and a new vocal pitch (stems up) which resolves (m. 18) as a plagal neighbor ($\hat{2}$, $\hat{4}$, ♭$\hat{6}$) to tonic triad pitches. The upper staff of example 5-9a also shows how vocal elements (stems up) merge with accompanimental pitches (stems down) to reinforce the cadential voice leading as the vocal fifth becomes a keyboard tenth in the next chord (5-10's). The fusion of voice-leading elements in the upper- and lower-neighboring pitches G and F♮ (flagged) resolves to the piano's F♯ of m. 18, and the vocal D of m. 18 recalls the initial vocal E of m. 11. The lower staff of example 5-9b indicates how the third-chain bass pitches all resolve stepwise to members of the closing D major tonic triad.

Ex. 5-9. "In der Frühe": Dominant Replacement and Third Chain, mm. 11-22

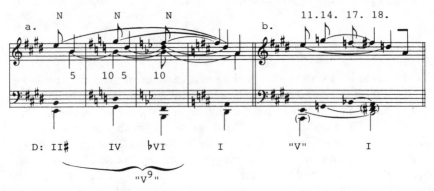

In example 5-9b, a supposition of the dominant chord's root beneath the plagal third chain suggests that the series of plagal harmonies within the third chain replaces a prolonged, incomplete V^{-9} (i.e., with supposed root and no third). While it is feasible to consider the third chain as a component of a V^{-9} chord, the absence of the actual dominant root, the functions of G and $B_\flat$ major as passing chords and the chromaticism that results from the third chain all contribute to hearing a complex plagal cadence.

Plagal Middleground

In light of the unusual but convincing close in D major, the tonal confusion of the song's opening must be reevaluated and related to the stable conclusion. Example 5-5 already demonstrated how the vocal line begins A minor, and the opening accompanimental D minor harmony is heard as IV/A minor. However, if one invokes a variation on the transformation of tonic function, one could consider the opening IV-I/A minor as I-$V_\flat$/D minor, with the opening A minor vocal line functioning as a tonal dichotomy that anticipates the arrival on $V_\flat$ in mm. 6-7. In general, a functional transformation acknowledges a harmonic ambiguity and, in this case, functional transformation allows the opening to be in both A minor (D=IV/A minor) and D minor (A=$V_\flat$/D minor). This interprets the beginning partly in D minor and ending clearly in D major, with a large-scale shift from $V_\flat$ (m. 6-7) to II$\sharp$5 (mm. 8-10). The E major section in mm. 11ff. can be considered an altered II, the modal shift reflecting the textual change of mood. In regard to the interpolated B dominant in mm. 3-5, its double function remains in effect: first, in a musical counterpart to initial textual confusion, the B dominant (hopeful day) undermines D minor (nocturnal despair) at the song's opening; and second, the V of B alludes to the middleground goal of II$\sharp$/D minor, which occurs tentatively in mm. 8-10 and more precisely in mm. 11-13. In reinforcing II (E minor) as a structural goal, the V chord on B gives ironic dominant emphasis to an element of a middleground plagal axis.

Example 5-10 shows a middleground reading where II replaces the more conventional V (or, in minor, $\flat$III) as the main structural polarity to the tonic D minor/major. It is possible to consider the B dominant as a compensatory element reinforcing II as a structural goal. In addition, the most pronounced compensatory factor of this plagal middleground is the motivic repetition, which interrelates the various ambiguous sections into one motivically coherent whole. The plagal axis of example 5-11 shows "In der Frühe" to be akin to those plagal structures examined in chapter 2; the Kopfton* A ($\hat{5}$) does not descend and the I-II-I structure may be considered a symmetrical structure: the D-A-E transposition scheme on one side of II is counterbalanced by the third-chain transposition scheme. The long-range melodic goal E ($\hat{2}$) of m. 6 to

D (Î) of m. 18 helps reinforce the D major close, thus countering the lack of Kopfton* descent.

Ex. 5-10. "In der Frühe": Plagal Middleground

D: I   V   II   II♯ IV♭VI I

Ex. 5-11. "In der Frühe": Plagal Axis

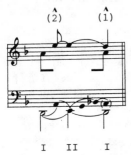

I   II   I

Combination of All Categories of Extended-Tonal Techniques: "An den Schlaf"

The present study of extended-tonal technique ends with an analysis that combines all three categories of such techniques: the plagal domain of chapter 2, the chromatic third relations of chapter 3, and the directional tonality of chapter 4. "An den Schlaf" is a relatively early song from the *Mörikelieder* (4 October 1888). It depicts a terse poetic discussion of sleep, life, and death with several characteristically Wolfian *Lied* techniques. To convey textual progression, Wolf replaces traditional harmonic progression with an ambiguous transposition scheme; and to convey textual conflict, he separates the vocal line from the accompaniment, thereby allowing each part to represent a different component of poetic opposition.

"An den Schlaf" begins in A♭ major and ends in E major.[4] While the opening tonality of A♭(G♯) might be understood as an altered mediant in the closing tonality of E major, such a retrospective hearing is problematic. Both the functional transformation and the chromatic third relations complicate the use of Schenkerian analysis. The song has a directional tonal design: it begins and ends in two different keys (each of which has its own network of harmonic relations), and these two networks remain distinct from one another at the song's conclusion.

The text of "An den Schlaf" is a laconic four lines that bespeak a commingling of sleep and death. The subtle shifts in textual meaning made this text well-suited to Wolf's transformation of tonic function and use of directional tonality.

Text to "An den Schlaf"
[Mörike, 4 October 1888]

Schlaf! süsser Schlaf! obwohl dem Tod, wie du, nichts gleicht, Auf diesem Lager doch willkommen heiss' ich dich! Denn ohne Leben so, wie lieblich lebt es sich! So weit vom Sterben, ach, wie stirbt es sich so leicht!	Sleep! Sweet Sleep! 'though nothing resembles death as you do. To this couch I bid thee welcome! For removed from life, so lovely is living! So far from death, ah, so easy is dying!

The beginning, "Schlaf! süsser Schlaf!" presents the subject of the poem: sleep. The second half of line 1, "obwohl dem Tod wie du nichts gleicht," places sleep into a comparison with death. The music of sleep ($A\flat$) is transposed to B minor on the word "Tod." In line 2, the singer embraces sleep: "auf diesem Lager doch willkommen heiss' ich dich," and the tonality shifts on the text "willkommen heiss'." The welcoming of sleep/death is associated with the new key of $D\flat(C\sharp)$, and the first half of the text occurs within the composite tonal realm of $A\flat/D\flat$. While the main harmonic motion in mm. 1–15 seems to be I-$\flat$III$\flat$-IV of $A\flat$, the sleep key is transformed to a V/$D\flat$ in m. 16, with $D\flat$ emerging as the acceptance key. In the second half, the tonality shifts dramatically, on the text "denn ohne Leben" from $A\flat/D\flat$ to E major. The word "Leben" is set to V^7/E. The connection between the two tonalities ($A\flat$ major and E major) is the enharmonic pitch class $A\flat/G\sharp$. In m. 17, $A\flat$ is dramatically projected in the unaccompanied voice and in m. 18, $A\flat$ becomes $G\sharp$ above a B^7 chord. The pitch $A\flat(G\sharp)$ thus functions as both the root of the opening sonority and as the pivotal common tone between the opening and closing tonalities. The remainder of the text: "wie lieblich lebt es . . . so leicht!" is cast unequivocally in E major. The instability resulting from the tonal shifts of the first half is replaced by chromaticism in the second half. The chromaticism exploits modal mixture ($\natural\hat{3}$, $\natural\hat{6}$), and most of the second half prolongs V/E, which resolves in m. 28. The final cadence reiterates the earlier modal mixture with a prolonged cadence IV$\flat$-I in mm. 28–34.

The Harmonic Structure

Example 5-12 shows the song beginning clearly in A♭ major. The piano introduction, mm. 1-4, is in A♭; the last beat of m. 4 is a V/A♭, whose function is intensified by its B♮ alteration to an augmented triad. The B♮ directs the ear to the melodic note C, on which the vocal line begins in m. 5. The section in B minor (m. 9) is heard initially as a transposition of the opening material to ♭III♭ which embellishes the opening material. The main melodic pitch is flagged as a neighbor to Kopfton* neighbor C♯. The motion to D♭ is heard less as a transposition and more as a progression to IV/A♭. In m. 16, the half cadence in D♭ offers the functional transformation of A♭: I becomes V/IV. The functional transformation in the first half prepares the listener for the tonal transformation in the remainder of the song. The transformation of A♭ major casts the opening tonality into doubt: is it A♭ major or D♭ major? When the tonality shifts to V⁷/E major in m. 18, the dramatically simple vocal gesture of mm. 17-18 leads the listener into the tonal realm of E through another transformation—the melodic A♭ becomes G♯ over V⁷/E. The tonalities of A♭ major, B minor, and D♭ major can now be recast retrospectively into E major (as III♯, ♭III♭/III, and VI♯, respectively), and the song can be considered an expanded and highly chromatic III♯-♭III♭/III-V♯-V-I progression in E major.

Ex. 5-12. "An den Schlaf": Detailed Sketch of First Half

Ab: I (IIb5)   V♮5   I   V/♭IIIb   ♭IIIb (VII)
E: III♯   N   ♭IIIb/III

♭III   IV (IIb5)   V/IV
♭IIIb/III   VI♯   V/VI♯   V7   I

Compared to what has come before, the second half of the song is relatively straightforward. The key is clearly E major. Only one chromatically altered chord occurs in mm. 22-23, functioning as V^9/II resolving to II^6 in m. 24. Wolf intensifies the simple harmonic progression with melodic chromaticism (especially in a staggered resolution pattern) and modal mixture. The song's formal symmetry is depicted in example 5-13a. While on one level this song presents a large-scale third progression, III♯-I (dotted beam), it also projects a series of fifth relations. The fifth relationship between III♯ and VI♯ in mm. 1-17 is reiterated by the large-scale V-I progression in mm. 18ff. Conversely, the large-scale V-I progression of the song's second half—mm. 18ff.—which denotes the surrendering of life is anticipated by the large-scale III♯-VI♯ progression of the first half—mm. 1-13—which depicts the welcoming of death. At the same time, the fifth relations are conjoined by overlapping minor thirds, A♭-B♮ and D♭/C♯-E, which are beamed in example 5-13b. The B minor section of mm. 9-11 foreshadows the V of mm. 18ff., and the C♯ of mm. 22-24 (V^9/II) alludes back to the D♭ section (mm. 13-17). Example 5-13c demonstrates the extensive use of fifth relations in the first half of the song, mm. 1-16.

Ex. 5-13. "An den Schlaf": Symmetry and Fifth Relations in the Middleground

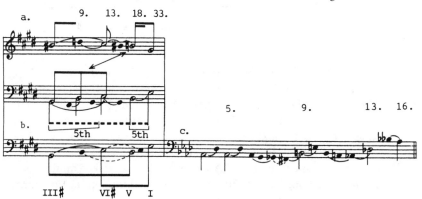

Inapplicability of Schenker

In Schenkerian analysis, the overall harmonic motion of "An den Schlaf" would be a large-scale progression (II♯-V-I—an interpolation of the progression ♭III♭/III (mm. 9-11) to VI♯ (mm. 12-17) enlarging a simple tonic arpeggiation. However, the extensive chromaticism on the middleground level undermines coherence through tonic arpeggiation. Example 5-14a shows that although the bass arpeggiation G♯-B-E could be heard as prolonging the E major tonic triad, the *Urlinie* above that bass diverges away from E major. The song's melodic chromaticism thus obfuscates the *Ursatz,* and the altered mediant results in a chromatic displacement of the *Kopfton* (in the strict Schenkerian sense) from B♮ to B♯. When, in example 5-14b, the function of B♯ is adjusted from Kopfton* to upper neighbor, the *Urlinie* becomes highly idiosyncratic. All melodic pitches for the song's first half are embellishments of a *Kopfton* that does not appear until m. 18. While embellishments can be understood as foreground elements that prolong a middleground harmony, these neighboring pitches (B♯, D♮, C♯) occur on the middleground and thus blur the tonic prolongation.

Ex. 5-14.   "An den Schlaf": Schenkerian Reading

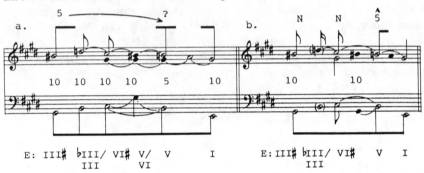

The conflict between the opening and closing keys in "An den Schlaf" is all but irreparable. The initial bass, A♭/G♯, is heard as III♯ in E major, but the opening Kopfton*, C♮/B♯, is at best an altered $\hat{5}$ or $\hat{6}$ and at worst a chromatic displacement of E major's main tonic elements. Furthermore, just as the poetic conflicts linger on after the text has been presented, so the two tonalities of A♭ major and E major remain in opposition at the end of the song.

To call the middleground in "An den Schlaf" a III♯-I motion is a misnomer. The underlying bass motion spans a major third, but the functional relationship of A♭ to E major is not that of mediant to tonic. The symbol III♯-I suggests the harmonic structure functions as some variant or analog to a diatonic III-I progression. When the piece is understood in the context of directional tonality, both the middleground chromaticism and the harmonic tension between the opening and closing tonalities cease to be problematical.

Coherence in a Directional Tonal Reading

Example 5-15a shows a middleground directional tonal reading.[5] The song begins in A♭(G♯) major, a section in ♭III♭ occurs in m. 9 and, as a result of the functional transformation, the first half ends on V/IV in mm. 16-17. The opening Kopfton* B♯ is given a single incomplete beam; and the main melodic pitch of mm. 13-17, C♯, is flagged to show its neighbor function to the Kopfton*. The main melodic motion of mm. 9-12 is complicated: the Kopfton* B♯ is temporarily displaced by the melodic B♮, which anticipates its function as Kopfton* in the song's second half. Meanwhile, the D♮-C♯ motion of the piano RH projects an *Übergreifen* above the B♮, and the D♮ functions as a neighbor to the C♯ neighbor of mm. 13ff. (The D♮ is given a double flag to show its role as embedded neighbor to C♯.) Measures 1-8 and 13-17 are related by the functional transformation. The section in B minor (mm. 9-12) connects the opening tonic with the subdominant of m. 13 and intensifies (through the melodic neighbor-note function) the arrival upon IV in m. 13. This section also underscores the poetic conflict of life vs. death as the B minor section occurs on the word "Tod" and the B major section half occurs on the word "Leben." Whereas the latter setting is that of dominant, the analogous function of the former setting is that of altered mediant. Wolf is symbolically stating here that the force of life is clear and powerful, and that of death is obscure and imprecise.

Ex. 5-15a. "An den Schlaf": Middleground Directional Tonal Reading

Anticipation of Middleground Events in Foreground Detail

Example 5-15b illustrates in detail how the song's first half prefigures many later middleground structures.[6] The piano introduction (mm. 1-4) includes a subtle reference to the B minor section of mm. 9ff. as melodic pitch D♮ aligns with bass B (m. 3, beat 3) within a series of chromatic tenths. This is especially important since it foreshadows the use of B♮ as a second Kopfton* during the song's latter half. The sketch in example 5-15b also shows two reiterated motives that connect foreground and middleground levels in both the bass and treble. The symbol "N" denotes the C♯ neighbor note in diverse contexts. The foreground B♭(C♯) occurring in the bass of mm. 1, 2, 5, and 6 alludes to the middleground harmonic prolongation in mm. 13ff. Here the bass D♭(C♯) functions as a neighbor to the prolonged V/E of mm. 18ff. The pitch C♯ also occurs in the treble as a neighbor to both opening and closing *Kopftöne*, B♯ and B♮.

Ex. 5-15b. "An den Schlaf": Middleground Directional Tonal Reading (cont.)

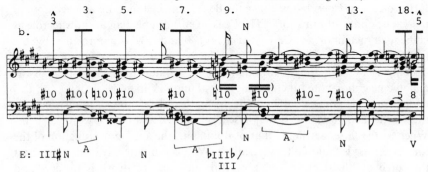

Similarly, the symbol "A" denotes a repeated arpeggiation element, the third G♯-B. Motive A first occurs in m. 3, where the bass third foreshadows both the connection of the opening G♯ to the section in B minor (mm. 9ff.) and the large-scale relationship of the opening G♯ to the section in V/E in mm. 18ff. Motive A also recurs in mm. 18-20 (where E major is established as a new tonic) and in mm. 22-27 as the final cadence in E. Finally, motive A is integrated into the section in B minor where it connects the preceding G♯ material to the following C♯ section. The many occurrences of motive A in the vocal line and RH piano part will be explored in the discussion of motivic repetition that follows (see ex. 5-18). Suffice it to say here that the two important motives (N and A) recur in both the bass and treble, and in both surface detail and large-scale design.

Motivic Repetition in the Second Half

Just as elements of the second half were anticipated in the song's first half, important aspects of mm. 1-17 are echoed in mm. 18-34. In mm. 22-23, the crucial D♮ neighbor recurs above the recurring C♯ harmony (IV/G♯ → VI/E); the text once more articulates death ("Sterben") before the song concludes in the life-symbolizing key (E major). The important subdominant of mm. 1-17 also recurs in the song's second half: in mm. 24ff. the subdominant or its plagal substitutes all but replace the dominant cadential function. Where the transformation of tonic function created harmonic ambiguity in the song's first half, the use of the plagal domain in the second half helps clarify the new tonic and also recalls some of the first half's somberness (mm. 9-12) through use of the minor mode.

Compensation for Ambiguity of Harmonic Design: Rhythmic Repetition

As in many extended-tonal songs, the complex harmonic structure of "An den Schlaf" is reinforced by nonharmonic elements of continuity. Wolf uses repetition of both rhythmic and melodic motives in addition to a carefully constructed vocal line to compensate for the song's unusual harmonic design. Coherence in "An den Schlaf" is created partially through harmonic rhythm, where various key areas interrelate through a rhythmic reiteration pattern. The song is grouped into two-bar units, a pair of two-bars forming a phrase. Measures 1-4 set up the pattern: the first two bars reiterate the basic, cellular harmonic and melodic gestures and recur in the next two bars with chromatic counterpoint (see example 5-16). The vocal line enters in m. 5, and the ensuing four bars repeat the opening material. When measures 7-8 shift to B minor (through the common tone G♭-F♯), the phrase is repeated, with slight alteration, a minor third higher. The four-bar phrase in B (mm. 9-12) modulates to D♭ in m. 13.

Ex. 5-16. "An den Schlaf": Rhythmic Repetition

The first change in harmonic rhythm occurs in the second transposition (D♭) of the original material: a 2 + 2 phrase grouping is replaced by 2 + 3 (mm. 13-17). This rhythmic change signals an important shift in harmonic direction. In m. 13, the bass moves up a minor sixth rather than a perfect fourth, and the phrase ends on V/D♭ rather than in a new key. The change in rhythm is an accompaniment to a shift in harmonic design. The song's four-bar modulatory phrases are replaced by a five-bar phrase that emphasizes a cadence within D♭; thus the emphasis on D♭ breaks the pattern of continuously changing harmonic motion. Example 5-17 shows how the section in D♭ could easily have modulated to V/E, following the model of the A♭ major-B minor modulation. Since V/E does appear in m. 18, the fact that the D♭ section did not modulate earlier to E emphasizes the fundamental opposition of A♭/D♭ and E major.

The implications of the A♭ half cadence at the end of the song's first half, mm. 16-17, are complicated. The transformation of A♭ from I to V/VI has

Ex. 5-17.   "An den Schlaf": Relationship of D♭ Major to E Major

taken place; sleep (and/or death) has been embraced. The ensuing melodic common tone A♭(G♯) connects the two sections as it underscores the division of the song into two sections. The half cadence sets up the expectation of resolving to D♭(C♯), but this resolution is elided. Instead, V/C♯/D♭ becomes V⁷/E, and the song concludes in E major. However one understands the elided resolution to D♭, the effect is the same: as the bass G♯ moves to B, the melodic A♭ becomes G♯, and the tonality shifts from A♭/D♭ to E major.

The ambiguity of tonal focus due to the continuous harmonic shifts (A♭ major-B minor-D♭ major) is somewhat alleviated by the regular rhythmic grouping. The repetition of two-bar phrases (with the exception of the dramatic phrasal expansion, 2 < 3 bars, in mm. 15-17) creates a rhythmic momentum that propels the obscure harmonic relationships forward. Even if the harmonic relationships themselves do not cohere by m. 17, the rhythmic continuity has created a semblance of cohesion in the song's first half. The rupture of harmonic rhythm in m. 17 serves to emphasize the shift in tonal focus, but returns in mm. 18-21. The two-bar phrase of mm. 22-23 suggests the return of regular four-bar phrases (2 + 2), but mm. 24-27 breaks the pattern with a four-bar cadential phrase. The final phrase is six measures long, and the harmonic rhythm of the second half results in a highly irregular pattern: 4 + 2 + 4 + 6 (+1) or 4 + 6 + 7.

The phrasal changes in the second half of the song coincide with a simplification of harmonic relationships, with the asymmetric phrase lengths allowing it to come to a conclusion with a steady decelerando of harmonic activity. The rhythmic expansion of phrase length underscores the overriding V-I relationship of the song's second half.

Melodic Motivic Repetition

Melodic repetition of a one-bar motive is also used to achieve coherence in "An den Schlaf." Even the prolonged phrases in the second half incorporate the one-bar motivic unit that has recurred in one- and/or two-bar groupings throughout the song. While mm. 18-34 present a deceleration of harmonic rhythm and a lengthening of phrase structure, they also involve an intensification of contrapuntal motion as the one-bar motive is continually projected over different harmonic contexts. Measures 18-19 display exact repetition in two-bar phrases, while mm. 20-21 have different one-bar melodic units within a two-bar voice exchange (B-G♯). Moreover, mm. 22-23 repeat a two-bar phrase and mm. 24-27 demonstrate a prolonged melodic ascent in one-bar units (RH piano) over a II-V$^6_4$ progression, while the vocal line makes a four-bar melodic descent from F♯ to A.

The prolongation of a large-scale V-I motion in mm. 18ff. thus incorporates a careful manipulation of reiterated motivic elements. The broad cadential gesture is further embellished by an expansive use of register in the piano RH. The vocal line connects the tessituras of the two halves, as the high F♯-E gestures in mm. 19-21 and 24-25 recall mm. 6-7 and 13, and the final descent to A (thence to G♯) in m. 28ff. recalls m. 14.

Coherence in the Vocal Line

A third means of cohesion in "An den Schlaf" is built into the melodic profile of the vocal line. The rupture of rhythmic flow caused by the extended phrase in mm. 13-17 creates a climax of expectation in m. 17. The connection of the first half of the song with the second is dependent largely upon perception of the progression from A♭ to B^7 (mm. 17-18). The vocal line offers some clarification of the song's harmonic ambiguity. Example 5-18 isolates the vocal line above the bass progression. The opening Kopfton* C ultimately traverses a major third to A♯ (spelled G♯). The motion C or C♭ to A♭ occurs twice. The pitch C first occurs in m. 5; C♭ (as B♮) is found in mm. 9ff. as the harmony shifts from A♭ major to B minor. The progression to V/D♭ brings the melody line down to A♭ (lower beam) for the conclusion of the song's first half. Note that the singer stops on B♭♭ in m. 14 and the piano RH concludes the motion to A♭. The A♭(G♯) connector then occurs in mm. 17-18. As the first melodic descent ends, a second melodic line begins in the voice, and G♯ moves back up to the second Kopfton* B♮ (C♭). The original line from C begins again a half step lower on C♭ (or B♮): B

Ex. 5-18. "An den Schlaf": Motivic Repetition in Vocal Line

moves down to A (m. 27) and finally G♯ (m. 33). Again, the vocal line is interrupted a half-step before its conclusion (A♮, m. 27), and the RH piano part concludes the linear descent to G♯. The symmetrical ascending fourth bass motions cited earlier accompany a pair of melodic descending thirds, C-A♭, B-G♯, and the common tone A♭(G♯) is the goal of both descents. Included in the sketch of example 5-18 is a notation of the recurring third G♯-B, (motive A) from example 5-15b, which occurs in both the bass and treble parts.

The foregoing analysis has shown that the third relation III♯-I creates an unusual harmonic structure that defies Schenker's monotonal system and suggests instead a directional tonal reading. As already mentioned, the large-scale motion from A♭ major to E major is heard less as a mediant to a tonic and more as a connection of two distantly related harmonies that simulates a III-I progression. This weakened connection between chromatic, third-related opening and closing tonalities is enhanced by the transformation of tonic function in mm. 1-17, which undermines the opening tonality function of A♭. The functional transformation is therefore the pivot between the opening and closing tonalities, and the functional alteration of A♭ undermines the opening tonality role and necessitates the assertion of a clear tonal focus in the song's second half. When the song concludes in E major, its opening (A♭ or D♭) is understood retrospectively as being in a key different from and irreconcilable to the closing tonic.

Conclusion

The three songs chosen to illustrate the combination of extended-tonal techniques display several similarities. All three use third relations, the transformation of tonic function, and the ambiguity principle. Furthermore, none is readily analyzed in Schenkerian terms.

Third Relations

The use of third relations in "In der Frühe" is unusual since the third chain replaces the dominant with a series of plagal harmonies (II♯-IV-♭VI). The third relations in "Wir haben beide" and "An den Schlaf" are similar to one another; occurring as ♭III-I (in major) and III♯-I (in major) respectively, they utilize chromatic third relations that are altogether different from third relations of the common-practice period. In addition, both large-scale third relations occur within larger contexts of musical complexity: the third relation in "Wir haben beide" is a third substitute for V, and the third relation in "An den Schlaf" is part of a transformation of tonic function occurring in the song's first half. Finally, the use of large-scale third relations involving altered mediant-tonic relationships in the major mode illustrates the innovativeness of such structures. These chromatic third relations suggest a form of double tonality.

Transformation of Tonic Function

The most important element of the plagal domain used in these songs was the transformation of tonic function. "In der Frühe" used this technique in a somewhat modified form: each new transposition of the opening material became a tonic while the preceding section became a subdominant. In both "Wir haben beide" and "An den Schlaf," the use of the extended-tonal technique was more precise: in the former the functional transformation undermined the initial tonic, initiating the first of several text repetitions. In "An den Schlaf," it obscured the opening tonality, preparing a shift in tonal focus within the context of directional tonality. Wolf's exploitation of the inherent ambiguity of the tonic and subdominant is a powerful resource, and his use of functional transformation demonstrates the immense variety of formal effects afforded by the technique.

Ambiguity Principle and Motivic Repetition

Two other characteristic Wolfian formal techniques found in all the songs of this chapter are his use of the ambiguity principle and the resulting compensation for ambiguity through extensive motivic repetition. The need for ambiguity invariably is prompted by the text. Textual conflicts are vividly conveyed by the extended-tonal techniques of functional transformation and directional tonality.

As compensation for extensive harmonic ambiguity, Wolf consistently uses motivic repetition for inner coherence and continuity. As we have seen, repetition schemes have included complete phrases of music. In "Wir haben beide," each of three harmonic areas presents the same harmonic progression, with the only slight variation in the vocal line. Meanwhile, in "In der Frühe" and "An den Schlaf," the four-bar opening phrases are repeated with minimal alteration throughout the rest of the song, repetition being used to counterbalance the transposition to remote harmonic areas.

Wolf's use of motivic repetition is an essential accompaniment to his exploitation of harmonic ambiguity. As motivic reiteration compensates for ambiguous harmonic relationships, motivic recurrence interrelates seemingly irreconcilable harmonic relations into a coherent whole. Whereas Wolf's need for motivic coherence seems necessitated by an inherent weakness or an instable harmonic design, his use of motivic repetition can be understood in a more positive way: it is a compositional resource in its own right that he explored continuously alongside other tonal expansion techniques.

Inapplicability of Schenkerian Analysis: The Problem of Structural Coherence

The application of Schenker's system to songs that combine several extended-tonal techniques is problematical. Indeed, every song ultimately proves to be more clearly depicted in a directional tonal reading. The final analytical problem is that of determining formal coherence. Where Schenkerian analysis prescribes coherence through simple and predictable harmonic relationships, coherence in some extended-tonal music derives from a different premise. The "ambiguity principle" that emerges from this study is that of establishing structural dissonance (i.e., harmonic ambiguity) and then resolving that dissonance over time to structural consonance (i.e., harmonic clarification). It is thus a resolution of an expanded concept of dissonance that creates stability in a given work and enables the piece to come to a close. Whereas this formal design of creating and resolving various forms of dissonance is not as precise as Schenker's comprehensive system, it does describe how some pieces can be heard and understood. Furthermore, the creation and resolving of dissonance corresponds vividly to Wolf's response to poetic texts, and underscores the relationship of his harmonic innovation to his fidelity of text depiction.

Wir haben beide lange Zeit geschwiegen
(In silence each the other passed unheeding)

In der Frühe
(In the early morning)

An den Schlaf
(Song to sleep)

Somne levis! Quamquam certissima mortis imago,
Consortem cupio te tamen esse tori.
Alma quies, optata, veni! Nam sic sine vita
Vivere, quam suave est, sic sine morte mori!
Meibom

Sehr ruhig

Schlaf!__ sü - sser Schlaf! ob - wohl dem Tod, wie du, nichts

Sleep!__ sweet - est sleep! the fore - taste of e - ter - i -

gleicht, auf die - sem La - ger doch will - kom - men heiss'__ ich dich!

ly,__ un - to this couch of mine I glad - ly wel - - come thee!

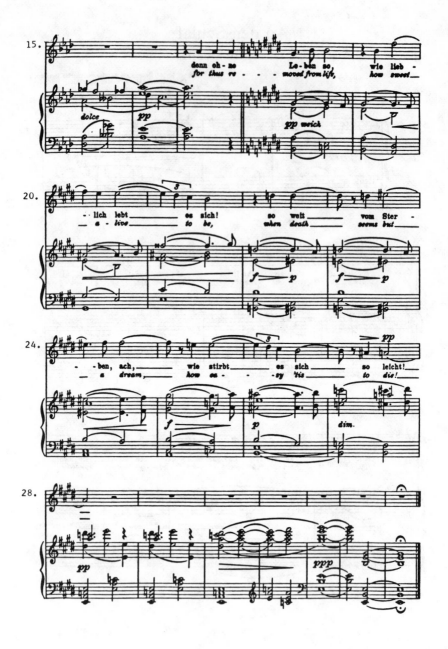

Epilogue

This study of Wolf's late-nineteenth-century harmonic language has demonstrated how one composer expanded upon or replaced common-practice tonal syntax with innovative extended-tonal structures. Chapter 2 showed how the plagal domain enabled Wolf to explore the harmonic ambiguity inherent in the traditional subdominant function and even led to a replacement of the tonic-dominant axis with an analogous but more problematic plagal axis. Chapter 3 demonstrated that while Wolf's exploration of third relations was relatively tame, he did not hesitate to use more radical chromatic third relations—those, for instance, suggesting a form of double tonality—when confronted with unyielding poetic conflicts. Wolf's use of double tonal schemes was not confined solely to pieces using third relations. Songs examined in chapters 4 and 5 exemplified the use of directional tonality in connection with both plagal and third relations, and combinations of these structures.

Two issues recur throughout every chapter of this study. These are the ubiquitous ambiguity created by the various forms of tonal expansion, and the need on the part of the composer to compensate for this structural ambiguity—both through rhythmic and melodic motivic patterns and through some kind of formal symmetry. Whereas Wolf's experimentation with formal ambiguity seems prompted by textual concerns, his ability to create compensatory motivic continuity proves masterful, and his music transcended both the formal and the harmonic context out of which it emerged.

This brings us to the general issue of Wolf's innovation with regard to musical form. While it is possible to view Wolf's formal designs as resulting from tonal ambiguity—that is, that the extended-tonal structures created formal problems—it is perhaps more instructive to consider the reverse: that Wolf chose weak and ambiguous tonal structures in order to vividly reflect the tensions and conflicts within the poetry he set. The ambiguity principle offered in chapter 1 proposes such a thesis of form: that the creation of formal dissonance and its complementary resolution through formal consonance is a design used by Wolf to a heightened level of compositional purpose. Since the ambiguity principle is inextricably bound to text depiction, this study has needed to distinguish between Wolf's exploration of musical structure and his depiction of poetic text. While it is known that Wolf's musical language was dedicated first and foremost to responding to the poetic text, I have maintained here that Wolf's extended-tonal structures were also comprehensible solely on musical terms. The present study thus has continuously challenged the tendency to dismiss a seeming lack of musical coherence as "resulting from textual concerns." Every Wolf song was scrutinized in extreme detail, and in the end a carefully constructed musical logic, both harmonic and linear, was discernable in every song studied. Ultimately, a fluid concept of form was adopted that combined musical innovation and poetic depiction. Each piece revealed itself to be a uniquely whole and coherent musical structure as well as an essential musical distillation of the poetic text.

The application of Schenkerian analysis to this study of tonal expansion has shown a great deal about both Wolf's harmonic language and Schenker's analytical system. Much of Schenker's methodology remained appropriate, even within double tonal pieces. This attests both to the success of Wolf's harmonic exploration and the remarkable breadth of Schenker's conceptualization of the tonal language. Using Schenkerian analysis as both a model and a gauge was equally revealing. Not only could we determine where harmonic expansion diverged from tonal logic, but we were also able to focus on why this was so.

Finally, in the introduction to this study it was suggested that many of the discoveries about Hugo Wolf's harmonic language would be applicable to his contemporaries and successors, especially to the music of Richard Wagner. Indeed, each chapter could be rewritten with examples from other late-nineteenth-century composers and the use of plagal relations, chromatic third relations, and double tonality would continue to recur. That Wolf's harmonic language was influenced by Wagner's seems certain enough. What is perhaps even more impressive, however, is how Wagner's operas influenced Wolf's *Lieder* in the depiction of poetic text. If history has recorded that Wolf believed Wagner's operas to be an unparalleled synthesis of text and music at the most dramatic and expressive level, then Wolf's music in turn has shown how the young Wagnerite translated his master's operatic craft into an extraordinary language of richness and imagination within the miniature world of the art song.

Notes

Chapter 1

1. Both standard biographies of Wolf chronicle in considerable detail Wolf's meeting with Wagner, his numerous trips to performances of Wagner's operas at Bayreuth, and his insistent preoccupation with Wagner's music. See Ernest Newman, *Hugo Wolf* (London, 1907) and Frank Walker, *Hugo Wolf: A Biography* (New York, 1968).

2. Most readers will probably be familiar with Schenker's theory and analytical methodology. Any who are not wholly comfortable with the Schenkerian material discussed in this study are referred to the now standard bibliographical sources: *Readings in Schenker Analysis and Other Approaches,* Maury Yeston, ed. (New Haven and London, 1977); Sylvan Kalib, "Thirteen Essays from the Three Yearbooks 'Das Meisterwerk in der Musik'" (Ph.D. dissertation, Northwestern University, 1973); Sonia Slatin, "The Theories of Heinrich Schenker in Perspective" (Ph.D. dissertation, Columbia University, 1967); Adele Katz, *Challenge to Musical Tradition* (New York, 1945); David Beach, "A Schenker Bibliography" (Published in two segments, the first reprinted from the *Journal of Music Theory* 13/1 [1969] in *Readings in Schenker* and the second appearing in the *Journal of Music Theory* 23/2 [1979]); Carl E. Schachter, David Epstein, and William E. Benjamin, "Review Symposium: Schenker's Free Composition," *Journal of Music Theory* 25/1 (1981) [hereafter cited as JMT] and *Aspects of Schenkerian Theory*. ed., David Beach (New Haven & London, 1983). The most relevant of Schenker's own writing is *Free Composition.* [*Der Freie Satz*] Vol. III of *Neue Musikalische Theorien und Phantasien,* trans. and ed., Ernst Oster. New York, 1979.

3. For a more detailed discussion of Schenker's concept of monotonality, see pp. 143-45 of chapter 4.

4. Allen Forte coined the term "tonic-dominant axis" in his text *Tonal Harmony in Concept and Practice* (3rd edition, New York, 1962).

5. The German terminology for Schenkerian concepts is retained in order to emphasize the deliberate and careful invocation of Schenker's theory in the strictest sense of the terms and concepts.

6. For a few such examples, see sections of David Beach, *A Schenker Bibliography;* Adele Katz, *Challenge;* and Felix Salzer, *Structural Hearing: Tonal Coherence in Music* 2 vols. (New York, 1962). A more recent application of Schenker to several late-nineteenth-century composers is a 1981 Yale University dissertation by David Allen Damschroder, "The Structural Foundations of 'The Music of the Future'."

7. A compelling case is made for this view by Wolf's biographer Ernest Newman. See *Hugo Wolf*, pp. 153ff. In addition, several other notable comparative studies of Wolf and other composers of *Lieder* are: Paul Boylan, "The Lieder of Hugo Wolf: Zenith of the German Art Song" (Ph.D. dissertation, University of Michigan, 1968); Ellen Carole Bruna, "The Relationship of Text and Music in the Lieder of Hugo Wolf and Gustav Mahler" (Ph.D. dissertation, Syracuse University, 1974); Eric Sams, *The Songs of Hugo Wolf* (London, 1961); Jack Stein, *Poem and Music in The German Lied from Gluck to Hugo Wolf* (Cambridge, 1971); Jurgen Thym, "The Solo Song Settings of Eichendorff's Poems by Schumann and Wolf" (Ph.D. dissertation, Case Western Reserve University, 1974); and Frank Walker, *Hugo Wolf*.

8. See Newmann, *Hugo Wolf*, p. 185.

9. See Walker, *Hugo Wolf*, p. 238.

10. The analysis of "In der Frühe" in chapter 5 exemplifies this practice.

11. The concept of modulation as dissonance can be traced as far back as Riemann, "Die Natur der Harmonik," in *Sammlund musikalischer Vortrage*, ed. Paul Graf von Waldersee (Leipzig, 1882), who considered modulation to be a dissonant removal from the tonic which was resolved with a return to the only consonance, the original tonic. See William C. Mickelsen, *Hugo Riemann's Theory of Harmony and History of Music, Book III* (Lincoln & London, 1977), p. 67. This issue is discussed in greater detail in chapter 4.

12. Charles Rosen, *The Classical Style: Haydn, Mozart, Beethoven* (New York, 1972); *Sonata Forms* (New York, 1980); and Sir Donald Tovey, *Beethoven* (London, New York, Oxford, 1945). A recent article by Leo Treitler casts the issue of ambiguous openings into a particularly striking context. See "History, Criticism, and Beethoven's Ninth Symphony," *19th Century Music* III/3 (March 1980), pp. 193-210, and a recent study by Jonathan Dunsby explores harmonic and rhythmic ambiguity in the music of Brahms, see *Structural Ambiguity in Brahms: Analytical Approaches to Four Works*. (Ann Arbor, Michigan, 1981).

13. Placement of ♭, ♯, or ♮ after a Roman numeral designates an alteration of that triad's third; placement of an accidental before a Roman numeral indicates an alteration of that chord's root.

14. Jean Philippe Rameau, *Traite de l'harmonie réduite à principes naturels* (Paris, 1772) and *Nouveau système de musique théorique* (Paris, 1726); Hugo Riemann, "Die Natur" and *Vereinfachte Harmonielehre oder die Lehre von den Tonalen Funktionen der Accorde* (*London*, 1896). See also Johann Friedrich Daube, *Generalbass in drey Accorden* (Leipzig, 1756), Heinrich Christoph Koch, *Handbuch bey dem Studium der Harmonie* (Leipzig, 1811), and Moritz Hauptmann, *Die Natur der Harmonik und der Metrik*, 2nd edition (Berlin, 1873). For a detailed account of Riemann's theories, see Willian Mickelsen, *Hugo Riemann's Theory*.

15. Riemann presents his system of chord derivation in *Vereinfachte*. It is described by Mickelsen, in *Hugo Riemann's Theory*, pp. 60-67 and 75-84.

16. Rudolph Louis and Ludwig Thuille, *Harmonielehre* (Stuttgart, 1906), paragraph 23, pp. 92ff.

17. Text translations are by the author and are as literal as possible to ensure the most precise understanding of the original German.

18. For a discussion of this unusual sonority, see Wallace Berry's *Structural Functions in Music* (Englewood Cliffs, N.J., 1976), p. 141.

Chapter 2

1. Jean Philippe Rameau, *Nouveau système de musique théoretique* (Paris, 1726), p. 38.

2. Matthew Shirlaw, *The Theory of Harmony* (London, 1917), p. 140.

3. Mortiz Hauptmann, *Die Natur der Harmonik und der Metrik*, 2nd. edition (Berlin, 1873), pp. 8-14.

4. Schenker's personal reluctance to apply his analytical system to late-nineteenth-century music has not deterred many of his followers. Among the many applications of Schenker's theories to late-nineteenth-century music, the most notable are Felix Salzer's *Structural Hearing: Tonal Coherence in Music*, 2 vols. (New York, 1962), Adele Katz's *Challenge to Musical Tradition* (New York, 1945), and William Mitchell's analysis, "The *Tristan* Prelude: Techniques and Structure," *Music Forum I* (New York, 1967).

5. While theorists such as Riemann claim that III can substitute for V, there are few musical examples of such substitution at structural or cadential points. In the case of the plagal domain, however, the theoretical possibility of substitution is borne out in musical practice.

6. Heinrich Schenker, *Free Composition* [*Der Freie Satz*], Vol. III of *Neue Musikalische Theoren und Phantagien*, trans. and ed. Ernst Oster (New York, 1979), paragraph 89, p. 37: "divider... serves as a reminder that the bass, like the fundamental line, aims at only one arpeggiation, the quintal division of the triad."

7. Many examples of the plagal cadence as a tonic extension or prolongation occur in the nineteenth-century music of composers such as Brahms and Chopin; Brahms's Symphony No. 1 (first and fourth movements) and Chopin's *Etude*, Op. 25, No. 8 and *Nocturne*, Op. 27, No. 1 are a few examples. Many examples of plagal extension of the tonic after a middleground authentic cadence may be found in Wolf's songs. In the Mörike collection alone, five songs use this technique in a clear and dramatic fashion: "Der Genesene an die Hoffnung," "Er ist's," "Gebet," "An den Schlaf," and "Neue Liebe."

8. This exact progression occurs in the opening—and closing—of Mendelssohn's *Overture to a Midsummer Night's Dream*, the only difference being that Mendelssohn uses a minor subdominant as part of a general exploitation of modal mixture. Many of the points about Wolf's song will also be relevant to Mendelssohn's *Overture*.

9. The "weakness" of the plagal cadence has long been noted by theorists. Riemann called the plagal cadence weak and cold (see Mickelsen, *Hugo Riemann's Theory of Harmony and History of Music, Book III* [Lincoln and London, 1977], p. 28), and Schoenberg stated: "plagal cadences... are only a means of stylistic expression and are structurally of no importance." (See Arnold Schoenberg, *Structural Functions of Harmony* [New York, 1954], p. 14.)

10. The fact that $\hat{1}$ can be posited as a tonic pedal above a I-IV-I progression does not mitigate the lack of melodic motion toward $\hat{1}$ such as $\hat{7}$-$\hat{8}$ or $\hat{2}$-$\hat{1}$.

11. It is indeed part of Schenker's genius that he was able to discern different levels of structure and, at the same time, coordinate these levels into one comprehensive system.

12. The fact that the ostinato begins on the subdominant of A♭ indicates that the subdominant is used on both the foreground and middleground levels—a most Schenkerian feature!

13. The harmonic ambiguity between the members of the relative major and minor is most commonly understood when the tonic is minor and its relative major is ♭III. The natural minor scale of the minor tonic incorporates the relative major in its entirety without

chromatic interpolation. The most common means of distinguishing one key from the other is through the dominant of the minor key (the dominant of the relative major being ♭VII of the natural minor) and the plagal members of the two keys for the most part exchange places: in the G minor/B♭ major pair, for example: IV/G minor = II/B♭ major and IV/B♭ major = ♭VI/G minor. In the nineteenth century, the Neapolitan ♭II emerges as the one plagal element that does emphasize one key over the other, as ♭II/G minor does not exist in B♭ major.

14.   Both the minor mode and the plagal domain offer a degree of harmonic ambiguity unequalled in the major mode or within the harmonic domain of the dominant.

15.   Robert Bailey, "The Genesis of *Tristan und Isolde* and a Study of Wagner's Sketches and Drafts for the First Act" (Ph.D. dissertation, Princeton University, 1969). The article appeared in *Nineteenth Century Music*, I/1, (July, 1977), p. 51.

16.   The unusual power of a major triad to sound like a dominant rather than a tonic is stated succinctly in Tovey: "if you approach any major triad from some remote quarter or from nowhere, and harp upon it for a considerable time, it is more likely to sound like a dominant than a tonic." Sir Donald Tovey, *Beethoven* (London, New York, Oxford, 1945), p. 14.

17.   The contrapuntal structure supercedes the inherent harmonic symmetry of the *Ursatz* of example 2-28a.

Chapter 3

1.   *The Art of Counterpoint*, trans., Guy A. Marco and Claude V. Palisca (New York: 1968), part I, chapter 14.

2.   Marin Mersenne, *Harmonie universelle contenant la théorie et la pratique de la musique*. Paris, 1636-37 and Joseph Sauveur, *Acoustical Essays in Histoire de l'Académie Royale des Sciences*. Ed., Fontenelle. Paris, 1700-1713.

3.   Hermann von Helmholtz, *Die Lehre von den Tonempfindungen als physiologische Grundlage für die Theorie der Musik*. Brunswick: 1863. Trans., John Alexander Ellis, 1877 *(On the Sensations of Tone as a Physiological Basis for the Theory of Music)*, 6th ed., New York: Peter Smith, 1948, and Hugo Riemann, "Die Natur der Harmonik," *Sammlund musikalischer Vortrage*, ed. Paul Graf von Waldersee (Leipzig, 1882), and *Verienfachte Harmonielehre, odor die Lehre von den Tonalen Funktionen der Akkorde*, 1893, trans. H. Bewerung (London, 1896).

4.   Moritz Hauptmann, *Die Natur der Harmonik und der Metrik*, trans. W.E. Heathcole (London, 1888).

5.   The impact of Riemann's teachings can be measured by a variety of textbooks by subsequent theorists, including some of Riemann's students, e.g., Hermann Erpf, *Studien zur Harmonie- und Klangtechnik der neueren Musik* (Leipzig, 1927).

6.   Hugo Riemann, *Grosse Kompositionslehre*, 1902, Vol. I, p. 481: "seit Beethoven, Schubert und Liszt ist die Terzverwandschaft der Tonarten in der praktischen Komposition zu unbedingter Anerkennung gelangt."

7.   Rudolph Louis and Ludwig Thuille, *Harmonielehre* (Stuttgart, 1906).

8.   Ibid., pp. 343-46. Louis and Thuille's discussion of third chains *(Terzencirkel)* will be particularly relevant to pp. 87-91.

9.   Heinrich Schenker, *Harmony*, ed., and anno., Oswald Jonas; trans. Elisabeth Mann Borgese (Chicago, 1954), p. 232.

10. Heinrich Schenker, *Free Composition,* trans and ed. Ernst Oster (New York, 1979), pp. 29-30.

11. Harald Krebs, "Third Relations and Dominant" (Ph.D. dissertation, Yale University, 1980) and "Alternatives to Monotonality in Early Nineteenth-Century Music," *JMT* 25/1 (Spring, 1981), 1-16.

12. The concept of harmonic substitution was discussed in chapter 1, p. 6-12.

13. The fact that C major occurs not as a triad, but rather as a V^7 chord, does not preclude the possibility of C major being a potential harmonic area, with its own domain of harmonic relations.

14. While ♮VI is not a dissonant harmony *per se*, the interrelationships of the harmonic domains of F minor and D minor does create a certain level of tonal ambiguity.

15. An example of a piece utilizing a circular progression outside any middleground tonic-dominant axis is Liszt's 1849 piano work *Consolation #3* in D♭. A reading of this work would be:

    mm.   25 31   33   39   41   43
    D♭:   I-III(♭)-♮→♭VI/A minor-V^{6-5}_{4-3}-I/A minor-A major→♭VI/D♭-V^{6-5}_{4-3}/D♭-I/D♭

    The score of the Liszt work is located in the appendix to chapter 3.

16. Heinrich Schenker, *Free Composition.* Trans., Oster.

17. Ibid., trans., Oster, p. 135.

18. Ibid., see figs. 154/4 and 114/8 for Schenker's analysis of Beethoven's Op. 57/1.

19. Ibid., pp. 139-40.

20. Ibid., p. 82. Oster cites a comparison of this to fig. 114/8, Beethoven's Op. 57/1 (Development).

21. Sonia Slatin, "The Theories of Heinrich Schenker in Perspective" (Ph.D. dissertation, Columbia University, 1967), pp. 275-76.

22. Gregory Michael Proctor, "Technical Bases of Nineteenth-Century Chromatic Tonality: A Study in Chromaticism" (Ph.D. dissertation, Princeton University, 1978), p. 181.

23. The F♮ of mm. 1-2 also suggests the key of C major. Furthermore, the clash between the F♮ of mm. 1-2 and the F♯ of mm. 6ff. evokes a sense of the past in a subtle reference to the aged minstrel's lute which, being unused, is as out of tune as the F♮.

24. While an adequate study of thematic correspondence and harmonic opposition is beyond the scope of the present analysis, it is noteworthy that Wolf's manipulation of thematic recurrence is a formidable element of coherence in a song that is predicated upon harmonic ambivalence.

25. Once again, the manipulation of thematic elements must at least be mentioned: the D chord of m. 26 is equivalent to m. 4 (V/F) and m. 6 (V/G minor?), while the abrupt B♭ of m. 27 is analogous to the interruptive D major of m. 5.

26. The third relation ♭VI-I depicted here foreshadows a use of third relations that will become increasingly commonplace in the later nineteenth century. Through its constant association with V (as a neighbor-note extension), ♭VI came to replace V, the plagal replacing the

authentic cadence. Third relations not only disrupted the governance of the tonic-dominant axis, but eventually they supplanted the fifth relation altogether. The Liszt piano piece cited on pp. 122-24 exemplifies such a replacement of ♭VI for V. See also the discussion of dominant replacement in chapter 2, pp. 26-28.

27. Felix Salzer, *Structural Hearing: Tonal Coherence in Music* (New York, 1962), fig. 382, pp. 178-79.

28. For a more thorough discussion of Wolf's harmonic language and double tonality, see chapter 4.

29. The "instability" of a third chain becomes clear when a third chain is compared to its circle-of-fifths counterpart. While a fifth chain ultimately resolves in a clearly definable key (with the progression ending on a V or a I) the third chain has no inherent tonal direction or focus and neither resolves to nor confirms a particular key.

30. This idea was suggested in a conversation with David Lewin.

Chapter 4

1. Arnold Schoenberg coined the term "monotonality" in *Structural Functions of Harmony,* (New York, 1954), p. 19.

2. "Once we determine that a certain note will be used at the beginning and at the end, . . . " Jean Philippe Rameau, *Traité de l'harmonie réduite à ses principes naturels* (Paris, 1722), Book III, chapters 8 and 23, including example III.64. Trans., Philip Gossett. (New York, 1971), p. 163.

3. C.P.E. Bach, *Essay on the True Art of Playing Keyboard Instruments,* trans. and ed. William F. Mitchell (New York, 1949), pp. 431-34.

4. Johann Phillip Kirnberger, *Die Kunst des reinen Satzes in der Musik* (Berlin, 1771-79).

5. Heinrich Christoph Koch, *Versuch einer Anleitung zur Composition* (Leipzig, 1782-93).

6. William C. Mickelsen, *Hugo Riemann's Theory of Harmony and History of Music, Book III* (Lincoln and London, 1977), pp. 30-31.

7. Ibid., p. 67.

8. Heinrich Schenker, *Free Composition,* trans. and ed. Ernst Oster (New York, 1979), p. 5.

9. Ibid., p. 112.

10. Ibid., see sections 56-59 (The Background), 10-112 (Middleground, First Level), 186 and 196-202 (The Later Structural Levels), and 280 (The Foreground).

11. Schoenberg, *Structural Functions,* p. 19.

12. Few scholars have examined in a systematic way late-nineteenth-century music that begins and ends in different keys. Robert Bailey coined the term "Directional Tonality" in his lectures at Yale University and the Eastman School of Music; and Jim Samson discussed what he calls "progressive tonality" in *Music in Transition: A Study of Tonal Expansion and Atonality, 1900-1920* (London, 1977). Bailey's conceptualization of late-nineteenth-century double tonality includes two distinct types: tonal pairing and directional tonality. While Wolf's songs do not appear to involve tonal pairing, they do indeed exemplify directional tonality. More recent studies of early-nineteenth-century third relations that allude to the techniques discussed here are Harald Krebs, "Third Relations and Dominant" (Ph.D.

dissertation, Yale University, 1980), and "Alternatives to Monotonality in Early-Nineteenth-Century Music," *JMT* 25/1 (Spring, 1981).

13.   This is not to say, however, that extramusical factors justify or explicate the use of double tonality in the absence of purely musical explanations, a position taken by Krebs in the research cited above. The textual and dramatic element may be a special impetus toward using directional tonality, but such a double tonal scheme must be comprehensible on purely musical terms as well. While it is beyond the scope of this study to explore other late-nineteenth-century genres, it is worth noting that directional tonality may be found in some symphonies of Mahler (e.g., Symphony no. 1) and Bruckner, (e.g., Symphony no. 9), as well as in some earlier nineteenth-century keyboard works, for instance, Chopin's *Prelude, Op. 28/2, Scherzo,* Op. 31, and *Ballade,* Op. 38. Chopin's Op. 28/2 will be discussed briefly in chapter 4.

14.   See *Free Composition,* fig. 110/3(a), which is presented in example 4-3a. In addition, Schenker's musings on another Chopin piece, the *Mazurka,* Op. 30, No. 2, are instructive. Referring to his fig. 152/7, Schenker states: "A fundamental line and V♯ ³⁻¹ in the bass are also lacking here; the uncertainty which rises about the tonality . . . almost prevents us from calling this Mazurka a completed composition. (This peculiarity was pointed out by Schumann.)" The sketch of the *Mazurka* (which shows the bass line only) reflects Schenker's frustration, as he cites both B minor and F♯ minor as potential tonics. (Trans. by Oster.)

15.   Ibid., paragraph 304, p. 129: "With the arrival of 1̂ the work is at an end. Whatever follows this can only be a reinforcement of the close—a coda—no matter what its extent or purpose may be." Schenker adds his own footnote: "If recent musical products have almost no end or seem to find no end, it is because they do not derive from a fundamental structure and hence do not arrive at a genuine 1̂; without this 1̂ a work is bound to give the effect of incompleteness." (Trans. by Oster.)

16.   Because the context of this discussion is, by definition, modified-Schenkerian, all usage of the term Kopfton will be accompanied by the asterisk which denotes modified-Schenkerian usage of that term.

17.   Heinrich Schenker, *Free Composition,* fig. 110/3(a).

18.   Ibid., pp. 40-41.

19.   The change from Schenker's *Kopfton* designation is, in part, necessitated by considering the opening in E minor rather than A minor, the treble E thus being 1̂ of the opening key. The opening melodic motion E-D is viewed as part of a long-range third, E-D-C, that does not resolve to C until the final measure of the piece. Note how the arrival on C is underscored by a recurrence of the motive in the bass clef, mm. 22-23 (bracketed in example 4-3b).

20.   The aesthetic and psychological effect of the opening of the *Prelude* is studied in detail by Leonard B. Meyer, *Emotion and Meaning in Music* (Chicago and London, 1956), pp. 93-97.

21.   An interesting colloquy about chromaticism in extended-tonality in twentieth-century music is found in several issues of *In Theory Only.* Responding in part to an article by Robert P. Morgan, ("Dissonant Prolongations: Theoretical and Compositional Precedents," *JMT* 20/1, Spring, 1976), William Benjamin discusses Stravinsky's *Concerto for Piano and Winds* in "Tonality without Fifths" (*ITO* 2/11-12 [Feb./Mar. 1977] and 3/2 [May 1977]). In a later issue, Morgan replies to Benjamin: "Dissonant Prolongations, Perfect Fifths, and Major Thirds in Stravinsky's Piano Concerto" (*ITO* 4/4 [Aug./Sept. 1978]) Both theorists allude to Schenker's famous commentary on the Stravinsky *Piano Concerto,* and consider the applicability of some Schenkerian principles in their own analyses of Stravinsky.

22.   Transformation of tonic function was explained in chapter 2. See pp. 22-25.

23.   The lower case e and b signify the minor mode, the upper case G, the major mode.

24.   This is a vivid example of Wolf's ability to align an independent vocal line with an almost unrelated piano part.

25.   This notion of correspondence between structural levels is implied or indirectly suggested at various times throughout *Free Composition*. See, for instance, paragraph 26 ("The fundamental structure can even be the content of the foreground," p. 16) or paragraphs 242-43 ("Transference of the Forms of the Fundamental Structure of Individual Harmonies," pp. 87ff.). Oster's comments on paragraph 26 (note 8, p. 16) explicate in considerable detail Schenker's fig. 7a, b, which show how various foreground details "preview" middleground structures in Beethoven's *Sonata*, Op. 27/2, first movement, and Chopin's *Etude*, Op. 10/8. Oster's interest in this phenomenon is echoed in his article, "Register and the Large-Scale Connection," in Maury Yeston, ed., *Readings. In Schenker Analysis and other Approaches* (New Haven and London, 1977). Several studies of motivic parallelism are worth nothing. The earliest is by Charles Burkhart, "Schenker's 'Motivic Parallelisms," *JMT* 22/2 (Fall, 1978) 145-75. More recent articles include David Beach, "A Recurring Pattern in Mozart's Music." *JMT* 27/1 (Spring, 1983) 1-29 and three essays from Beach's anthology, *Aspects of Schenkerian Theory* (New Haven and London, 1983): Charles Burkhart, "Schenker's Theory of Levels and Musical Performance," (pp. 95-112); John Rothgeb, "Thematic Content: A Schenkerian View," (pp. 39-60); and Carl Schachter, "Motive and Text in Four Schubert Songs" (pp. 61-76).

26.   It is also noteworthy that even though Wolf's opera, *Der Corregidor*, (1895) follows an adventurous tonal scheme between and within acts, the opera both begins and ends in the key of C major.

Chapter 5

1.   "Wir haben beide" was composed in 1891, "In der Frühe" and "An den Schlaf" in 1888.

2.   For a discussion of the use of compensatory elements in extended-tonal techniques, see chapter 2, pages 31-38.

3.   Readings of this song have been offered by Felix Salzer, *Structural Hearing: Tonal Coherence in Music* (New York, 1962), figure 488, pp. 238-39, and Gregory Proctor, "Technical Bases of Nineteenth-Century Chromatic Tonality: A Study of Chromaticism" (Ph.D. dissertation, Princeton University, 1978), pp. 220ff. Neither theorist adequately addresses the complexity of the harmonic language, and thus neither will be discussed further.

4.   Enharmonic equivalence is invoked here. Unless otherwise stated, A♭ represents both itself and G♯, D♭ both itself and C♯, and so forth.

5.   Some of the ideas in this reading were suggested to the present author in a conversation with David Lewin.

6.   See chapter 4, note 25 on correspondence between structural levels.

Selected Bibliography

Works about Hugo Wolf

Boylan, Paul C. "The Lieder of Hugo Wolf: Zenith of the German Art Song." Ph.D. dissertation, University of Michigan, 1968.

Bruna, Ellen Carol. "The Relationship of Text and Music in the Lieder of Hugo Wolf and Gustav Mahler." Ph.D. dissertation, Syracuse University, 1974.

Newman, Ernest. *Hugo Wolf*. London: Methuen & Co., Ltd., 1907.

Sams, Eric. *The Songs of Hugo Wolf*. London: Methuen & Co., Ltd., 1961.

Stein, Jack. *Poem and Music in the German Lied from Gluck to Hugo Wolf*. Cambridge: Harvard University Press, 1971.

Thym, Jurgen. "The Solo Song Settings of Eichendorff's Poems by Schumann and Wolf." Ph.D. dissertation, Case Western Reserve University, 1974.

Walker, Frank. *Hugo Wolf: A Biography*. New York: Alfred A. Knopf, 1968.

Works Related to Heinrich Schenker

Beach, David. "A Schenker Bibliography." Published in two parts: *Journal of Music Theory 13/1 (hereafter cited as JMT]* (Spring, 1969): 2-37 [Reprinted in *Readings in Schenker*, ed., Yeston, Maury, 275-311] and *JMT* 23/2 (Fall, 1979): 275-86.

———. *Aspects of Schenkerian Theory*. ed., David Beach. New Haven and London: Yale University Press, 1983.

Burkhart, Charles. "Schenker's 'Motivic Parallelisms'." *JMT* 22/2 (Fall, 1978): 145-75.

Kalib, Sylvan. "Thirteen Essays from the Three Yearbooks 'Das Meisterwerk in der Musik'." 3 vols. Ph.D. dissertation, Northwestern University, 1973.

Katz, Adele. *Challenge to Musical Tradition*. New York: Alfred A. Knopf, 1945.

Salzer, Felix. *Structural Hearing: Tonal Coherence in Music*. 2 vols. New York: Dover Publications, Inc., 1962.

Schachter, Carl E., Epstein, David, and Benjamin, William E. "Review Symposium: Schenker, Free Composition." *JMT* 25/1 (Spring, 1981): 113-73.

Schenker, Heinrich. *Free Composition [Der Freie Satz]*. Vol. III of *Neue Musikalische Theorien und Phantasien*. Trans. and ed., Ernst Oster. New York: Longman Publishers, Inc., 1979.

———. *Harmony [Harmonielehre]*. Vol. 1 of *Neue Musikalische Theorien und Phantasien*. Trans., Elisabeth Mann Borgese; ed. and anno., Oswald Jonas. Chicago: University of Chicago Press, 1954; Boston: MIT Press, 1973.

Slatin, Sonia. "The Theories of Heinrich Schenker in Perspective." Ph.D. dissertation, Columbia University, 1967.

Yeston, Maury, ed. *Readings in Schenker Analysis and other Approaches.* New Haven and London: Yale University Press, 1977.

Works about Music Other Than Hugo Wolf's Lieder

Bailey, Robert. "The Genesis of *Tristan und Isolde* and a Study of Wagner's Sketches and Drafts for the First Act." Ph.D. dissertation, Princeton University, 1969.

_____. "The Structure of the Ring and Its Evolution." *19th Century Music* I/1 (July, 1977): 48-61.

Beach, David. "A Recurring Pattern in Mozart's Music." *JMT* 27/1 (Spring, 1983): 1-29.

Benjamin, William E. "Tonality without Fifths." *In Theory Only* 2/11-12 (Feb./Mar., 1977): 53-70 and 3/2 (May, 1977): 9-31.

Damschroder, David Allen. "The Structural Foundations of 'The Music of the Future'." Ph.D. dissertation, Yale University, 1981.

Dunsby, Jonathan. *Structural Ambiguity in Brahms: Analytical Approaches to Four Works.* Ann Arbor, Michigan: UMI Research Press, 1981.

Krebs, Harald. "Alternatives to Monotonality in Early Nineteenth-Century Music." *JMT* 25/1 (Spring, 1981): 1-16.

_____. "Third Relations and Dominant." Ph.D. dissertation, Yale University, 1980.

Levenson, Irene. "Motivic-Harmonic Transfer in the Late Works of Schubert: Chromaticism in Large and Small Spans." Ph.D. dissertation, Yale University, 1981.

Meyer, Leonard B. *Emotion and Meaning in Music.* Chicago and London: University of Chicago Press, 1956.

Mitchell, William F. "The *Tristan* Prelude: Techniques and Structure." *Music Forum I.* New York: Columbia University Press, 1967: 162-203.

Morgan, Robert P. "Dissonant Prolongations, Perfect Fifths, and Major Thirds in Stravinsky's Piano Concerto." *ITO* 4/4 (Aug./Sept., 1978): 3-7.

_____. "Dissonant Prolongations: Theoretical and Compositional Precedents." *JMT* 20/1 (Spring, 1976): 49-91.

Proctor, Gregory Michael. "Technical Bases of Nineteenth-Century Chromatic Tonality: A Study in Chromaticism." Ph.D. dissertation, Princeton University, 1978.

Rosen, Charles. *The Classical Style: Haydn, Mozart, Beethoven.* New York: W.W. Norton & Co., Inc., 1972.

_____. *Sonata Forms.* New York: W.W. Norton & Co., Inc., 1980.

Samson, Jim. *Music in Transition: A Study of Tonal Expansion and Atonality, 1900-1920.* London: J.M. Dent & Songs, Ltd., 1977.

Tovey, Sir Donald. *Beethoven.* London, New York, Oxford: Oxford University Press, 1945.

Treitler, Leo. "History, Criticism, and Beethoven's Ninth Symphony." *19th Century Music* III/3 (March, 1980): 193-210.

Works about the History of Theory

Bach, C.P.E. *Versuch über die wahre Art des Clavier zu spielen* [*Essay on the True Art of Playing Keyboard Instruments*]. Trans. and ed., William F. Mitchell. New York: W.W. Norton & Co., Inc., 1949.

Daube, Johann Fredrich. *Generalbass in drey Accorden.* Leipzig: Johann Benjamin Andra, 1756.

Erpf, Hermann. *Studien zur Harmonie- und Klangtechnik der neueren Musik.* Leipzig: Breitkopf und Härtel, 1927.

Hauptmann, Moritz. *Die Natur der Harmonik und der Metrik* [*The Nature of Harmony and Meter*]. 2nd ed. Berlin: Breitkopf und Härtel, 1873. Trans., W.E. Heathcote. London: Swan Sonnenschein & Co., 1888.

Helmholtz, Hermann von. *Die Lehre von den Tonempfindungen als physiologische Grundlage für die Theorie der Musik.* Brunswick: 1863. Trans. John Alexander Ellis, 1877, 6th ed., New York: Peter Smith, 1948.

Kirnberger, Johann Phillip. *Die Kunst des reinen Satzes in der Musik [The Art of Strict Musical Composition].* 2 parts. Berlin, 1771-79; Trans., David Beach and Jurgen Thym. New Haven: Yale University Press, 1982.

Koch, Heinrich Christoph. *Handbuch bey dem Studium der Harmonie.* Leipzig: J.P. Hartknoch, 1811.

———. *Versuch einer Anleitung zur Composition.* 3 vols. Leipzig: A.F. Böhme, 1782-93.

Louis, Rudolph and Thuille, Ludwig. *Harmonielehre.* Stuttgart: Carl Grüninger, 1906.

Marco, Guy A. and Palisca, Claude V., trans. *The Art of Counterpoint.* New York: W.W. Norton & Co., Inc., 1968.

Marpurg, Friedrich Wilhelm. *Handbuch bey dem Generalbass und der Composition.* 4 vols. Berlin: G.A. Lange, 1755-60.

Mersenne, Marin. *Harmonie universelle contenant la théorie et la pratique de la musique.* Paris: S. Cramoisy, 1636-37.

Mickelsen, William C. *Hugo Riemann's Theory of Harmony and History of Music, Book III.* Lincoln and London: University of Nebraska Press, 1977.

Rameau, Jean Philippe. *Nouveau système de musique théorique.* Paris: J.B.C. Ballard, 1726; Reprint edition, New York: Broude Brothers, 1965.

———. *Traité de l'harmonie réduite à ses principes naturels. [Treatise on Harmony, Reduced to its Natural Principles].* 4 vols. Paris: J.B.C. Ballard, 1722; Trans., Philip Gosset. New York: Dover Publications, Inc., 1971.

Riemann, Hugo. "Die Natur der Harmonik." *Sammlung musikalischer Vortrage.* Ed., Paul Graf von Waldersee. Series 4, no. 40. Leipzig: Breitkopf und Härtel, 1882, pp. 157-90. Trans., John Comfort Fillmore as "The Nature of Harmony." In *New Lessons in Harmony.* Philadelphia: T. Presser, 1887.

———. *Grosse Kompositionslehre.* Vol. I: *Der Homophone Satz.* Berlin, 1902.

———. *Vereinfachte Harmonielehre, oder die Lehre von den Tonalen Funktionen der Akkorde [Harmony Simplified or the Theory of the Tonal Functions of Chords].* Trans., H. Bewerung. London: Augener & Co., 1896. Reprint, Ann Arbor: University Microfilms, 1968.

Sauveur, Joseph. *Acoustical Essays in Histoire de l'Academie Royale des Sciences.* Paris: Ed., Fontenelle, 1700-13.

Shirlaw, Matthew. *The Theory of Harmony.* London: Novello & Co., Ltd., 1917. Da Capo Press Reprint Edition, 1969.

Sorge, Georg Andreas. *Vorgemach der musikalischen Composition.* 3 vols. Lobenstein: privately published, 1745-47.

Zarlino, Gioseffo. *Le Istituzioni harmoniche.* Venice, 1558. Part III trans., Guy A. Marco and Claude V. Palisca. *The Art of Counterpoint.* New York and London: Yale University Press, 1968.

General Theoretical Works

Berry, Wallace T. *Structural Functions in Music.* Englewood Cliffs, New Jersey: Prentice-Hall, Inc., 1976.

Forte, Allen. *Tonal Harmony in Concept and Practice.* 3rd edition. New York: Holt, Rinehart & Winston, 1962.

Schoenberg, Arnold. *Structural Functions of Harmony.* New York: W.W. Norton & Co., Inc., 1954.

Index